INSIDE THE
BRITISH LIBRARY

INSIDE THE BRITISH LIBRARY

Alan Day

Library Association Publishing

London

© Alan Day 1998

Published by
Library Association Publishing
7 Ridgmount Street
London WC1E 7AE

Library Association Publishing is wholly owned by The Library Association.

Except as otherwise permitted under the Copyright Designs and Patents Act 1988 this publication may only be reproduced, stored or transmitted in any form or by any means, with the prior permission of the publisher, or, in the case of reprographic reproduction, in accordance with the terms of a licence issued by The Copyright Licensing Agency. Enquiries concerning reproduction outside those terms should be sent to Library Association Publishing, 7 Ridgmount Street, London WC1E 7AE.

First published 1998

British Library Cataloguing in Publication Data

A catalogue record for this book is available from the British Library.

ISBN 1-85604-280-4

LEEDS METROPOLITAN
UNIVERSITY LIBRARY

1701783455

16-BV

947279 26.5.99

2) 027.541 DAY

Typeset in 11/13pt Goudy Old Style and Humanist 521 by Library Association Publishing.
Printed and made in Great Britain by Bookcraft (Bath) Ltd, Midsomer Norton, Somerset.

CONTENTS

. . . it is possible to foresee that when the new home for it on St Pancras railway yard has finally been topped-off, it will be inhabited by a single and tolerably unified organism.

(Editorial, *New Library World*, **77** (907), January 1976, p. 4)

PREFACE

Twelve years ago, when preparing my first book on the British Library, a senior colleague remarked with some asperity that 'you cannot possibly write an entire book about just one library'. In the event, the difficulty was to compress all the Library's activities and services within the confines of a single volume. It soon became apparent that if the progress of the St Pancras project was to be adequately chronicled while, at the same time, recording the Library's role in the national library and information context, until it settled into its long planned twin-site operation, then at some point a second book would be required. And so *The British Library: a guide to its structure, publications, collections and services* (1988) was followed by *The New British Library* six years later. This present book carries the story to just beyond the Library's long-delayed but triumphant partial arrival at St Pancras. But if one book could be justified without too much effort, a second might appear barely tolerable, and a third might justly be regarded as extravagant or self-indulgent.

Of course the circumstances to a large extent exculpated the author from criticism on this score. The seemingly interminable saga of St Pancras stretched on and on, and it was not as if the British Library stood still, patiently waiting for its long nightmare to be relieved by a new dawn. Vibrant new policies, new structures and publications, new technology and, at last, a new building, interacted to the point where the British Library of 1998 bears little resemblance to the British Library of ten years earlier. Hence this third book. In treatment and content it follows the pattern of the previous two in following the Library's fluctuating fortunes through the media of parliamentary enquiries and reports, policy documents, newspaper and journal articles, and material first printed in the Library's own newsletters, and attempting to present the information collected, with a comment or two, in a coherent and integrated narrative. Contrary to what has privately been suggested to me by professional colleagues, I have not sought to peddle the official British Library line. No doubt, when the time is ripe, the British Library will publish its own review of events, but this is not it.

ACKNOWLEDGEMENTS

I owe a debt of gratitude to numerous British Library staff who answered my frequent enquiries with invaluable documentation.

Dr Bart Smith not only put me on the mailing list for press releases, information sheets and *Annual reports*, but also without hesitation allowed me to reproduce *Facts and figures 1996/7*, whilst his colleague, Ken Shirreffs, was assiduous in ensuring that I should have an early sight of St Pancras related brochures.

David Beech, Head of Philatelic Collections, provided copies of journal articles and other material, so that I might make amends for my previous cursory account of his department.

Chris Clark gave valuable detail on the origins of the National Sound Archive's CADENSA system.

Michael Crump sketched in pencil a diagram of Reader Services and Collection Development's structure when confronted by importunate demands for information at a BLISS reception.

Arthur Cunningham cheerfully gave me permission to reproduce a table from the National Bibliographic Service's consultation paper, *The future of the National Bibliography*.

Richard Hill elucidated some of the finer distinctions between the responsibilities of the National Bibliographic Service and Acquisitions, Processing and Cataloguing when I was in serious danger of floundering.

Graham Jefcoate and John Draper dispelled my confusion as to the full extent of the Digital Library Programme.

Amanda King, Document Supply Centre's visit organizer, procured for me welcome documentation on the British Library's response to the Public Library Review.

Fiona McLean enlightened me on the Health Care Information Service; Marie-Laure Manigand swiftly sent copies of *International Music Connection* when requested; Richard Ranft responded to a message on his answerphone for a copy of *Wildlife Section Newsletter*; Simon Shaw stayed calm when responding to frequent telephone calls concerning the publication date of *Towards the Digital Library*; and Dr Susan Whitfield saw to it that I should have a complete file of *IDP News*.

I also took full advantage of the enlightened policy of the editors of almost 20 British Library newsletters of allowing material to be freely reproduced provided it was acknowledged.

To Jane Simister and her colleagues in the Manchester Metropolitan University Library interlibrary loans office a special debt is owed for the countless journal articles obtained for me with minimum fuss and maximum efficiency.

At Library Association Publishing, my editor, Helen Carley, possessed the happy knack of knowing exactly when to prod, when to listen and when to sympathize. The editorial team also kindly agreed once again to relax their normal citation and capitalization practices.

Alan Day

PART I

GENERAL

I

HISTORIC BOOK MOVE

Sunny intervals were forecast for the London region, Monday, 2 December 1996, but whatever the weather it was a bright morning for the British Library. The storm clouds which for too long had circled around Bloomsbury and St Pancras were at last breaking up and dispersing. After innumerable disappointments and delays, the biggest transfer of books the world had ever seen was under way as the first of 5600 vanloads departed from the British Museum's Bloomsbury site to their new home a short distance away. Although the St Pancras building would not be officially handed over before July 1997, the British Library was entering into possession of 96 Euston Road, an absolute bargain at £511 million. Of course there had been a little gazumping along the way, the basements were not always immune to flooding, the extensions to the North problematical, and if any rewiring needed to be done in the future it would cost a pretty penny, but it was a landmark, an auspicious occasion nevertheless.

The Library's Chief Executive, Dr Brian Lang, celebrated it by placing the first book, *The Oxford Book of English Traditional Verse*, on a deep basement shelf for the benefit of press photographers, although it was reliably reported the next day that this was hastily produced 'to replace a rather more obscure offering from the first crate' (Damian Whitworth, 'Book opens new chapter for library', *The Times*, 65751, 3 December 1996, p. 8). Whatever, there it was, blazoned across the front page of the *Guardian*.

To mark the occasion the Library came up with a few interesting facts:

1   Material to be moved includes 39 million patents, 12 million monographs and serials, 8 million stamps, 2 million maps and over 1 million sound recordings.

2   The total shelved stock to be moved would stretch from St Pancras in London to the Boston Spa site in West Yorkshire.

3   The removal vans will travel the equivalent of one journey around the world (over 24,000 miles) moving the stock from the British Museum site at Bloomsbury and about a dozen other smaller sites to the new building at St Pancras.

4   The largest item to be moved will be the Klenke Atlas which stands over 5 ft 9 in high and 3 ft 4in wide.

5   The smallest item to be moved will be a thumb-sized edition of the New Testament.

6   The historical treasures of the British Library such as the Magna Carta, Lindisfarne Gospels and the Gutenberg Bible will move from the Bloomsbury galleries to the purpose-built Treasures Gallery in the new building at St Pancras, where they will be on display to the public from Spring 1998.

7   Many of the treasures have not left the British Museum building site since it was founded in 1753. The King's Library, given to the nation by George IV, has been housed in the current gallery since 1828. ('Library Begins Biggest Book Move In History', *British Library News*, no. 208, November 1996, p. 1).

The whole move consumed 275,000 staff hours, engaged 35 full-time staff and directly involved 30 different contractors over a 30-month period. Humanities material was moved at an average of 300 linear metres a day, packed in crates, in sequential order, each crate holding approximately 90 cm of stock, roughly 27 items, lined with bubble plastic, then sealed for security reasons. These crates, meticulously ordered and controlled, using labels provided by the Library's Book Move Control System, were transported in small, unmarked, sealed vans. Meticulously planned, the scheduled occupation timetable for the new building allowed for the Library's House Management team to assume responsibility both for the cleaning and the security of the building, from the Department of National Heritage in January 1997. An integrated cataloguing system to support the Humanities, Rare Books and Music collections was initiated in January to anticipate the second stage of the move. At this point the cataloguing system to support Maps, Manuscripts and the Oriental and India Office Collections was in place. And then, in November 1997, the first Reading Room, for Humanities, opened, followed by a second, the Rare Books and Music Reading Room in March 1998. The exhibition galleries and the Library Bookshop opened to the public in April and in May the recorded sound service began. The Map Library and the OIOC reading rooms are scheduled to open in August, the Manuscripts reading room in January 1999 and, finally, the Science reading rooms in mid-1999..

Readers were informed of the scheduled timetable on an information sheet, *Moving to St Pancras*, dated November 1996, posted in the reading rooms. Besides giving key dates, the broad details of the proposed move sequence, and the special arrangements for rare books, there was also an assurance that the Library would contrive to keep services running normally during the relocation but, inevitably, the Book Delivery Service would be affected. A monthly bulletin from December onwards listed the pressmarks of the books to be removed for the current and two succeeding months. The closely integrated operation ensured that the period of unavailability of material from the date it became inaccessible would be no more than two to three weeks, although most of the material moved to St Pancras would still be available for consultation in the current reading rooms until the relevant reading room was opened in the new building.

By mid-February 1997 the contractors had moved 18 km (c. 500,000) of books of the general humanities stock and the target rate of 300 metres of books to be moved daily was comfortably being exceeded. A month later the daily rate had risen to 330 metres. Rare books, music, National Sound Archive stock, and philatelic material joined the exodus in July, by which time the move was three weeks ahead of schedule. Harrow Green, the contractors for the initial stage, were asked to continue for the second stage. As more and more stock was transferred, so the number of reading room requests for material now safely ensconced in the St Pancras basements had risen to 400 requests per day or 4000 book movements per week.

If the move from Bloomsbury to St Pancras was proceeding without a hitch, it was back to makeshift time on the first day at the Woolwich outhouse.

> Problems in the Blackwall Tunnel made the trip impossible for the vans
> . . . Not wishing to get behind schedule on the first day of the two-and-
> a-half year move, the BL resorted to the Woolwich ferry to bring its pre-
> cious cargo to the other side. ('Ferry funny incident', *Library Association
> Record*, **99** (2), February 1997, p. 61).

But nothing was allowed to mar the occasion, the bright day was not to be dimmed by minor irritations. A few vanloads had to switch routes; staff had displayed their resourcefulness, that was all. The British Library was on the march.

DRESS REHEARSAL

A full-scale dress rehearsal for the St Pancras move had taken place two years earlier when 25 km of material stored at Woolwich, in South London, was moved to purpose-built accommodation at the Library's northern site at Boston Spa. From July to September 1995, two articulated lorries ferried 450 crates full of books up the A1 in a five-hour journey every day. The move allowed the Library to try out its special new computer software, the Book Move Control System, developed to assist the move to St Pancras. This was used to notify staff exactly how and where the Woolwich stock should be shelved at Boston Spa.

'YOU ARE ALL VERY WELCOME'

The next milestone on the long journey to an integrated twin-site operation came on Monday, 24 November 1997 when, at 9.30 am precisely, the Chief Executive opened the central doors of the St Pancras building to 60 or so expectant readers and researchers with the words 'You are all very welcome.' To excited staff applause, readers filed in somewhat sheepishly and made their way by lift to the two Humanities Reading Rooms.

Press coverage of the big event was muted. The *Daily Telegraph* editorial, 'Overdue Books', resurrected all the time-honoured adverse criticism and recalled the inefficiencies and costs of its construction before advocating that the Library should free itself from future mismanagement by becoming financially independent through a mixture of sponsorship and charging readers.

> Substantial funds could be raised by levying charges on the many patent agents and other commercial users of the library as well as on individuals. The consequences are plainly visible in the bricks and mortar of the building. It cannot now be right to administer the library on such an outdated principle. (*Daily Telegraph*, 44302, 24 November 1997, p. 21).

'New Day Of The Book', *The Times*, 66055, 24 November 1997, p. 23 was less grudging and more forward-looking. Conceding that the new Library could not compete with the Round Reading Room's legends and romance, it pronounced it as rather 'a modern workshop of the book . . . The first readers today will find themselves in a 21st-century laboratory . . . efficient as well as beautiful.' That the laboratory could deliver is indicated by the fact that 2000 books were issued to readers within the first two hours of opening, as Erica Wagner reported in 'Readers' acclaim speaks volumes', *The Times*, 66056, 25 November 1997, p. 10.

> A few taps on the keyboard and the computer ordered my book. It was 11 am. At 11.40 the little light on my desk told me to collect my book . . . It did seem that the new British Library had met its first invasion of readers with order, efficiency and books on demand.

2

THE WASTED YEARS

It had not always been like that of course. Publication of the 1990 National Audit Office report, *New Building for the British Library*, by no means signalled the end of the Library's trials and tribulations at St Pancras. Over the next three years what could go wrong inevitably did, with horrendous implications in terms of time and money for the construction of the new library. One by one problems surfaced. In May 1991 tests on the prototype mechanical mobile shelving system indicated that books were creeping on the shelves; further tests over a three-month period uncovered more serious problems with the driving mechanism jamming the shelves and rendering them inoperative. In addition paintwork on the shelves and uprights was judged not to be of the quality expected, while in August 50 faulty cogs had to be replaced after an inspection. Worse was to follow. Inspections of the above-ceiling voids in the basements revealed ductwork and air-conditioning faults.

According to the Regular Readers Group, always stern critics of the St Pancras project, water penetrated the basements following heavy rain, entering map cabinets and the book-handling machinery in July 1992. Eighteen months later 2000 miles of faulty wiring involving the plastic coating of the heating and lighting power cabling was brought to light during a routine inspection. Susannah Herbert, Arts Correspondent of the *Daily Telegraph*, informed her readers that

> the new problem – which has been exacerbated by blurred chains of command on site – is strongly reminiscent of the great shelves disaster of 1991–92 . . . officials at the Department of National Heritage [she continued] have commissioned a report from the consultants Kennedy and Donkin. But an interim report indicates that the problem may affect 80% of the wiring . . . The cost of replacing it has yet to be calculated, but is likely to run into millions of pounds.

An insider is quoted as explaining that

> as the cabling was drawn through the metal trays which carry it round
> the building, the insulation was stripped off here and there . . . Every
> time anyone finds a bit of bare wiring, they have to examine the rest of
> the cable in that area as well. It's a big issue because it affects the timing
> and it is now holding everything else up. It's sheer chaos.

He added that the building also faced difficulties with ageing mechanical
and electrical components. 'A lot of stuff is just sitting there getting
older – but it all needs to be renewed before we open' ('New British
Library hit by blunders over wiring', *Daily Telegraph*, no.43084, 30
December 1993, p. 2).

Problems with the water sprinkling fire prevention system were
revealed in January.

> Sections of the galvanised steel pipework supplying water to the build-
> ings' 2000 sprinkler heads, which would protect the library's collection
> of 11 million books, are prone to internal condensation. Consultants
> fear that in the long term this could cause corrosion in the pipes (James
> Macneil, 'Sprinkler fears hit library', *Builder*, **259** (7827), 21 January
> 1994, p. 12).

Susannah Herbert reported that Robert Dennis, for the contractors, estimated that adjustments would cost at least £250,000 and take six
months. 'The ceilings are finished but they will have to be taken down
again. It doesn't just involve us, it will involve the ceiling contractor and
the lighting contractor.' She quoted Brian Lake, of the Regular Readers
Group, never far away when another St Pancras disaster was reported,
who remarked that 'the library will never be fit for its intended purpose.
It's like the Tower of Babel – it seems it will never be finished.' ('British
Library faces new delay over sprinklers', *Daily Telegraph*, 43099, 17
January 1994, p. 3).

A stern editorial called for changes in the project's management:

> This sorry tale is unlikely to end well. Even the project's on-site man-
> agers admit they have no idea how much the building will cost or when
> it will be ready for occupation. The Regular Readers Group wants an
> independent review of this blighted project. It is surely right. Many of
> the problems on site have been caused by an unwillingness to account
> for past errors. None of those in charge of the building has resigned or

even offered to do so. They prefer to treat each fresh problem as a freak of fortune. These difficulties stem from complacency and a deep-seated failure of leadership. It may be far too late to start again, but there is still time for the Heritage Department to reconsider its approach. A public audit of errors to date would be an ideal start ('Bringing To Book', *Daily Telegraph*, 43099, 17 January 1994, p. 6).

These were portentous words.

REGULAR READERS GROUP

Against this sort of background the Regular Readers Group was quick to exploit the rising anger and frustration. It prepared a second edition of its 36-page document, *The Great British Library Disaster*, first issued in the autumn of 1993, addressed to the Prime Minister, the Chancellor of the Exchequer, the Secretary of State for National Heritage, the Chairman of the British Library Board, and the readers and staff of the British Library, to coincide with the day appointed for a meeting of the House of Commons National Heritage Committee to inquire into the progress of the St Pancras project. Still obsessed with the library's evacuation from the Round Reading Room, and seemingly possessed by an inability, later mirrored by the Select Committee, to view the British Library as anything more than the old British Museum Library, the aims of its report were fivefold:

1   to avert disaster in the National Library;
2   to review the present state of the British Library, including current management policies, and the development of the new buildings at St Pancras;
3   to urge the Government to publish results of the study of the development at St Pancras commissioned by David Mellor, and to consider carefully current library strategy in relation to policy changes outlined in the strategic review, the current position at St Pancras, and the autumn budget;
4   to make specific proposals: that there should be a refocusing on the basic functions of the Library – making available for study primary source materials, books and manuscripts, free of charge – rather than the redefined aim of the recent Review – 'the capture and storage and transmission of electronic documents' – for a fee;

5 and to show that Bloomsbury facilities – the Reading Rooms and storage – should be retained by the BL in tandem with St Pancras, because the new building will be full of books as soon as it is opened.

Following an introductory review of the St Pancras project – a diary of events, March 1991–June 1994, a tale of misfortune, woe and calamity, based on attributed press sources and its own response to the British Library's Third Strategic Plan – the Regular Readers Group called for a clear statement on the recurring annual costs of running St Pancras; for a thorough reappraisal of the mobile book shelving system which it claimed to be unsuitable for frequent use; for detailed reports on the failings of the mechanical and electrical systems, their short life expectancy, the extent of the remedial work needed, and the estimated costs of their replacement every 20 years. St Pancras should be the main storage depot for the Bloomsbury reading rooms. (This, of course, would lead to the absurdity of spending up to £450 million on a storage outhouse!)

Sooner or later the National Heritage Committee, charged with the task of scrutinizing the expenditure, administration and policy of the Department of National Heritage and other public bodies, was bound to turn its attention to the St Pancras project. So persistent had the Regular Readers Group been in advocating the retention of the Round Reading Room in the British Museum and opposing the relocation to St Pancras that it was invited, along with the British Library, and the Department of National Heritage, to submit a memorandum, attend and give evidence.

PRESS DISCLOSURES

Two ominous press reports which appeared on the fateful day of reckoning reinforced the atmosphere of doom and gloom. Chris Blackhurst and Sailesh Ramakrishnan's 'Library's trilogy of delay, bills and blame' (*The Independent* 30 June 1994, p. 3) claimed that what should have been the most prestigious new building in Britain this century had become bogged down in delay, cost over-runs and accusations of mismanagement and fraud, so much so that the National Audit Office had decided to launch a second inquiry within four years.

> The plan is beset with problems: too many chiefs; blurred reporting lines; a contract that is open-ended and based on a 'cost plus' formula – whatever it costs to build the contractors receive, plus their agreed mar-

gin . . . One sub-contractor in his twenties had made so much money from the project – from supplying at any one time, up to 250 electricians and engineers – that he boasts of being able to retire. He is reckoned to have made over £500,000 in two years from the Library.

The principal building constructor, the design team, and Library staff

oversee rafts of sub-contractors including construction giants and also one-man band operators. Determining who is responsible for final decisions is one of the problems investigators would face . . . In all, 27 building firms are profiting from the library, employing between them 1,000 people on the project. Part of that small army is devoted to 'quality assurance' – a euphemism, claim insiders, for delaying the project as long as possible . . . In most large-scale projects only 10 per cent of service fittings are checked – yet at the British Library it is 100 per cent, and conducted not only by Laing's quality assurance department but by teams from SVM, other companies and the Property Services Agency. One former site worker said the only reason he could see for such a tough regime was the desire to keep the project going for as long as possible. He blamed civil servants whose jobs depend on the project as much as private sector workers.

Even allowing for journalistic hyperbole, incipient sensationalism, and reliance on anonymous sources of uncertain authority, this was a damning indictment. Blackhurst and Ramakrishnan continued to distinguish eight examples of unrestrained extravagance: every fitting inside phase one of the building was checked and replaced; ceramic tiles were brought down because one was out of line – 'by the width of a five pence piece', said a site engineer; hand-made bricks also received the same treatment; miles of electrical cables were ripped out because their outer castings were the wrong colour – even though they would eventually be housed in boxes and not be seen by anyone; a hundred cabling boxes costing £1000 each were bought, found to be unnecessary and were eventually tucked away under the floorboards; a ceiling was ordered to be remade after a quality checker noticed a piece of insulation tape hanging down; the £400,000 corridor linking the book loading bay and the library was replaced because the mortar did not exactly equal the design specification; and a total of 27,000 slates were ordered for the roof and rejected because the quality control team was not happy with their natural markings – this meant sieving through another 100,000 slates!

Secrecy and the suppression of facts, two perennially favourite

Independent targets, were also evident.

> Establishing the scale of the disaster is difficult because the exact progress of the library remains a closely guarded secret. Its detailed plans and specifications are too commercially confidential to be shown to taxpayers according to the department.

Two reports had been suppressed,

> building firms refused to discuss their work, saying they had signed confidentiality clauses and needed government permission. When the Independent attempted to talk to a site manager he agreed to a meeting but failed to appear. His telephone number was suddenly disconnected.

Susannah Herbert's 'British Library Costs to Pass £450 Million Mark' (*Daily Telegraph*, 43240, 30 June 1994, p. 11) concentrated on the costs of the government's single most expensive post-war building project, 'now officially out of control on both timetable and cost', quoting a Department of National Heritage spokesman as saying, 'as of today we have spent £336 million and committed £439 million of the £450 million budget. There will certainly be an overshoot, though we cannot say how big it will be.' However,

> the inquiry is not expected to uncover much: largely because the people most closely involved with the site will not be required to answer questions. This week, an insider said: 'Nobody is facing the issues. The Heritage department is weak and will not stand up to the library's people, while the library's people are holding everything up by insisting on perfection whatever the price in time or money. Meanwhile the contractors are sitting back and coining it. No one is in control.

Clearly, it was not an auspicious backdrop to the Select Committee's proceedings that morning.

NATIONAL HERITAGE COMMITTEE

First to appear before the Select Committee, chaired by Mr Gerald Kaufman, was the Regular Readers Group. Its memorandum was stark and uncompromising and was formulated on the perception that major changes had taken place in the way the British Library's senior staff regarded the public institution in its charge.

Instead of defending one of the centres of excellence in our culture, it seems that 'The Library as Profit Centre' is more of a driving force. Instead of fighting to maintain basic services – collecting and preserving the written and printed word, and making that collection freely available for scholars – there has been a shift of emphasis towards digitization, the capture, storage and transmission of electronic documents, which can be sold for a fee.

This has created a new situation with decisions to be made that cannot be left entirely to the British Library management. Guidance from Parliament on new policy decisions was essential. The Group outlined its own proposals.

The St Pancras delays might just be a simple matter of frustration if the end result was going to be magnificent. We all know this cannot be the case because of the building's truncated size and consequent shortage of space for books and Readers, the practical problems resulting from the length of time that project has taken, poor management, outdated technology and the planned split-site operation with Yorkshire. St Pancras has gone desperately wrong . . . The British Library will continue to need outhousing, but Boston Spa is not a sensible long-term option and should not be pursued just because someone made a mistake about property prices in the late 1980s. Use the storage at St Pancras as soon as practicable. Move in the post-1850 books, which are most vulnerable. Maximize the storage potential of St Pancras – see it as an outhouse, while holding on to Bloomsbury for its Reading Rooms and substantial storage. Instead of allowing standards of both service and maintenance at Bloomsbury to fall, argue for the mere peppercorns (cf. St Pancras costs) on upgrading storage areas and introducing air-conditioning. The British Library will then have perfectly adequate storage for its pre-1850 collections for many years to come. This approach is workable and pragmatic. The British Library and the government cannot continue to defend the indefensible, or claim magnificence for the second-rate and uncompleted.

With this farrago of nonsense out of the way, Mr Brian Lake, Secretary of the Regular Readers Group, touched upon the possibility of on-site corruption:

The open ended way in which phase one has been built has led to a massive waste of public money. That is still going on in an environment which, ideal or not for books, is one in which corruption could flourish and the project become literally endless. Certain component parts of the building seem to be in a constant state of removal, renovation or replacement and someone is having to pay.

Asked to enlarge on this, and on comments in the *Independent*, he could only refer to 'at least the possibility of self-interest among the people who are involved on the site to continue work on the site because they will continue to have an income from it'. Additionally, the Group had received 'various pieces of paper from people who work on the site which tie together'. Asked for concrete evidence, he offered none. It was not the bombshell which might have been anticipated.

Altogether it was not a propitious occasion for the Group, not one of its better days. No doubt to its chagrin, much of its time was diverted into the debate whether readers should be charged for access to the British Library, until the Chairman intervened to allow the discussion to move forward. In reply to some hard questioning on the wisdom of retaining a conservationally unsuitable environment at the British Museum, and would it not waste still more money to go into reverse, and put it all into improving the Museum's atmospheric conditions, all that the Group could dredge up was a plea to look at it as a possibility at least in the short to medium term.

Some down-to-earth questioning on how representative the Regular Readers Group was in terms of numbers of readers elicited that there were 600 members, 300 of whom had arrived *en bloc* from the London Archive Users Forum. As to the total number of registered readers to the British Library's Bloomsbury collection, the Group could not be absolutely sure, although the number was increasing all the time. The Chairman pithily summed up: 'What they are is like members of most political parties – a collection of busybodies and I do not say that in a pejorative way!' And with that they had to be content.

Next in was the British Library team which lined up with Sir Anthony Kenny (Chairman, The British Library Board), Dr Brian Lang (Chief Executive), and Mr Mike Smethurst (Director General London Services). Their pre-submitted memorandum was predictably comprehensive in scope, with no pretensions to modesty, and left the Select Committee in no doubt that it was now taking evidence from the professionals. In turn, the British Library's role as the national library, its collections and services were enumerated: the current pattern of its London operations; the new building at St Pancras which 'will enable the Library to provide a faster and more efficient service to readers both by the concentration of material on one site and the installation of a mechanical book handling system and electronic book requesting'. The intention was that 80 per cent of material held on site would be delivered to readers within 30 minutes of request. Readers would also enjoy the use of online catalogues including electronic access to the world's major databases.

Emphasizing that there could be no turning back at this late stage, that the planned relocation was irreversible, the Library pointed out that it would release 40 per cent of the total space on the British Museum site at Bloomsbury and that the Museum's trustees were maturing plans to reunite their collections under one roof and to undertake long-needed reorganization and refurbishment of the exhibition galleries, student rooms, public areas and visitor services.

The Library's projects were outlined after the Committee was reminded that it was the Department of National Heritage that was responsible for the construction of the St Pancras building, whereas the Library was accountable only for the use of its grant-in-aid for its own St Pancras operational planning, occupation and information systems. Operational planning was concerned with policy, decision-making, and service provision during and after the move to St Pancras; the Occupation Project's objectives were to plan the occupancy, to effect the move of stock, staff and equipment, to meet the operational and organizational targets, involving the relocation of 1200 staff, 12 million volumes, and the establishment of 70 operational units. Three major automation projects were being undertaken in preparation for occupying and operating at St Pancras: a Reader Admission System for issuing reader passes and for controlling access to different parts of the building; an Online Catalogue to the Library's main collections on site for which no previous knowledge of computers or online catalogues was required; and an Automated Book Request System to request materials from the basement stores.

Other topics touched upon were the consequences of the delays in construction, causing the Library much uncertainty and frustration; meeting the Library's needs in the light of only a modest increase of 130 readers' desks and of the need to retain the land to the north of the site for the Library Conservation Bindery, various photographic processing units and developments for the National Sound Archive. Finally, the memorandum firmly closed the lid on speculation that the Library should retain reader and storage accommodation in the British Museum, quoting the Minister of Arts 1991 statement that 'there can be no question of the British Library continuing to use the Round Reading Room or other major areas of the British Museum building after 1996'.

An equally strong opening statement underlined the Library's responsibilities and clarified the relationships between the British Library, the British Museum and the Department of National Heritage. The Select Committee's initial line of questioning was directed towards the St Pancras building's capacity about which doubts had already been expressed. Surely, the Committee argued, after spending hundreds of millions of pounds, 'the country ought to have a National Library which accommodates the books of the National Library', which should not be forced to provide alternative accommodation at Boston Spa which 'when last heard of was 200 miles away from London?' Explanations that with eight kilometres of books being added every year the building was bound to be full within a very short period – and that, in any case, it made economic and operational sense to store the most valuable and heavily used books at St Pancras and material less in demand at Boston Spa – appeared to fall on deaf ears.

'If we are going to have a huge quantity of books . . . which are going to be at Boston Spa, you are not going to be able to fulfil your desideratum of delivering every book that anyone might want within twenty minutes,' the Committee's chairman persisted. 'Would it not be better,' he continued, 'if the Library had its whole collection of books, as distinct from newspapers and . . . ?'

'Yes, it would indeed,' interjected Sir Anthony Kenny.

'So in fact you are not getting a satisfactory deal,' the Chairman remarked, satisfied at establishing the point he had been striving for. 'What you are having, in getting a great new building, provided at vast and unquantifiable cost, is yet another site with which you are going to have to make do rather than which will fulfil what is appropriate?'

Questioning moved on to the possibility of corruption. Mr Jim Callaghan was perturbed:

> We have been told that this building could have been completed in four years and we are 15 years on. Surely, there is something wrong? The amount of money that has been spent on it would suggest there is something wrong. Is it not time that we had an independent inquiry into the amount of money and the time it has taken to put this building into its present condition?

If it knew what was wrong, the Library was not telling, and yet another inquiry would have had little appeal at this stage, but it welcomed the opportunity of nailing the canard that it was the prime suspect for extravagance and wasting time.

> We are obviously very interested in the quality of the product which is delivered to us at the end of the day. In the article from the *Independent* . . . it was suggested that some of the delay could be blamed on the British Library for being excessively perfectionist in its demands. I would like to categorically deny that and I can also say that the Department itself is on record as agreeing that the Library has not been excessively perfectionist. We have been very anxious to make sure that the product we eventually receive is safe, is healthy, is operable and is maintainable within likely levels of grant in aid. (Sir Anthony Kenny).

How far the Library participated in drawing up the original specification of the building project was put under close scrutiny. This, of course, was in the distant past but the Committee showed a measure of disbelief that the Library effectively distanced itself from the management of the project in 1976/77, in 1982 and in 1985. Suspicious of the constant plea of *mea non culpa* (it wasn't me, guv) Mr Michael Fabricant strove, with some energetic and determined questioning, to establish what was the ongoing involvement of the Library with the Property Services Agency and the Department of National Heritage in actually changing the specification over the previous 15 years.

Eventually the Chief Executive revealed that what happened in 1982 was that the Library 'described in broad terms what it wished to provide from a new building. They supplied a very long list of requirements which went to several thousand which was turned into a specification by the PSA', but added that he had never actually seen the specification. In the event Fabricant had to be satisfied that

> in no way has any input from the Library itself contributed to any delays or contributed to any cost overrun because you have not varied a great deal from the original specification which you may or may not have contributed to in the original design of the Library.

Sir John Gorst again raised the question of free access especially in the case of works of entertainment but the Library held the line that, while 27% of its income was generated from priced services, great importance was attached to maintaining free access to the basic book service. At the end Sir Anthony Kenny was forced to repeat his denials that the Library was responsible for holding up the construction project by insisting on perfection at no matter what cost in time and money. It had been a full and frank exchange but its value was hard to determine. A discussion between underbriefed MPs, to some extent responding to scare headlines in the press, and experienced and knowledgeable managers and administrators, was bound to sail perilously close to cross-purposed stalemate.

Represented by the Secretary of State, Peter Brooke, and Miss Margaret O'Mara, Head, Libraries, Galleries and Museums' Group, the Department of National Heritage was the third body to give evidence. Its submitted memorandum rehearsed the establishment of the British Library, and reviewed its responsibilities, the building project, the Government's responsibility for its construction, the various proposed opening dates, and the reasons why these failed to materialize, the project's management, the project costs, and ended with an annex giving annual and cumulative cost figures. Its conclusion was that

> The building project is extremely large and complex and, over the years has faced a number of significant problems. As a newly formed department, DNH has taken a number of steps to identify problem areas, to find cost effective solutions . . . and to introduce a management regime which [provided] effective communication and which sets out responsibilities and accountabilities clearly. We believe that we have done as much as we can to uncover the full extent of the problems and are well on the way to finding and implementing technical solutions . . . The liability for the cost of implementing the solutions still needs to be resolved. We are confident that, when the building is complete it will be a fitting place for the national library and its priceless collections and will enable the BL to provide an excellent and cost effective service to its users.

Dominating the examination of the Department of National Heritage team was the question of cost. Some confusion on the part of the Select Committee members is understandable when faced with the Secretary of State's explanation that

> the commitments that have so far been entered into are £439 million. We have authority from the Treasury to go above £450 million prior to the exercise of claims and counter claims. The basic figure has to come out underneath £450 million.

Clearly puzzled and perplexed, the Committee's chairman endeavoured to clarify matters: 'If you have authority to exceed £450 million and if you do exceed £450 million, then how do you come out at £450 million and no more?' His question deserved a less opaque answer than:

> The final figure on the building, when all the accounts are in, has to be below £450 million but we have authority from the Treasury because of the nature of the difficulties into which we have come in certain technical capacities, when there is recognition there will be a subsequent exercise of claim recognised by everybody involved in the process, that the consequences of those subsequent claims will reduce the total cost below £450 million.

Around that the discussion flowed without moving much further forward.

Mr Jim Callaghan attempted to skewer the Secretary of State on the question of the long, dismal history of government funding, cuts, compromises, delay, splitting the project into stages, building work being forced on to a stop-go basis, successive Chancellors of the Exchequer and Treasury Secretaries constantly attempting to scupper the whole project, which culminated in an exchange of 'the original wonder library plans for the mini-library which is now being built'. Quoting David Mellor, a former Secretary of State, as describing the project as 'a wretched fiasco, £450 million of public money on a building nobody wants and which may never be completed. I was all for mothballing the bloody thing while they sorted it out. Who is going to be made accountable for all this? On any view it is a scandal', Callaghan asked Peter Brooke outright, 'is it a scandal and who is responsible?' But, sadly, this awesome question elicited nothing more than a reference to the 1990 National Audit Office report and a reluctant admission that, with hindsight, 'the drip feeding of the contract during the 1980s did constitute part of the problem'.

Dave Parker's 'The Plot Thickens' (*New Civil Engineer*, 14 July 1994, p. 10) provided an instructive balance to the question of too pernickety checking by quality control inspectors, and to the possibility of corruption, both matters which had exercised the Heritage Committee.

> Expecting the highest possible standards for the buildings distinctive facing brickwork is defensible, contractors will grudgingly acknowledge. But applying the same degree of expectation to such short-lived items as

the air conditioning, or even the internal paintwork, is very different. It seems every contractor has a fund of stories about minor, barely visible defects causing whole sections of work to be rejected. [He continued], some outsiders find corruption a more likely explanation. . . A sophisticated snagging system was installed in 1992 which reduces the risk of traditional 'arrangements' between inspectors and workers. What is known is that the 200,000 plus deficits now registered in the snagging computer's memory are largely minor 'scratches, smears and spots', to quote one bemused insider.

NATIONAL HERITAGE COMMITTEE REPORT

Venting parliamentary outrage at the whole sorry episode, the National Heritage Committee Fifth Report, *The British Library. Together with the Proceedings of the Committee and Minutes of Evidence*, published by HMSO, 20 July 1994, was prefaced in candid and outspoken terms:

1   The saga of the new British Library is a sorry story. What governments (of both main parties) set out to provide was a suitable headquarters for one of the greatest libraries in the world. It should have been an example to the world of how a great project can be achieved at acceptable cost, can be appropriate for its purpose, and can moreover be an adornment to the capital city in which it is situated.

2   Instead, more than sixteen years after the project was launched and twelve years after construction was started, there sprawls next to St Pancras station a messy building site in which there lurks an edifice that resembles a Babylonian ziggurat seen through a fun-fair distorting mirror.

3   No-one – Ministers, library staff, building contractors, anyone at all – has more than the faintest idea when the building will be completed, when it will open for use, or how much it will cost. What is certain is that, unlike the sublimely beautiful British Museum reading room, which it is intended to supplant, the new building's interior will be at best clinically utilitarian and at worst actively unattractive. It will not be big enough to house the books the British Library already possesses, let alone those it is certain to acquire. It will not accommodate many more readers than the present premises in Bloomsbury.

4   The Committee already knew the rough outline of this shambles when it decided to conduct its enquiry; that, indeed, was why it

decided on an inquiry. But, until it had taken evidence and seen the site for itself, the Committee has no true idea of just what a shambles the story of the British Library has turned out to be.

The Committee made three recommendations. As facilities in the new building seemed unlikely to meet public demand, the Committee was of the opinion that the British Library should not evacuate the Round Reading Room, 'undoubtedly one of the most beautiful reading rooms in the world', which was 'an aesthetic pleasure just to walk in. It also has a rich history which ought not to be wantonly discarded.' Accordingly, the Committee strongly recommended that it *should be retained in perpetuity as a public reading room that is an integral part of the British Library*. Secondly, the Committee agreed with the Library that its planned innovative Multimedia Centre should not be jeopardized by the disposal of the land to the north of the St Pancras site, recommending the Government to

> retain that land at least until the British Library has been operating from its new site for several years so as to allow its future needs to be accurately assessed. Should the case for future development be established, the Committee further recommends that the land be retained for the British Library's future use even if there are insufficient funds available at that time for its development.

But the Committee was not at all sure that the problems of the new British Library could be eased by mere panaceas. What was needed was a full public inquiry, chaired by a former Ombudsman, to establish whether there had been maladministration and incompetence. It should also seek answers to a number of urgent questions, *viz.*

> Who approved the design? What were the costs quoted? What allowances were made for cost increases to allow for inflation? What control was kept of the progress of the building in terms of the timescale and of costs? How was the money provided, and to what extent did this contribute to the increase in costs and the length of construction? What continuing consideration did the Government give to the suitability of the building for its intended use? Responsibility for the building was passed from one department to another over the years. Was there ever anyone in specific charge? To what extent can this continual transfer of responsibility be blamed for the project's failings? What provision is being made for the books of the future and where are they going to be

stored? To underline the urgency of the situation, the inquiry should report within three months!

What a veritable curate's egg of a report this was. To suggest that the Round Reading Room should be retained was a nonsense: the British Library had made it abundantly clear that it had no interest in providing duplicate and therefore expensive services on two nearby sites while the British Museum was nurturing its own plans. It must charitably be classed as an aberration. The National Heritage Committee's chairman, Gerald Kaufman, made his position clear three days after the Report was published:

> That the Reading Room is beautiful, that it is aesthetically captivating, that it could be argued to have a soul, does not seem to enter into the British Library's pragmatic considerations . . . modern technology, as it too often replaces lovely libraries with utilitarian storehouses, is not necessarily doing so with the efficiency that is claimed as justification . . . The handsome catalogues in the British Museum library, which adorned every photograph of the Reading Room, have long been discontinued. Now readers wanting to consult an index have to jostle for access to insufficient microfiche machines . . . Books and libraries are a trust which we hand on to the future. We must not impoverish future learning and research for the sake of fleeting efficiency, which may not even be efficient ('Read the riot act at the British Library', *The Times*, no. 65014, 23 July 1994, p. 14).

By contrast, the recommendation that the spare land should not be sold off was far-sighted and eminently sensible; the British Library had long earmarked this site as the location for its future Conservation Bindery and for new premises for the National Sound Archive. As for the third recommendation, the public inquiry to report within three months, this was worthy, commendable, ambitious and totally unrealistic. It was inconceivable that the Government would relish an expensive public inquiry into a project which more or less had to be completed to avoid even more embarrassment. No doubt answers to the questions proposed by the Heritage Committee would have proved of immense public interest, but the Government may have decided that it would be more convenient to leave such questions to historians in the distant future.

But after all the Heritage Committee's sound and fury it exercised no long-term influence or effect. The Government's response, *British Library St Pancras* (Cm 2709), a six-page White Paper, published in November

1994, rejected all three recommendations. First,

> the Government does not accept that the benefits of access to the Round Reading Room as an undoubted part of the nation's history and architectural heritage should necessarily be confined in future to those who need to use the Library's collections (located, as these will be, elsewhere). Those readers will be better served in the new St Pancras building.

(a masterly dismissal in the best tradition of the Civil Service). Second,

> when the British Library presents its final proposals for further development on the site, they, and the assessment of the Library's needs embodied in them, will nevertheless be carefully considered. The Government will obviously need to pay regard to the income foregone from delaying the sale of the land, given the very substantial public expenditure already undertaken on the rest of the project, and will also need to take full account of the public expenditure implications to any proposals involving further public investment in extending the Library's estate at St Pancras

(in other words, the Government was frit of watching yet more colossal sums disappearing from view and sinking into the porous clay at St Pancras).

Third,

> the Government does not agree that there is a case for a public inquiry . . . The Committee will be aware that the NAO is currently undertaking a further investigation of the project, and many of the questions which it suggests as issues for the inquiry are one which the NAO examined in an earlier study

(so everyone could look forward to the next gripping instalment). The White Paper also revealed that the cost of delays and remedial work had forced a revision of the budget to £496 million. The faulty cabling would be protected by automatic fire switches; the sprinkler system would be converted from a pre-action dry system to a less complex and more reliable wet one; and a fire barrier would provide high-level protection.

PRESS REACTION

In the mean time the Press made hay with the *Report*'s headline-catching preface. Dalya Alberge's 'British Library saga a shambles, says MP's report' (*The Times*, no. 65012, 21 July 1994, p. 7) and Anthony Doran's 'MP's throw the book at British Library fiasco' (*Daily Mail*, no. 30512, 21 July 1994, p. 18) are two examples. But the most thoughtful appraisal was unquestionably James Buchan's gloriously illustrated article, 'The Library Fiasco' (*Independent on Sunday*, 24 July 1994, Sunday Review, pp. 4–7). Peering deep into the Library's psyche, avoiding all semblance of sensationalism, Buchan contrives to analyse the St Pancras débâcle within its historical, political and technological context.

After a generation of effort, and with the total capital expenditure nearing half a billion pounds, the completion of the new library was still out of sight. In the mean time,

> the very basis of knowledge – its preservation and transmission through systems of moveable type invented by Gutenberg and others in the 15th century – has cracked under the assault of electronic processes . . . in the new world, people will no doubt read text, but on personal computers linked to highways of information.

For them the heart of the library is not St Pancras 'but a dreary set of warehouses at a disused ordnance factory at Boston Spa, where the library earns £18 million a year photocopying articles from learned journals for academics and business people from Cuernavaca to Seoul'. They would argue that the solution to the Library's problems is to convert its collection into digital form. But even this drastic step is a chimera: the Library estimates it would cost £12 billion and this money would have to be spent again and again, reformatting the text to accommodate advancing technology.

On the political side Buchan is dismissive of 'Thatcherite philistinism and Treasury penny-pinching, things best forgotten', outlining the depressing sequence of events, from the purchase of a 12.5 acre derelict London & Midland Railway goods yard to the west of St Pancras Station, to the fragmenting of the original blueprint, and the end of the Library's dream of housing all its collections in perfect atmospheric conditions at a single location. 'The delays and extra costs are largely the fault of the Government, or rather the ideological chaos which was the British public administration in the Thatcher years' when 'the largest public building attempted this century, with its complex and expensive plant designed to protect the books for another couple, was shuffled between powerless and unstable administrative entities'. Crucially to blame was the political decision to build the new library by instalments.

'Because nobody knew what was actually going to be built, or when, it was not possible to put out work for tender at fixed prices and penalties and many of the hundreds of contractors on site were working on only vaguely defined packages, with every temptation to spin the work out.' At the very least, as one government official put it, 'the nature of the contractual arrangements encouraged a motivation of delay'. For the architect, Colin St John Wilson, Buchan had considerable sympathy. His only mistake, if he made one, 'was to design a building of free asymmetries, expected to grow over time, rather than a Classical building; not because of any superiority of the Classical style, but because a Classical building can't be cut in half'.

In summary, St Pancras has been a dual catastrophe for the British Library. 'First, it has discredited the library in the eyes of government and public for the best part of a generation' and, secondly, the building 'will cost perhaps three times as much to light, heat, operate, air-condition and guard as the iron reading-room and other stores it will vacate: perhaps £20m a year, according to one contractor.' Yet,

> curiously, it has been a blessing as well as a curse. For it has forced the library and its users (though not, it appears, the Government) to think hard about what the whole thing is for. What is clear is that the library still believes it is a public good, that should be free at the point of use . . . anything fancier, such as home delivery of information, should be paid for. Above all, the practice of research, though it leaves no audit trail that you can follow and often leads nowhere but the grave, is seen as a worthwhile activity.

In the end,

> as more and more people have electronic access to the collection, its almost unbelievable splendour . . . will endear it to the Government and public, who'll pay for it. The library, under fire from two directions, will be vindicated in pursuing its middle course.

It was an informed, level-headed and fluent piece of journalism.

PERIOD OF CALM

For a short while the British Library enjoyed a period of relative calm following the announcement in the November 1994 White Paper that the project budget had been revised upward to £496 million. Published the next day, Sir Anthony Kenny's widely distributed 26 page pamphlet, *The British Library and The St Pancras Building*, provided a long-needed authoritative summary of the entire St Pancras project, correcting the widely held misconception that the alarming escalation of costs and delays on site had been due to ineptness and incompetence of the British Library Board and senior management, and explaining why the move to St Pancras was essential for the library to provide the highest possible level of service to its readers, rather than to pander to the desire of over-zealous library technocrats impatient to play with their computerized and digitalized electronic marvels. The pamphlet was in two parts.

In the first, the Chairman relates the complex history of the St Pancras project which began in the 1960s when storage space at Bloomsbury began to run out and relocation became imperative in the years following the formation of the British Library in 1972. The various plans for the new library, the different stages and substages of its construction, the lack of constant supervision on site, and of an overall budget, the scaling down of the original plan, are all outlined with apparent ease. A schematic diagram of the St Pancras building clarifies just which parts comprised Phases 1AA, 1AB, 1B and 3A Reading Rooms in the original stages, or the current Phase 1A and completion phase. Next, the author attempted to put the project's escalating costs into some sort of convincing perspective, a difficult task when figures of hundreds of millions of pounds are being bandied about:

> the escalation in cost estimate from £116 million to £300 million was in fact less dramatic than it appeared . . . nearly £7 million was due to changes in VAT and building codes, £6 million was due to redefinements of the design . . . and some £2 million to increased staff costs . . . £6.5 million (after a misapportionment by PSA between sub-stages 1AA and 1AB) was spent on the employment of Laing Management. The total increase in the basic cost of phase 1A was some £22 million, an increase of 14.4% in real terms . . . By far the largest part of the increase in the estimate was due to inflation past and future: £60 million for inflation between 1979 and 1985 and £92.5 million built into the cash limits to allow for inflation (at 7% per annum) during the period up to the completion of the project.

Part 2, 'The present and the future', is equally absorbing. Sir Anthony begins with an identification of the friends and enemies of St Pancras.

He discerns the latter as forming two communities: the traditionalists and the futurists. Of the traditionalists, resisting all attempts to drag them from the reading room,

> some are single-minded admirers of its architecture. Others are lifelong researchers who feel their work patterns have become woven into the building. There is also the local commercial community which could lose custom if readers migrated northwards [and] those who have expressed aesthetic distaste for Colin St John Wilson's design.

He also looks closely at the original architect's brief: was it too ambitious? Will the scaled-down version meet the library's needs? His common-sense approach, as compared to shrill self-interest, and contrived wisdom, is refreshingly evident, nowhere more so than in his analysis of readers' seat numbers. The original plan would have provided 3440 seats, more than three times the total provision in the widely dispersed London reading rooms; the scaled-down version allows 1176, an increase of only 73. At the moment, taking into account the removal of Oriental Collections to the India Office Library, the plans allow for an increase of 11% over the current provision. Again, there is some slight indication of special pleading, as he remarks that the comparison is always drawn between the number of seats in the new library and the total number in British Library's present scattered London accommodation. He prefers to talk of more efficient use and the calculation that the seat occupancy will rise to 85% at St Pancras. That does not get over the fact that the original plans were much more ambitious. For all the scope that a single-site operation gives for more efficient use of the reader seats available, it is still easy for critics and dissenters to cry 'all that money for just 73 more seats'.

Well-ordered arguments are deployed for the futurists: even if, by the year 2000, hard-copy monographs are no longer published and all journals appear only in electronic form,

> it cannot be supposed that the human race will lose all interest in its intellectual history prior to the electronic age. There will still be readers who will want access to the volumes now held by the British Library for reading in Bloomsbury.

As for digitalized facsimiles replacing books,

> such a scenario is a triumph of technological hope over economic experience. The cost of scanning the eighteen million volumes of the British

Library would be quite prohibitive [and] even if we imagine this gigantic operation successfully completed, it would be the act of a barbarian then to destroy all the scanned volumes to be relieved of the need to store them. [In addition] given the rapid obsolescence of information technology, the electronic replicas once made would constantly need costly retranscription . . . old fashioned books may fade and decay, but the technology for human access to their contents . . . has not changed since the invention of spectacles.

Perhaps the hardest nut for the chairman to crack was to convince the die-hards why it is necessary to vacate their cherished reading room. He presented a stark choice: besides providing higher levels of service,

the proposal to keep pre-1850 books in Bloomsbury would mean that some of the most precious and vulnerable of the Library's collections would remain in the poor and deteriorating conditions of stacks where there is inadequate control over temperature, humidity and pollution. It would also have the regrettable effect of introducing an artificial date boundary between the early printed and modern book collection, thus creating exasperating problems for the many scholars who use older and recent materials at the same time.

As for the dual storage operation, with Boston Spa being used for storing little-used material, there could be little doubt that a single site in central London would be infinitely preferable, but its costs would be unreasonably extravagant for the taxpayer.

We estimate that the cost of storing a linear metre of books at St Pancras will be more than double the equivalent cost at Boston Spa. It is no longer a sensible policy for a national library to aim to place each of its acquisitions in a particular place on a particular shelf and leave it there in perpetuity. The most appropriate policy is to store those books most frequently used for reference as close as possible to the reading rooms, and to remove those that are rarely consulted – and in an archival library there will be many books which are consulted only once in twenty years – in safe and cheap storage at a distance.

The Library's main responsibilities, he concluded, are to preserve its historical collection, to continue to build the national printed archive, and to make its holdings available to present and future users. 'Only when it has moved to St Pancras will the library be able to provide a service worthy of a great national institution.'

At the turn of the year library planners could look forward to a less troubled period. If the Department of National Heritage's construction dates were met, and the building was handed over to the Library some time during 1996, the Library could see the possibility of offering reader services in its new library before the end of 1997. Following the Government's rejection of the Heritage Committee's recommendation of a public inquiry there was nothing to worry about on that score. The only blot on the Euston Road landscape was that the Library had still not secured the spare land to the north of the building's completion phase. But the British Library was never destined to experience more than a few weeks' uneasy peace.

In January 1995 it was announced that the Library had learned more about Union Railways' plans to develop St Pancras Station into an international rail terminus. In detail, these included a London terminus for the Channel Tunnel Rail Link; a new Thameslink station beneath Midland Road; maintained midland main-line services; additional capacity for Kent trains to the Rail Link; links to east and west coast main-line services; and enhanced interchange facilities with the Underground and other transport facilities. The likelihood was that some of the early engineering work would coincide with the Library's move to its new location. Discussions were reported to be underway with Union Railways to assess problems relating to possible disruption of the Library's massive transfer of books and with the opening of the new library to readers.

Following discussions with Camden Council, the Library petitioned Parliament, expressing its concerns about its proximity to the site, namely the use of land to the north during the construction period; continuity of access during construction works, to ensure that book moves, vehicle deliveries and pedestrians could use entrances on the Midland Road side of the library; traffic movement around the site; and issues such as dust, security and the provision of utilities. Thankfully, by the end of the year, the Library reached agreement with Union Railways on access arrangements during construction of the rail terminus. The maintenance of existing emergency and evacuation arrangements, the retention by the Library of some temporary accommodation on the land at the back of the building, and access for book moves and general deliveries, was now assured.

BUDGET DIFFICULTIES

Severe pressure on the Library's financial resources emerged after the announcement of the 1996–97 budget. Initial reaction was one of relief when the figures were known; the Library had fared as reasonably as could be expected after a national budget had traded tax concessions for cuts in public spending, its grant-in-aid had been fixed at £88.124 million, i.e. £3.334 million short of the bid figure. Although significant, this shortfall was not disastrous even at a time when the Library was having to shoulder the burden of substantial costs for maintaining the new building, but when the advance planning figures for the following two years were carefully scrutinized, an alarming gap opened up between the Library's bid and the planning figure, amounting to £30 million in the three-year period 1996/97–1998/99.

The full implications of the budget shortfall and the Library's 1996/97 business plan were underlined in a *Message from the Chief Executive, The British Library*, issued internally to all British Library staff, 27 March 1996, but not disseminated outside the Library. It was eventually printed in the House of Commons Committee of Public Accounts Second Report, *Progress in Completing the New British Library*, published in October. In deciding how to operate within the constricted figures the Library sought primarily to protect the interests of its users; minimize the damage to the scope and quality of the collections; protect investment in developments critical to its future; achieve a rapid and successful move to St Pancras; and focus on efficiencies rather than cuts in services. Specifically, the protected areas would include not only the St Pancras opening but also 'investment in the Library's new awareness and document supply service, the "digital library" developments, the new finance system and the Corporate Bibliographic Programme'. (This last refers to the replacement and rationalization of bibliographic systems.) The Library would also continue to invest for future growth by developing its site at Boston Spa.

But safeguarding priorities in some areas inevitably signified economies elsewhere and long- and short-term strategies were devised to conform to government funding levels. An annual reduction in staff numbers would be necessary to ensure that pay increases could be absorbed. By the end of the century some 200 posts would be lost principally by natural wastage but some redundancies would be unavoidable, although posts in revenue earning areas might possibly increase and new posts for St Pancras would also be required. Many of the redundancies would involve senior posts.

The rationalization and relocation of a small number of acquisition and processing posts from London to Boston Spa would also be necessary. In the short term, cuts in the acquisition budget, notably in the duplication of foreign serial titles, would mean that several thousand titles currently held at the Document Supply Centre and at the Science Reference and Information Service would be stocked at only one site. A cut of almost 50% would also be made in the funds allocated to the purchase of manuscripts with other significant reductions in the funds for report literature and monograph acquisition. Urgent preservation work and that requiring high levels of skill would be protected although approximately £1 million would be chopped off conservation work in the year. The operational budget for computing and telecommunications was to be reduced to fund only basic IT operations while the budgets of the National Sound Archive and Oriental and India Office Collections, where costs per use were higher than in other service areas, would also be pruned. Planned changes to the structure of the Research and Development Department, based on a review of its aims and operations, were hastened by a 13% reduction in its 1996–97 research budget.

NATIONAL AUDIT OFFICE

Advance warning that the National Audit Office second report would likely fuel the controversy that constantly hovered over the St Pancras building project surfaced in November 1995 when there was a brief flurry of speculation in the press that its opening would be delayed until 1999. At least one newspaper seems to have obtained an early glimpse of the contents of a forthcoming National Audit Office (NAO) study, reporting that the latest delays in building work were due to disputes between contractors and unions, confusion among subcontractors and shoddy workmanship. An Amalgamated Engineering and Electricians Union official said that poor organization had demoralized the workforce and that 'the situation down there is chaotic and morale and production are at rock bottom. The men all know the project cannot be completed in time. It's a fiasco.' Similarly, a sub-contractor remarked that it would be a miracle if the library was finished before the millennium: 'it's complete pandemonium, nobody has a clue what's going on' (John Harlow and Rajeev Syal, 'British Library not ready before 2000', *Sunday Times*, no. 8935, 26 November 1995, section 1, p. 7).

By February the NAO report was comprehensively leaked. *The Times* quoted a Whitehall source as surmising 'this is possibly the most critical report the NAO has ever produced' and divulged that it had been

> the subject of much wrangling between the watchdogs and Virginia Bottomley, Secretary of State for National Heritage. The department has asked Sir John Bourn, head of the NAO, to tone down some criticisms. But the NAO will severely criticize aspects of the financial management and report that many of the technical problems that have contributed to the delays and increased costs were easily avoidable (Nigel Williamson, 'British Library will finally open nine years late', *The Times*, no. 65509, 22 February 1996, p. 4).

An editorial in the London *Evening Standard*, a formidable opinion moulder at Westminster, was incandescent as it fulminated against 'the long, mumbled litany of technical construction problems, costing mistakes, equipment failures and sheer bad management'. It demanded vengeance against 'the resolute refusal of those concerned to take the blame', and continued

> all that matters to civil servants from the Property Services Agency and elsewhere is to fudge the line of accountability so that none of them can be held responsible . . . if the Government wants to reverse the growing impression that it views concealment as synonymous with the public interest, it should take out one or two of the guiltiest civil servants and hang them at dawn from a turret of St Pancras Station ('The great Library fiasco', *Evening Standard*, no. 52034, 23 February 1996).

Doubtless this draconian verdict attracted a good deal of sympathy.

Clearly it was an unpropitious moment to put in a bid for £30 million of National Lottery cash for an extension to the St Pancras building. But, undeterred, the British Library was still determined to retain the land to the rear of the St Pancras site in defiance of the Department of National Heritage which had long nurtured plans to sell it off. According to the *Sunday Times* the plan submitted featured tunnels or covered walkways to connect an annexe with the main complex. Officialdom's response was both immediate and unanimous. An aghast official at the Department of National Heritage commented: 'All we want is for Dr Lang to open his doors without further foul-ups. He should not even dare to dream of expanding his empire until that task is completed – and that still feels a long way off.' Gerald Kaufman, chairman of the House

of Commons National Heritage Committee, and long-standing oppo-
nent of the St Pancras building, was equally forthright: 'enough money
has been wasted on this dreadful place already. I hope it does not get a
penny from lottery funds to build an ugly extension to an already
unpleasant building.' Etienne Lymbery, chairman of the Regular
Readers Group, added more fuel to the inferno of outrage: 'it is ridicu-
lous to trust these people with any more money for their white elephant
at a time when the day-to-day service at the current sites is falling apart.
Now is the time to say enough is enough' (John Harlow, 'British Library
puts Bottomley in lottery bind', *Sunday Times*, no. 8949, 3 March 1996,
section 1, p. 5).

The long-heralded, heavily leaked, National Audit Office Report by
the Comptroller and Auditor General, *Progress in Completing the New
British Library* fully lived up to its advance billing when it was finally
published on 15 May 1996. Focusing on events since the publication of
its earlier report in 1990, the NAO examined progress towards completing the building to time, cost and quality; how the Department of
National Heritage and its predecessors, the Office of Arts and Libraries,
managed the project since 1988; and how far the completed building is
expected to meet the demand for reader seats.

'Part 1: introduction' covers the origins and early development of the
project; the NAO's report of October 1990, the subsequent report by
the Committee of Public Accounts in May 1991, and the Government's
response of August 1991; the key events in the progress of the project
since 1988, including changes in responsibility; an overview of the
method used to procure phase 1; and the scope of the NAO examination. What emerges most clearly is that many of the project's present
troubles stemmed from Government decisions and budget arrangements
during the period 1972–80.

> The splitting of phase 1A into two substages, in order to defer a com-
> mitment to the full phase, had resulted in more complex management, a
> loss of momentum and some abortive costs. It also extended the con-
> struction period, with attendant commercial and technical risks such as
> claims, extended maintenance, increased resource costs and the need to
> replace parts.

Moreover, the NAO's previous report had concluded that

> management had lacked a clear definition of the project's requirements,
> specialist staff experienced in project sponsorship and regular and reli-

able management information. Uncertainties about the design and funding of the building had extended the construction timetable significantly.

Another key factor that had constantly plagued the project since its inception was the frequent changes in departmental responsibilities. A significant turn of events came in April 1988 when the Office of Arts and Libraries assumed financial responsibility for construction, and the Property Services Agency retained its responsibilities for its management. At the same time the British Library, although it at no time had any management or contractual responsibility for the construction of its new building, took over its maintenance and, nine months later, appointed its own chief engineer and recruited managers for its own projects relating to the building's future occupation, operation and the automation of various reader services. Further developments in this Byzantine hierarchy of responsibilities were the subsuming of OAL into the Department of National Heritage (April 1992); the transfer of project contracts to the Department which established a contracts board, and negotiated and signed a commercial agreement with PSA Projects for continued project management services (September 1992); the privatization of PSA Projects (December 1992) and a consequent translation to TBV Consult (October 1993). The evident lack of continuity, coupled with the Department's delegation of its responsibility for the project's management, further loosened an already wayward control of the whole project. Compounding the confusion was the emergence of virtually two clients for the same project, with potentially conflicting objectives, resulting from the April 1988 division of responsibilities. 'The Department have [sic] sought to deliver the best possible building within the cash limits. The Library's main concern, as the eventual user of the building, has been to ensure safety, operability and maintainability.'

Undermining progress, and encouraging costs to spiral out of control, was the 1982 decision to adopt a 'construction management' procurement strategy whereby the client employs a design team and engages a construction manager to coordinate design and construction and to supervise site activity. Crucially, there is no main contractor and construction is divided into separate works packages carried out by different trade contractors. Unfortunately, there was little experience in the UK building industry of the construction management approach and, in this instance, the advantages of such a strategy were outweighed by the disadvantages: contract prices are not all known when construction starts, and price confidence is only achieved once packages are let; the client, through the construction manager, is responsible for overall coordination and suffers the risk of delays and disruption; and it requires the detailed and continuous involvement of the client who must be prepared to take quick and effective decisions. On the ground 'deficiencies in defining roles and responsibilities prevented the strategy from working effectively'. The NAO concluded that these deficiencies 'contributed to the Department's difficulties in controlling the project'.

'Part 2: Progress towards completion' examines why the construction timetable slipped and endeavours to determine the reasons for the cost increases. As late as July 1990 the objective was to hand over the new building to the Library in stages from July 1991 onwards, with a final completion date in March 1993, for the Library to open its doors to readers later that year. On three separate occasions each of these dates was postponed, principally because of the time taken to identify and resolve technical problems with the electronically operated mobile shelving, damaged cabling and the fire protection system. The time taken by the Department, the Library, the consultants and the contractors to agree on, and to implement, costly remedial work, and at whose charge, is judged to have delayed completion by two and a half years.

Even allowing for the fact that the St Pancras building was a large and complex project, and that some technical problems were bound to arise, nothing can conceal the horror story the NAO describes at length as it attempts to outline how the various faults were discovered, what action was taken and when, and, most dispiriting of all, the uncovering of further unsatisfactory work while remedial work was in progress. The jamming of the gear mechanisms of the mobile bookshelves, substantial non-compliance with specified standards, major damage to the electrical cabling insulation attributed to faulty installation practices, all caused considerable delays. So, too, did a prolonged disagreement on whether to install a 'dry' or 'wet' fire protection system. The scenario could hardly have been more dreary, especially if we reflect that this catalogue of incompetence does not include what the *Report* lumps together in an appendix as 'other technical problems', namely two floods caused by abnormal rainfall and four others due to leakages, modifications to the mechanical book handling system, the installation of chargeable battery units to improve emergency lighting, the additional work commissioned to replace damaged parts of the building energy management system, ductwork insulation and cleaning, remedial work to improve the information technology cabling, high and low voltage protection problems and less than optimal operation in the thermal storage system. No wonder the British Library lost all confidence in the quality and maintainability of its new building.

Not until March 1996 was the Library in a position to confirm that it had agreed with the Department an accelerated schedule of occupation, with the first book transfers into the new building in November 1996, and the opening of an Humanities reading room within another twelve months. But at what cost?

By September 1993 the Department of National Heritage had concluded that remedial work to the electrical cabling was likely to push the total costs over the 1991 £450 million cash limit. It therefore required its project management team to put in hand a cost-reduction exercise which identified savings of £16 million, permitting the Department to inform the Treasury that, although the limit would be breached, there was 'an even chance' that the final cost would fall within the set limit. However, four months later, TBV Consult provided the Department with updated estimates of the cost of work still outstanding resulting from the technical problems encountered and the consequent delays in completion. 'The Department considered various options for curtailing the works, *including stopping the project completely . . .* ' Why the Department should have ever relayed such a comment to the NAO remains a mystery. It beggars belief that 14 years and £450 million into the project the Minister, or the Government, should have contemplated pulling the plug at this late stage. The point of no return had long since passed. But it made a good headline. In the event the Treasury coffers were raided to the tune of a further £46 million bringing the total cost to a colossal £496 million.

Having dealt with the historical background, the reasons for the timetable slippage, and the consequent increase in the project's budget, the NAO turned its attention in Part 3 to the project's management, in particular to the relationship between the DNH and the British Library, the site organization, and its budgetary and quality control.

Following the 1990 NAO Report the OAL commissioned PA Consulting Group (PACG) to assess the effectiveness of existing management controls and to identify areas that might be improved. In April 1991 PACG recommended that OAL's project team and the Library should establish common objectives(!). This they attempted, but after a year their efforts lapsed, mainly because there were differences of opinion over the question of reconciling quality and cost objectives, and also because the bookshelving problems had undermined target dates and were preoccupying senior management's time and energy. The Department commissioned a second PACG report in July 1992 to establish whether the construction budget was adequate, to review that of the Library's own projects for the occupation and operation of the new building, and to examine certain (unspecified) aspects of the completion phase plans. By any standards this second study seems to have been put in train remarkably late in the day. Acting with commendable speed PACG reported in September that the £450 million budget was very tight, owing to cost increases brought about by the long timescale, problems encountered in completing the works and the uncertainty which would plague the project until all the various problems were finally identified.

The long-standing differences of opinion between the Department and the Library on the weighting given to cost, time and quality were also of concern to PACG, who emphasized that the benefits of the new building would only be realized if both the construction project and the Library's own projects were jointly successful. To this end PACG proposed a simplified organization structure, with the Library's assuming responsibility for the construction project, a policy which it had long advocated, but which proved impracticable at this advanced stage. Given PACG's recent introduction to the project, it appears to have summed up the situation with a degree of clarity and common sense that had not been evident at any stage previously. The Department and the Library redoubled their efforts to cooperate more effectively, a small steering committee was established, a draft memorandum of agreement attempted to harmonize their procedures, but in the event this was never completed. However, by March 1996 the two institutions had achieved a closer working relationship.

Getting to grips with overall site management and control is more difficult. The *Report* considers in turn its structure, the system of awarding contracts, relationships between the design team and the contractors, the budgetary controls of contracts for the different works packages, the cost of changes to the brief from 1988 onwards, inspection procedures, the management of contractors' claims, and the settlement of professional fees. After consulting all parties concerned, the Treasury, TBV Consult, Laing Management and the British Library, the Department of National Heritage instituted a new site management structure in April

1994, with the aims of creating a Departmental group responsible for all aspects of planning, operations and commercial issues; and of using the best TBV Consult and Laing Management personnel in an integrated site management team. But there were still elements of confusion in that, as compared to normal practice for the 'construction management' method in the private sector, there was an extra tier of administration between the project manager and the construction manager in the shape of the post of Superintending Officer. The close involvement of the British Library, which communicated directly with the site organization, instead of via a steering or policy group, also muddied the waters.

In the course of its investigation the NAO commissioned Coopers & Lybrand to examine the construction management contract, the architects' and engineers' contracts, and the standard conditions for works contractors, amounting to an intricate network which did not reflect best practice either in the 1980s or 1990s. Coopers & Lybrand identified four key weaknesses: although the project manager was directly responsible for delivery of the project to DNH, he had little formal contractual authority over the progress of construction; the superintending officer's responsibilities included many normally performed by the construction manager; some responsibilities were imprecisely defined, probably reflecting early inexperience in operating the 'construction management' strategy, especially in the area of financial control; and responsibilities for quality control and inspections were blurred.

NAO found it impossible to analyse the causes of a net increase of £58 million resulting from changes to the brief emanating from the design team or the contractors which were routed through the superintending officer to Laing, and thence to the works contractors. Although the 49,000 instructions issued by Laing in 1984–95 were categorized, the project management systems in place could not break them down by type or origin. But, from an analysis of Laing's correspondence, it was found that approximately 25% were related to the mechanical and electrical packages. For various reasons, budgetary control of the works packages proved difficult because of the uncertainties over the final scope of the project, particularly when it was split into 1A and completion phases. The potential costs of design development, or of technical modifications, planned to be covered by contingency funds, were also difficult to estimate. As the project progressed, variations in contract prices over time, the discovery of earlier underestimates and putting right underdesign all contributed to difficulties in controlling the project budget. Moreover, the repeated increases in work package budgets meant that the aggregate extent of cost movements on individual packages over time was not obvious. Not until January 1995 was the DNH able to introduce a new system of budgetary control.

Responsibility for quality control was equally diffuse: contractors were required to provide work conforming to contract, specifications and drawings, to the satisfaction of the construction manager; the design team was responsible for establishing the standards of quality of materials and workmanship, and also for supervising the site; construction managers ensured that contract specifications were adhered to, supervising the execution of the works and maintaining quality control; while the superintending officer had the ultimate responsibility for certifying that the works were completed to his satisfaction.

Similarly, responsibility for the inspection of work was ill-defined between Laing, the design team and the clerk of works. Other unsound practices were that Laing's inspections of work quality were carried out by the managers supervising the performance of the work and so judging themselves what they were responsible for; there had been insufficient planning; guidance on handover procedures had been confused; inspections generally encompassed too large an area at one time; there was inadequate identification and recording of work to be rectified which usually resulted in uncertainty over the amount of remedial work still outstanding; and insufficient time allowed to clear it. Revised inspection procedures were set in place in 1992–3 when a quality team inspection revealed that the previous system of inspection was not adequately recorded. The new procedures were much more rigorous, finding many defects in the mechanical and electrical works.

> By April 1995 the quality team had performed 3,810 inspections. They had identified over 230,000 items needing correction, of which 218,000 had been cleared, and 11,200 were still outstanding at April 1995. There was a computerised system, which listed in detail each of the defects. But there was no system to categorise and summarise defects by their severity. The Department considers, on the basis of selective examination, that the majority were minor. In the Library's view some, if not corrected, could have caused significant problems for the running of the building.

'Part 4: the completion phase' examines the progress in managing its construction. In contrast to the confusions that plagued stage 1A, the completion phase, at the rear of the St Pancras Building, which will accommodate the King's Library, the General Humanities Reading Room, the Oriental and India Office Collections and the restaurant, enjoyed a comparatively free ride. Construction of the concrete shell started in 1993 and was completed in mid-1994. Wisely, a different procurement strategy was employed, thus avoiding the earlier complexities. The Department of National Heritage contracted with a joint venture between a building contractor, Sir Robert McAlpine, and a mechanical and electrical contractor, Haden Young, and so side-stepped all the problems involved in dealing with a large number of contractors and, not least, those arising from the ill-starred mechanical and electrical services in stage 1A. The use of lump sum contracts, an improved budgeting strategy, a less complex management structure and a more clearly defined role for the British Library in the inspection of work, also expedited progress, although the completion date slipped from February 1996 to June 1996 mainly because of the late completion of phase 1A in November 1995, which caused some on-site congestion of stage 1A and completion phase contractors.

The NAO *Report* concludes with an examination of how far the new library is expected to meet the demand for reader seats. This was an issue that had perplexed and troubled both the 1991 Committee of Public Accounts and the National Heritage Committee in 1994. Although the new building as now designed will have 1206 reader seats, this represents only a 12% increase over existing London provision. In May 1993 the British Library commissioned TA Consultancy Services to examine current seat occupancy levels and to consider the effect of further growth in demand at the new library, and Kneller Market Research in July 1994 to forecast the likely demand for seats. Based on their conclusions the Library estimated that the new building could possibly attract an increase of between 10% and 19% in reader attendances over a number of years after opening and concluded, on more up-to-date information than was available to TA Consultancy, that the capacity of the Science and Oriental reading rooms would be exceeded either at, or shortly after opening. However,

> the Library plan to exploit the greater flexibility of the new buildings, with its automated book ordering and mechanical book handling systems, to match the allocation of seats with the varying demand from readers. In September 1995 they commissioned an internal study of seat

management techniques, and they are continuing to improve their information on seat occupancy levels.

Appendices to the *Report* include 'A summary of Treasury minute undertakings'; a chronology of project events since 1 April 1988; and the other technical problems already mentioned. There is also a glossary of terms and a fold-out diagram of the St Pancras building, distinguishing the division between phase 1A and the completion phase, and locating the various reading rooms and other facilities.

PRESS OUTRAGE

If the reaction of the national press to the 1994 National Heritage Committee report was predictably trenchant, the verdict now, partly based on their own investigations, and not entirely on the NAO report itself, was one of outrage and derision. Nigel Williamson, Whitehall Correspondent of *The Times*, set the tone: 'Squabbles and indecisions by civil servants over building the new British Library have trebled costs and caused a catalogue of technical disasters.' He continued,

> The report has been delayed for many months while Virginia Bottomley, the Heritage Secretary, tried to persuade the audit office to water down some of its criticisms. Yet the conclusion remains devastating: the library never had direct management or contractual responsibility for the construction and the Government's desire to secure short-term savings not only led to delays but eventually added to long-term costs. ('Whitehall lets bill run out of control at British Library', *The Times*, no. 65580, 15 May 1996, p. 9).

A scathing editorial in the *Daily Telegraph*, 'Catalogue of disasters', deplored that 'just about everything that could have gone wrong with it has' and pronounced that

> it seems extraordinary . . . that throughout this whole troubled project the one body that has never had any responsibility for the construction of the building is the British Library itself. If the library had been given a budget and left to get on with it, at least the lines of command and responsibility would have been clear.

That must have brought solace of some sort to the Chief Executive's office in Euston Road.

LEEDS METROPOLITAN UNIVERSITY LIBRARY

The *Evening Standard* returned to its theme of finding the culprits:

Angry demands grew today for the public unmasking of the bureaucrats at the centre of the £500 million new British Library scandal... there was widespread incredulity that those responsible for a staggering 230,000 building mistakes continue to escape accountability. Despite their unprecedented series of blunders, which have led to huge delays and needlessly added almost £200 million to the cost of the prestigious project, they are still in their jobs and drawing high salaries . . . in his report Auditor General Sir John Bourn uncovers a woeful saga of building errors, management failures and blurred responsibilities. The inspectors know who is to blame, but have refused to name names. (Colin Adamson and Robin Stringer, 'Name names call in £500m Library row', *Evening Standard*, no. 52089, 15 May 1996, p. 6).

Richard Morrison summed up the report better than most in his Week in the Arts column:

So many things were wrong, it seems, that 'a new computerised system was introduced at a cost of £49,000 to record all items to be rectified'. Yes, dear readers, that's the price of a small semi, just to find a machine capable of writing down all the mistakes without blowing itself up in a fit of indignation. But what is £49,000 in a budget of £496 million? I suppose it says something for the honesty of British public life that such a report has been published at all . . . But of course the honesty comes at a price: nobody is castigated by name. A handful of government departments and agencies sidle in and out of the 20-year story, plus some of the biggest names in the building trade, plus innumerable teams of management consultants. But when you reach the end of this messy tale, you feel as if you have ploughed through a complicated whodunit only to find the vital last chapter is missing. Who *are* the guilty men? We are not told. We never will be. ('A great read; pity about the library', *The Times*, no. 65583, 18 May 1996, p. 17).

COMMITTEE OF PUBLIC ACCOUNTS

On the basis of the Comptroller and Auditor-General's report, the House of Commons' Committee of Public Accounts returned to the project, 24 June 1996, when it received a memorandum from the Regular Readers Group and took evidence from the Department of National

Heritage (Mr G.H. Phillips, CB, Permanent Secretary) the British Library (Chief Executive) and Mr F. Martin, Treasury Office of Accounts. Its Second Report, *Progress in Completing the New British Library. Together with the Proceedings of the Committee relating to the Report, the Minutes of Evidence, and Appendices*, was published by the Stationery Office at the end of October.

Of the 477 column inches of the Minutes of Evidence, that involving the Chief Executive amounted to only a fraction over 25%, dealing with the date when all parts of the Library would be open to the public (June 1999); the logistics of the book move; book environmental conditions; the role of Boston Spa in the Library's operations; the relations between the Department and the Library; the interwoven nature of the management of the Library and the management of the building project; the political reasons for truncating the original plans and the consequent reduction in seating; the accessibility of the St Pancras to readers; the flexibility of the seating arrangements; future demand and the Library's plans to meet it; delivery times; relations with the Regular Readers Group; and the shelving, wiring and flooding problems.

Questioning directed against the Department was more obviously incisive, persistent, protracted and concentrated on the project's management, funding, remedial work on site, who had pointed out deficiencies to whom and when, and value for money (now £511.1 million of it). Eventually the Committee became entangled in the grey and dubious area of claims and counter-claims for compensation. The Department was reluctant to announce publicly specific sums spent on settling claims because this was commercially sensitive and because there was still a possibility of further litigation.

Andrew Alderson and Caroline Lees' 'Builders to be sued over bungled library' (*Sunday Times*, no. 8866, 24 July 1994, p. 16) reported that a team of financial trouble-shooters had been recruited by the Government to recover up to £60 million from companies involved in the installation of the wiring, sprinklers and the mechanical shelves. What might prove to be one of the more ominous and pivotal quotes of the entire saga came from an anonymous source: 'if the government sues companies, it will open a huge can of worms'.

Sub-contractors would not only deny allegations of poor workmanship, but also claim that repeated design changes brought about by construction delays continually hampered their operations. There was news in May 1996 that Steensen Varming Mulcahy (SMV), responsible for designing and supervising 3000 km of cabling underneath the floors, had been landed with a legal claim from the Department of National Heritage. 'It includes £4m for repairing the cable and £5m for the delay to the project' (John Waples, 'Engineer sued over delays at library', *Sunday Times*, no. 8961, 26 May 1996, section 2, p. 2).

Just four weeks later the Department was informing the Committee that its legal and commercial advice was that it should not put on record how much had been paid out so far either in settlement of claims con‑ tractors had on the Department or on claims it had on them. For its part, the Committee was rankled that major contractors were being allowed to evade their responsibilities because the Department could not establish sound charges of negligence and might face substantially increased costs in arbitration or litigation. It had to be satisfied that no contractor had actually been paid to rectify its own shortcomings.

Clearly, the Committee had undertaken a thorough investigation of the construction project – its progress and financial aspects; its manage‑ ment, the lack of shared objectives between Department and Library, the commercial agreements and quality control; the financial problems, budgetary control, professional fees and claims; the technical problems; and how far the new library reflected readers' needs – but, essentially, it was covering old ground. The real impact had been made five months earlier.

At length, to no great fanfare, after 15 years of construction, an undoubted landmark in the British Library's short but turbulent history materialized on 1 July 1997, when the Library's Chief Executive and the Permanent Secretary of the Department of National Heritage signed a formal transfer document in the Board Room at St Pancras, and the Library finally became the owner of the new St Pancras building.

3

THE ST PANCRAS BUILDING

EXTERIOR

Verdicts on the St Pancras building's design merits have been inconclusive: it would appear that contemporary architectural critics cannot agree on its aesthetic virtues or defects although, as the years have passed, a certain respect has emerged for its functional qualities. This, of course, could change. Stephen Fay, for one, perceived

> evidence – though it is still slender – that the British Library is a subject of one of those unfathomable shifts in public taste . . . suddenly, the clean 20th century Scandinavian lines of Wilson's building seem to complement rather than clash with Scott's pointed arches and decorative steeples' ('Story of bricks and brickbats', *Guardian*, no. 46238, 11 May 1995, Section 2, pp. 2–3).

But, writing in the *Independent*, Jonathan Glancey would have none of it.

> On the left, in tiers and slabs of salmon pink, the British Library. On the right, in spires and vaults of salmon pink, St., Pancras station. What an extraordinary pairing. Flanking Euston Road, one of London's most clotted arteries, two of Europe's greatest and most monstrous civic buildings brood . . . The hero of the piece, however, is undoubtedly St Pancras's architect, Sir George Gilbert Scott (1812–1880). The Goth has rescued Professor Wilson, for, without the heraldic glory of St Pancras, the British Library would look merely lumpen. ('A Marriage Made in NW1', *The Independent*, no. 2383, 9 June 1994, p. 21).

Hugh Pearman shared Fay's views:

> It is traditional to profess to hate such big public projects, but now the front of the library with its landscaped square and its clocktower is largely complete, one senses opinions changing. By the time the first

readers are let in . . . it will have passed through its slough of despond and be ripe for reappraisal. Real people – not just critics – are coming round to it ('Almost word perfect', *Sunday Times*, no. 8958, 5 May 1996, Section 10 The Culture, pp. 8–9).

Dan Conaghan, in the *Daily Telegraph* lined up with Glancey:

With the hoarding gone, the building is revealed in all its ugliness. The elegance of the piazza, the herbaceous borders and open-air amphitheatre does little to disguise the monstrosity towering over. Inside however, [he admitted], it is a different story. ('Décor speaks volumes but library books are overdue', *Daily Telegraph*, no. 43666, 10 November 1995, p. 12).

INTERIOR

In fact the design of the interior, especially that of the imposing entrance hall, commands unanimous approval. For example, conducting a tour of the building, Richard MacCormac remarked:

This room is sensational, not simply because it is unexpectedly big, but because the impact, like that of entering a cathedral, is visceral – surprising and unsettling at first and only then profoundly calm. Volumetrically, it develops up and away from the entrance doors in a series of great waves that appear to float on reflected daylight. This sense of natural expansion also finds expression in the broad flight of travertine marble steps which invite visitors to enter the reading rooms and other public areas of the building. It is also due to the divergent flanking walls of brick and stone which accelerate space away into the depth of the library, beyond the series of bridges linking the humanities reading rooms to the left with the science and technology libraries to the right.

He continued:

entering the rare book reading room, you pass under the upper reading gallery and experience a sense of temporary enclosure in a threshold between the volume of the entrance hall and that of the reading room you are about to enter. You arrive in a space which is lit by a kind of inverse lantern which you do not immediately see. The main reading area is furnished with leather-topped tables of American oak and around the perimeter panelled doors give access to study carrels. So there are three distinct places to read: the raised gallery under the central lantern; the main area under the sloping roof with its comfortable peripheral feel; and the privacy of the carrels.

The humanities reading room . . . is arranged in a similar way but on a more dramatic scale . . . Again, this environment for 500 readers . . . will consist of a range of different kinds of space. Neither of these two reading rooms is designed to compete with the volumetric blast of Smirke's circular room, but each will combine the dramatic and unexpected with a humanity appropriate to the subjects they sustain. Crossing the galleries . . . to the science and technology library you enter a different kind of space, where open-access shelving predominates and readers are arranged along the edges of the triple height, side-lit volume which, with its solar shading, forms the elevation along the eastern edge of the entrance courtyard. ('Don't knock it till you've seen it', *The Independent*, no. 2776, 11 September 1995, Section 2, p. 9).

Two commentators suggested the library could be registered as a listed building before it was completed. Kester Rattenbury:

There has been, it has been pointed out elsewhere, a miracle in the Euston Road. A minor public building project has been going on for so long (thirty-four years: a good age) that it has already passed through the stages of public protest, critical acclaim, critical reaction, general assumption of hatred, several major shifts of the canon of perceived popular and high-art taste and re-emerged back in to the forum of historical approbation. It may be a race against time, but the British Library looks set to be the first building to be grade I listed before it is even complete. ('Happily ever after in London', *Building Design*, no. 1328, 13 October 1995, p. 2).

And Hugh Pearman:

You could make out a convincing case for listing Colin St. John (Sandy) Wilson's building as historically and culturally important while the builders are still at work. The library was designed in the mid 1970s – a period stiff with recently listed buildings – though not begun, due to both Labour and Conservative hesitation, until 1982 and then with cruel parsimony. But there is something paradoxically satisfying about the fact that, by the time everything is done and dusted (everyone hopes) in 1998, it will have taken more than 20 years to build. Like a cathedral, it has gone through endless vicissitudes and changes even while it was being built. ('Almost word perfect', *Sunday Times*, no. 8958, 5 May 1996, Section 10 The Culture, pp. 8–9).

Fourteen colour photographs, some less familiar than others and four plans, illustrate Christine Deschamps' 'Londres British Library', pp. 209–31, *Nouvelles Alexandries. Les Grands chantiers de bibliothèques dans le monde*, edited by Michel Melot (Paris, Éditions du Cercle de la Librairie, 1996), a sumptuously attractive volume, available from DSC for reference use only, which examines the entire St Pancras project, its history, methods and procedures adopted, its architecture, its facilities and equipment, automation and computerization; ending with a selected bibliography of French and English sources. If an enterprising publisher this side of the Channel has issued an English-language version, it has successfully eluded the present writer.

A long-awaited milestone at St Pancras arrived 14 March 1997, Colin St John Wilson's 75th birthday, when the temporary wall separating the Entrance Hall from the six-storey glass tower, situated in the centre of the building, which houses the 60,000 rare volumes of the Kings Library, was removed, thus linking Phase 1A and the Completion Phase of the St Pancras building. The Completion Phase accommodates the General Humanities Reading Room, a restaurant for visitors, a café, the Cotton Room for readers and a large open-air terrace.

THIRTY-FIVE YEARS OF PLANNING, CONTROVERSY AND BITTER RECRIMINATION

Marking the British Library's departure from the Round Reading Room, 25 October 1997, Stephen Gardiner's 'Final Chapter' in that day's issue of *The Times Magazine* (pp. 42–4, 46), looks back at '35 years of planning, controversy and bitter recrimination' and peers forward to a month later when the Library would at last open its doors to readers. Gardiner first pays tribute to Colin St John Wilson for his determination, patience, flexibility, sheer effort and faith in the importance of the project in the face of cuts, changes and demoralizing criticism to see through the project to completion, before recounting the sequence of events from the time Wilson and Sir Leslie Martin's first design for a new library in Bloomsbury was accepted in 1964, to the eventual truncated design for the St Pancras building. He finds much to praise, notably 'the east wing's build-up of levels, strongly emphasised by the dark green sun screens over continuous windows and the layered red brick' withstanding the power and vitality of the neighbouring St Pancras hotel. And the transition from outside to inside – never easy, he remarks – but here successfully accomplished by 'slight changes of plane in the forecourt, the placing of walls and hedges around seating, an occasional shallow step and the enormous slate roof sweeping down to the delicate touch of a subtle canopy above a run of glass doors'. Like other critics and commentators, Gardiner is bowled over by the majestic entrance hall, which he describes as 'modern architecture at its cavernous best, so clean and sharp that it could have been cut from a cliff of chalk'.

Not the least beguiling feature of 'Final Chapter' is Wilson's own comments on Camden Council's requirements:

> on the West side, just to the north of the Euston Road, is the Shaw Theatre and they didn't want the view of that blocked. They wanted a line above that to be taken right across the site to act as a boundary in front of which I couldn't go. That was all right. It meant the Library was well away from the noise of Euston Road traffic and it created the forecourt. But I didn't want it right across – I wanted then to screen the forecourt from Midland Road, which at some point is to be turned into a four-lane highway. So I brought a wing forward along there. They saw the logic of that.

Gardiner signs off with the thought that 'if hundreds of millions can be produced for the inaccessible Millennium Dome, surely the Government can find enough to finish off a building of such immense importance to education', thus allowing the British Library to exploit the five acres of the site remaining. He might have added that, after all the harsh words, prevarications, cutbacks and delays, honour demanded no less.

Also sympathetic in tone, Paul Finch's magnificently illustrated 'Booking a place in history (*Architects Journal*, **206** (19), 20 November 1997, pp. 47–50, 52, 54) sums up the criticism levelled against the St Pancras building, that it is ugly, a verdict favoured by politicians; that the main frontage 'resembles a latter-day barn of the sort designed to win Tesco planning permission in rural Essex'; and that there is 'fiddly detailing', suggesting that the building is essentially suburban. 'In short', Finch avers, 'whatever critical axe one has to grind, one can find something in the BL on which to exercise it.' Fortunately for the architect, the huge time lapse between design and construction completion possibly means that 'the building will receive much greater popular support than it might have five years ago. It is very obviously *not* Lottery architecture . . . the building has spanned a series of changing cultural miniclimates in respect of planning, conservation, materials, aesthetics and technology.' Moreover, it 'is triumph for one man: the architect who is the sole survivor in a near-heroic struggle against the odds'.

Full justice is also accorded to Wilson's building, 'arguably the most important public building in the UK since the Royal Festival Hall in 1951', in Roger Stonehouse's 'Inside Story: the British Library at St Pancras', *Architecture Today*, no. 84, January 1998, pp.22–4, 27–8 and 31. Illustrated with some glorious colour photographs, including a striking view of the Entrance Hall on the front cover, with 18 other large and small interior and exterior shots, plus an annotated axonometric diagram, this forceful article asks a number of pertinent if figurative questions:

> How do you make a building of the greatest monumental significance in the latter part of the twentieth century? A building which has gravitas but is not pompous? Which is culturally accessible to all but not, in consequence, stripped to the bare bones of form or cloaked in the illusions of postmodernism? How do you make a building which is of its nature permanent and enclosing in a culture which is apparently fixated with change and the ephemeral? How do you make a building which is immense in size and cultural importance but which houses that most individual and introspective of activities, reading?

The answers are provided by means of a descriptive perambulation of the building enriched with appreciative comments, not only on the aesthetic effectiveness of its design, but also on how it impinges on its users: 'This is not an architecture of circulation pattern and system, but one of grace and ease based on a clear understanding of movement and orientation.' Perhaps the most apt and final word on the architecture of the St Pancras library is the knighthood conferred on Professor Colin Alexander St John Wilson for services to architecture in the 1998 New Years Honours List. His book, *The Design and Construction of The British Library* (The British Library, 1998) will no doubt attract a wide readership among visitors to the library, architects, designers, construction engineers and librarians.

4

POLICY MATTERS AND DOCUMENTS

CODE OF SERVICE

Responding to a request from the Department of National Heritage to review the extent to which its services upheld the principles outlined in the Prime Minister's Citizen's Charter, the British Library produced its own Code of Service dealing primarily with those service aspects it believed to be most relevant to users, namely delivery times of requested items and response times in answering enquiries. Introduced in February and April 1994, in the shape of 25 uniform A5 leaflets, the Code reflected the library's intention to clarify the level of service that could normally be expected. It also seized the opportunity to promise that it would at all times treat users with courtesy, professionalism and efficiency; to communicate in clear, straightforward language; to deal promptly with all verbal and written enquiries; and to welcome suggestions and comments. Considering the scale of the Library's operations, its 16 reading rooms and study areas, hosting half a million reader visits annually, the standards laid down for each service point represented a brave and confident approach that few other institutions or enterprises dared contemplate.

However, before joy becomes unconfined, it has to be said that certain of the standards are not exactly earth-moving in nature. Aspiring readers are assured that they will be given prompt, clear and accurate information on the arrangements for obtaining a Readers Pass (no more than they deserve, surely and no more than they would legitimately expect). They might be a little apprehensive to learn that the Library will require them to give certain information about themselves before they can be issued with a pass but will probably be reassured that this will be kept to a minimum and that any information they impart will remain confidential. That the Library will prepare an appropriate pass without delay will no doubt offer some consolation as they hurry away to obtain a photograph they didn't know they needed.

Despite a reservation or two over detail, some apparent confusion on the part of those who drew up the standards on the difference of responding to an enquiry, answering it and satisfying it; and the inexactitude of words and terms like 'promptly', 'as quickly as possible', 'normally' and 'seek to avoid', the standards at least indicate an awareness of possible service shortcomings and a commendable intention to improve matters. No doubt, from time to time, such as at the height of the summer season, when all the world's scholars seem to descend on the reading rooms simultaneously, delivery times might stretch a little and circumstances might conspire to defeat the best of intentions. As if aware of this, the standards all provide contact names for service complaints. In the last resort, those who are unhappy at the way their complaints have been handled are invited to write to the Chief Executive.

Evidence that the British Library itself took its Code of Service standards very seriously is to be found in the various divisional and departmental newsletters twelve months after their introduction. The published performance figures, which appear not to be 'sanitized', invariably offer a sentence or two of explanation in cases where the minus variance percentage figure requires it. For example, at DSC the actual response of the Urgent Action Service to requests received during the normal working day within two hours reached only 89% instead of the standard aim of 100%. A note states that 'this less than satisfactory result . . . reflects some early problems with anomalies in data collection. This has now been rectified and the Service is regularly achieving 100% response, with an average of 96%' ('Code of Service', *Document Supply News*, no. 47, Sep.1995, p. 4).

Similarly, Graham Cranfield, Manager of the Round Reading Room, reviewing the Code's progress, admitted that although the standard set for the Book Delivery Service was 80% of material held in the Great Russell Street main stock should be delivered to the Reading Room within 90 minutes; the figure reached during the Code's first year of operation was only 69%. This under-achievement was attributed to a long calendar of complex reasons:

> the level of staffing had not kept pace with the growth in demand; more and more stock has had to be retrieved from out-stations, which has a knock-on effect upon the onsite delivery services; the disruption caused by emergency fire precautions work in the stacks meant that staff were evicted from their usual offices; and some of the consequences of a

major reorganisation in staffing structure in 1993 were still being worked through (the restructuring itself having been carried out within terms that had to be approved by H.M. Treasury).

Successful remedial measures were taken in the following twelve months:

staffing levels were increased; changes in procedures were introduced; and management of the Book Delivery Service was transferred to the Humanities and Social Services directorate, thus integrating operations . . . Eventually, staff were able to move back into their stack offices.

Because of these measures the Book Delivery Service dramatically improved its performance and comfortably exceeded the standard, but at a cost. Demand on its services was threatening to outpace the resources available and in August and September 1995, at Easter 1996 and at times during the summer of 1996 the Reading Room was forced to readopt the policy (first employed in 1993) of restricting on a daily basis the number of readers' requests. 'While this did not meet with universal approval, many readers confirmed that they preferred a limited but reliable service to a service without limits which deteriorated when overloaded' (Graham Cranfield, 'Code Of Service Standards', *London-Services-Bloomsbury Newsletter*, no. 14, Summer 1996, pp. 1–2).

A full summary of how close the Library came to attaining its targets in the Code's first year is printed in *The British Library Twenty Second Annual Report 1994–95*, pp. 67–9. Deficiencies are not hidden and the true picture is presented warts and all. Staff shortages in the first six months accounted for most of the problems encountered.

While performing the same function as the original loose leaflets, *Code of Service 97–98* (30 pp.) reiterated that 'our primary aim is to provide a service that satisfies the fullest needs of the many people who use the Library's collection in a manner which is efficient, reliable, consistent and courteous'. Each of the Library's most heavily used reading-room, document-supply and information services now occupies a separate page outlining a collection profile, opening hours, address, telephone enquiries number, admission charge (if any), enquiry response time, material delivery time, contact point and complaint contact name. During the year staff dealing directly with users in person began to wear name badges for the first time and so making identification easier. This time round, the Reader Admissions Office disclosed that applicants for a pass must supply two recent passport-size colour photographs and proof of identity bearing a signature, thus saving time and aggravation, provided always of course that applicants obtained the Code beforehand. To avoid frustration and disgruntlement, the Library authorities really should signal this requirement more prominently.

PETERBOROUGH INITIATIVES

Targets listed in the Chief Executive's introduction to the British Library's third strategic plan, *For Scholarship, Research and Innovation. Strategic objectives for the Year 2000*, published in 1993 to present its vision of the Library's operations and services at the beginning of the twenty-first century, included a single library, operating a single collection, based on two major sites at St Pancras and Boston Spa; budgets for core programmes in acquisitions, preservation and research grants at levels appropriate to the Library's standing as a national library; a set of library services offering maximum access through full use of new technology on-site and over electronic networks; the Library established as a major centre for the capture, storage and transmission of electronic documents; and as a leader in the development of library systems and services.

In February 1994 the senior British Library management team, including all the directors, met at Peterborough, chosen no doubt because it is roughly equidistant from the Library's two main sites, to consider the issues involved in the implementation of the strategic objectives. Four key programmes, known as the Peterborough initiatives, were conceived: Collection Development Initiative (CDI); Collection Management Initiative (CMI); User Satisfaction Initiative (USI); and Access Improvement Initiative (AII). A senior corporate 'champion' was assigned to each initiative team, charged with developing in more detail the Library's role within each initiative area, formulating policies and developing workable practices. The 'champion's' responsibilities also encompassed advocating the initiative team's proposals within Library management and in their submission to the Board.

The Collection Development Initiative examined how the British Library's book purchases are developed and attempted to arrive at a realistic plan for creating a single collection, not necessarily a single-copy collection, but one that would most effectively support the Library's services. Even such an apparently simple exercise required concerted planning. First, the Library must decide what sort of material to collect, what sort of budgetary system would most efficiently coordinate the way in which its acquisition funds were spent and then allocate specialist staff to cooperate on the selection and location of stock. To facilitate less duplicate purchasing of new monographs and serials, improved systems were required to ensure the Library could cope with different demands for the same item in London and at Boston Spa. On site users needed reference copies while document supply services also needed readily available material. An action plan was prepared for coordinated selection, reduced duplication and better management information systems for collection development, the first practical evidence of which is the increased usage of material between sites.

The Collection Management Initiative espouses the British Library's processing, cataloguing, pressmarking and stamping of new acquisitions and deciding which books are to receive expensive preservation treatment, or, in other words, managing the processing of new stock from ordering it, to putting it on the shelves and deciding if and when it should be relegated to remote storage or discarded. Together, these operations account for over 25% of the Library's expenditure. Almost a quarter of a century after the British Library came into being, crucial policies, structures and procedures and budgets for effective collection management were, surprisingly, not in place. The CMI's aims are

> to develop and establish corporate policies (and procedures for executing those policies) for the cost-effective management of the Library's collection; to develop performance measures to monitor the management of the collection corporately; and to embed these in BL's wider planning and reporting mechanisms.

A Framework Study disclosed that, in many cases, policies were lacking or only partly documented, procedures were uncoordinated, responsibilities only partly defined and the basics for coordinated management of the collection totally absent. An intensive period of policy development and efficiency planning to promote rapid progress in collection management was recommended.

The User Satisfaction Initiative addressed whether the Library was providing the services expected of the national library in terms of effective delivery, timeliness, predictability, reliability, courtesy, simplicity, accuracy and responsiveness and whether the Library had in place appropriate and efficient mechanisms to monitor performance, users' expectations and satisfaction. Because of the Library's complex operations and services the USI team concentrated on how a number of external services ensured satisfaction, the standard and premium document supply services at DSC and Patent Express and the Bloomsbury, SRIS and Boston Spa reading rooms, scrutinizing how performance measures and the Code of Service are used, how users' expectations and requirements are surveyed and how the information is used to improve services and develop new ones. The conclusion was that the Library inclined to be product and service directed rather than be responsive to its users. A corporate approach, built around a new post responsible for coordinating user consultation, was recommended.

Key issues for the Access Improvement Initiative were to develop the concept of a single gateway to Library services (i.e. 'issues as diverse as catalogue provision, information services, ordering and delivery systems for reading room and remote users, collection policies, the provision of surrogates such as microfilm, user demands, user registration, relationships with other collections and public access'); to show how the Library could implement the automation infrastructure improvements required; to demonstrate how the Library can coordinate the development of services more effectively; to propose a concerted programme for improving access; and to show how all this allows the Library to implement its single collection strategy. A lack of coordination below Management Committee level and the absence of communication and prioritization, were identified as barriers to progress. At the centre of the AII team's report was a proposed structure that would allow the Library to improve its decision making.

Andy Stephens' 'Working towards the British Library's strategic objectives for the year 2000', *Library Management*, **16** (4), 1995, pp. 12–17 describes the background to the Peterborough initiatives and is particularly useful on the role of the 'champions'.

> This has the potential to be a more powerful and effective means of achieving clear analysis and problem solving than the conventional 'committee review', providing both a framework for decision making and also an authority and accountability for implementation of strategic initiatives. Its importance as a means of addressing and progressing corporate issues across the Library's structural boundaries is of great significance.

Stephens' and Marie Jackson's 'Working towards the millennium: the British Library's plans for the year 2000', *New Library World*, **97** (1126), 1996, pp. 33–7 covers much the same ground but includes a brief consideration of the Library's *Information Systems Strategy* published in November 1995.

INFORMATION SYSTEMS STRATEGY

Moving forward from its information technology strategies outlined in its third strategic document *For Scholarship, Research and Innovation* (1993), the British Library aims, by the year 2000 to become a major centre for the storage of and access to digital texts required for research and to provide access to the world's catalogues through a single gateway from its online catalogue, using the superhighway and other digital technology to supply documents to remote users faster and more efficiently. This aim was cogently expressed in *Information Systems Strategy*, a successor to the outdated *Automation Strategy* (1988). A three-route approach is adopted to explain how the Library will improve access to the collections and develop new services by exploiting digital information and networking.

First it sets the Library's strategy within a national and international context examining developments at the Library of Congress, the ambitious plans of the Bibliothèque Nationale de France, the strategic planning process at the Koninklijke Bibliotheek in Copenhagen and also European initiatives in which the British Library plays a conspicuous role, notably the Computerised Bibliographic Record Actions (COBRA). At home, the Report of the Higher Education Joint Funding Council's Library Review Group, the *Follett Report*, underlined the opportunities that information technology offered academic libraries over the next ten years. The British Library had responded positively to proposals concerning closer cooperation between libraries, increased networking and rapid electronic document supply. (Brian Lang's 'The British Library's Response to the Joint Funding Council's Library Review Group Report', *British Journal of Academic Librarianship*, 9 (1–2), 1994, pp. 16–22 prints its response verbatim). The Library had already offered assistance in establishing standards for digital library development to the Follett Implementation Group on Information Technology.

Clearly, national and international network facilities and technology were rapidly changing. The Information Superhighway, connecting end-users to digital information services through a direct high-speed global telecommunications network, was manifestly of direct concern and relevance to the Library's document supply services.

Users will expect easy access through this network to all the Library's services, including catalogues, document requesting and delivery and other information services. For those with direct access, the high capacity of the superhighway will make digital transmission of copies of items from the Library's collection technically practical, although copyright restrictions and the volume of digitisation that can be afforded will limit the range of items available (para.14, p. 12).

The Library was also monitoring commercial and technical developments in the Internet infrastructure, assessing their implications for future service provision and their impact on availability and costs.

The increasing use of personal computers with interactive access would inevitably place a heavier demand on the Library's resources; its services

will be expected to fit seamlessly into this environment, giving access both to identification and requesting of physical material and to digital information and documents. While access to physical material will always be a major requirement, users will increasingly require access to digital material and will expect common tools for access to both forms (para 21, pp. 13–14).

A unified catalogue database, common systems for access and a common information technology infrastructure, would be crucial in satisfying users' demands.

What exactly would be required and the Library's leading objectives are spelled out in Appendix A: Key Actions of the Information Systems Strategy, printed a disconcerting twelve pages on. First, the Library would secure improved access to its collections by means of more comprehensive information for its users including information on an item's specific location and availability. Extended catalogue records would indicate its availability, restrictions on its use, its retention status, its preservation status and possible surrogate or alternative forms. Online searching of the catalogue will use simpler data formats than those required for fiche or printed catalogues; scanned images will replace keying for some descriptive data and, in the longer term, searching the computer catalogue will be supplemented by facilities allowing searching for the full text of items stored in digitally encoded form. Optical character recognition techniques could then be utilized to convert a number of small card and book catalogues currently used for some material in the Library's collections and so provide access through the Online

Public Access Catalogue.

Further development of the OPAC will lead to improved searching methods. 'Extended services in the form of free-text searching, alerting services, sophisticated search algorithms, combined indexes and improved browsing methods will also be incorporated into the Library's services' (para. A4, p. 27). Hypertext documents, free-text searching of word-processed documents, networked information servers, bulletin boards, mail servers will be integrated with the computer-based catalogue. Guides to the collection, small specialized catalogues, enquiries, requests via electronic mail for help and the associated answers, topical bibliographies, overviews of collection policy, details of new acquisitions and discussion groups, are some of the ingredients flowing from the new technology into the catalogue and the requesting services and improving access to the collections.

Once these systems are in place the Library will more easily capture digital information in a number of different formats, perhaps on a CD-ROM, or perhaps as a digital file downloaded from another source. But visionary plans and far-seeing concepts of the rapid provision of information, based on a comprehensive collection of digital material, are accompanied by a practical realism that concomitant problems, legal deposit, copyright, preservation, costs etc. remain to be solved. Nevertheless the Library was confident that its information systems strategy will overcome these difficulties.

> The Library will develop an infrastructure of efficient and effective storage, retrieval and transmission systems based on open systems principles. It will also develop the necessary expertise to find, preserve and use this information. For example, an understanding of the manner in which digital information is created and used will be particularly important in establishing the Library's role in the possible legal deposit of digital materials (para. A9, p. 28).

At the heart of the strategy, of course, is a recognition of the need to create a corporate database to integrate all the Library's catalogue records. This will be

> the basis of a wide variety of systems that support the Library's processes and services. It will underpin systems used for acquisitions processing, cataloguing record supply, preservation, OPAC, information retrieval and alerting services. The development of the database will also be an

opportunity to replace existing catalogue and information systems which are dated and inefficient and so improve operational efficiency (para. A17, p. 30).

Completion of this corporate database would spread over the full term of the strategy period and it would also be related to a new National Bibliographic Database to be built in cooperation with the other copyright libraries.

It is evident, too, that the British Library was determined to apply the benefits of the new digital technology to its own administrative processes once staff had received training in appropriate information technology skills. The widespread use of computer and telecommunications systems was expected to lead to a development of management information systems to support many of the Library's routine administrative and processing activities, to collect information, financial and other resource data on use and performance, and to establish feedback between services and library processes, and so assist corporate planning at every level of service and administration. All these computer and telecommunications systems would of necessity be based on a common set of infrastructure systems, not only to optimize their efficiency, but also to support the concept of the single library and the single collection. It is strange to perceive here that the struggle for a corporate identity, both internally and externally, is still in evidence 23 years after Parliament summoned the British Library into being.

'British Library Information Systems Today', the *Strategy's* second section, outlines the Library's use of information technology over the past twenty years: catalogue access through OPAC terminals in the reading rooms, on CD-ROM, or through networks accessed from the user's own system and the transfer of massive printed catalogues to online access. More recently, the Initiatives for Access Programme harnesses digital and networking technologies to improve access to the Collection and to investigate conservation scanning of high-quality colour photographic transparencies of images of famous heritage items. Internal computer systems had long been in place for such activities as catalogue enquiry, recording stock information, receiving requests, while package software was widely used for planning and project management, financial administration and general library automation.

In addition, a wide-area telecommunications network links all the Library's sites and connects with JANET, the Internet and other external networks. A technical summary of the informations systems in use in

1995 occupies Appendix B (pp. 36–7). With current expenditure on the operation and development of automated systems running at 15% of the Library's total annual budget, the British Library had no doubt of its strong position to exploit the full potential of the latest information technology to support its strategic objectives for the year 2000.

What these objectives are and the crucial contribution of information technology to their achievement, notably in the provision of document supply and access to digital texts, are underlined in the third section, 'British Library Information Systems in the Year 2000'. Six areas are identified: the first, Standard Business-Support Technology, is for management, record-keeping and communications purposes, in common with other organizations of similar size and structure. 'Building, Cataloguing and Conserving the Collection' promises that a new automated system will make the acquisition and cataloguing of legal deposit material (a predicted 83,000+ titles to be catalogued in the year 2000) more timely and more cost-effective. This new system will also facilitate the operations of the Copyright Libraries Shared Cataloguing Programme (CLSCP) whose aims are to maximize the currency, quality and coverage of the national bibliographic service. And, in addition to its traditional holdings, the British Library aims by the year 2000 to be a major centre for the storage of and access to, digital texts required for research, an aim to be achieved by purchasing published material in digital form, ADONIS journals, patents on CD-ROM and full-text databases on CD-ROM.

If the case for the legal deposit of electronic materials is accepted, the Library will seek National Lottery support to develop the necessary infrastructure for long-term collection management systems. To enhance its digital collection building the Library will also proceed with the digitization of items in its own collection, rare and fragile materials, special collections such as the philatelic collection and ageing document surrogates on microfilm direct from the film without handling the original documents. This replacement of one outdated technology by a new technology provides a cautionary reminder that digital images themselves will probably require preservation at some point, perhaps by transfer to new formats or storage media as the technology of storage and retrieval evolves. 'We are seeking collaboration in digitization programmes through the British Library University Research Support Service, among other channels' (para. 36, p. 18).

'Serving Readers in the Reading Rooms' details the opportunities already grasped for piloting the Online Public Access Catalogue during the long run-in to occupying the St Pancras building and describes how users will have access to the Library's catalogue and also to the catalogues of other libraries, via an OPAC-led single gateway. 'At St Pancras we aim to have sufficient terminals, running fast easy-to-use software, to permit readers to consult the catalogue without delay. Even at times of peak usage the aim is that no reader will have to wait more than two minutes to consult the catalogue' (para. 40, p. 19). In the St Pancras reading rooms there will be scope for the provision of direct access to the Library's networked services for users with their own computers, although access to the Library's collection of digital material will be controlled because of the limited number of workstations available.

'Serving the Library's Remote Users' emphasizes the enhancement of remote document supply afforded by digital network technology. The Patent Express service will be extended by Internet access to the database and to premium electronic delivery of selected patents. Computer searching of Inside Information and other contents page databases will improve existing electronic document delivery services. Access to the Library's online catalogue via JANET, SuperJANET and the Internet will also be extended.

'Serving Other Libraries' reminds us that remote access to the Library's online catalogue will be via the Networked OPAC.

A National Bibliographic Resource will be developed which will offer access to the bibliographic data created by the British Library and related bodies and will enable users to search for and download bibliographic records either individually or in bulk. Users of this database will be libraries, systems suppliers and bibliographic utilities as well as members of the Copyright Libraries Shared Cataloguing Programme (para. 46, p. 21).

It is also envisaged that this resource will be a major source of the British Library's internal derived cataloguing requirements. An imminent direct connection to BLAISE-LINE is announced and advance notice is given that a World Wide Web interface is being developed.

'Serving the Wider Public' reiterates that information technology will contribute to the British Library's ability to provide the broadest possible awareness of and access to, the national record heritage and that, in the St Pancras Exhibition Galleries, 'interactive displays will provide platforms for interpretation of the collections, bringing together the knowledge of the Library's curatorial staff and images from the actual treasures on display' (para. 50, p. 22).

'Corporate Strategy, Corporate Systems, Corporate Objectives' provides reassurance that curatorial staff are well qualified in maintaining both traditional and electronic library services, that the Library expects to work with 'a broad alliance of other organisations which share its concerns and aspirations', that many of the developments described in this document have been fully cost-justified and budgeted within the Library's business plan, that although the Strategy as outlined is made up of many diverse elements, 'none of them are isolated strands' and that 'this is a corporate strategy for corporate systems supporting corporate objectives'. Without doubt ambitious, 'it is the Information Systems Strategy the Library must have in order to achieve its broader strategic objectives' (para. 56, p. 23).

Components of the new technical infrastructure for the Library's computer systems that will be created for the Strategy's implementation are outlined in 'Appendix C: Future British Library Information Systems: A Technical Summary' (p. 38–45). Each component is described under a number of headings (e.g. end-user systems, collection management, the delivery of digital material and personal systems for staff). Their interconnections and relationships are superbly illustrated by two colour diagrams contrasting existing and future systems. At a glance, or at least by prolonged and concentrated study, every computerized Library function can be discerned in relation to all the others. For readers who might conclude that these two detailed diagrams tell them more about the computerized systems than they will ever need to know, there is also an overview of future systems which might be more to their taste.

Examining *Information Systems Strategy* halfway through its relevant period and in the knowledge of subsequent developments, it is clearly a convenient yardstick by which to measure aspirations against achievements. Already the equation is impressive and will continue to be so, as will become apparent as this book unfolds.

REVIEW OF THE PUBLIC LIBRARY SERVICE

Alarm bells began ringing in Euston Road when the *Review of the Public Library Service in England and Wales for the Department of National Heritage Final Report* was published by Aslib in 1995. The Review was the largest-ever single research project into public libraries and the first major review in the UK since the epoch-making McColvin Report of 1942. While the British Library welcomed the Report's focus on strengthening public library services and wholeheartedly supported the premise that electronic networking was a key element in their future development, it was quick to play down the suggestion that the Department should encourage regional library bodies to put forward proposals for funding Regional Library Centres (or hyperlibraries), with the British Library and private, voluntary and public sector partners cooperating in joint ventures.

Not wishing to watch its already overstretched resources vanishing into regional black holes, the British Library dismissed all such half-baked notions in its response to the Report.

> The British Library believes that it is in a better position to provide reference services and document supply services to the users of public libraries if its *national* collections are kept intact and maintained to standards that a number of regional hyperlibraries would be unlikely to maintain. Moreover, since its foundation, the National Lending Library for Science and Technology, now the British Library Document Supply Centre, has been a model for document supply around the world. With increasing emphasis on 'just-in-time' rather than 'just-in-case' library policies, the need for an efficient and cost-effective service arguably points to a single national back-up library of last resort, particularly bearing in mind the way in which IT is developing. We do not believe the concept of the hyperlibrary should be taken any further.

There are echoes here of the debate as to DSC's future which occupied centre-stage in the years 1989–92.

EXTENDING LEGAL DEPOSIT

Engaging the constant attention of the British Library during the period 1995–7 was the extension of legal deposit to electronic and other non-print publications. Sir Anthony Kenny, then Chairman of the British Library Board, took the initiative when he opened the 1995 Libtech International Exhibition. At the time the Library was preparing proposals, presented to the Department of National Heritage in January 1996, recommending that UK publishers should be required to deposit all existing and future forms of non-print materials like CD-ROMs, films and slide programmes, with a number of national archives and repositories under the supervision of a minister of the Crown. In the course of his address the Chairman stated that his main concern was 'the effect of the electronic age on national research libraries. The collection of the British Library and other great libraries in the world and this country depend very heavily on the system of legal deposit' and continued 'now that much material is being published in electronic forms as well as or instead of book form, there is a danger the national public archive might wither away' ('Electronic Publications Should Be Deposited with British Library', *Assistant Librarian*, 88 (10), Nov.–Dec. 1995, p. 153).

Issues raised by the Library working group responsible for formulating the proposals were already being investigated by staff in the various directorates. The National Bibliographic Service was examining the bibliographic control of non-print materials; Humanities and Social Sciences was preparing selection guidelines; Research and Development Department was funding a study of overseas legal deposit arrangements; and Computing and Telecommunications was studying how the British Library could contrive to provide access to non-print materials when the hardware and software required to read them became obsolete.

Sir Anthony expanded upon his remarks in a *THES* article. Essentially it was the inadequacies of the 1911 Copyright Act and how best these could be remedied, that troubled him. As the Act stood there was no provision for building up national archives for sound recordings or films; the British Library's National Sound Archive and the British Film Institute, had to rely on purchase and voluntary deposits to maintain their collections. But how most efficiently to amend the legal deposit legislation? One possibility would be to change the definition of a book to include CD-ROMs, for example, but, in the British Library's view, proceeding piecemeal in this fashion would be to invite future legislative chaos as repeated amendments would be required to update the Copyright Act. Rather than attempting to precisely define a 'book' or 'publication', it would be better by far for Parliament to adopt flexible statutory procedures for widening the categories of material to be deposited.

> The statute should provide for subsidiary regulations to be drawn up as appropriate to bring specific media and forms of publication within the ambit of the legal deposit system. In this way it will be possible to cope with media as yet unimagined. New regulations will be able to amend or repeal previous regulations without the governing primary legislation requiring amendment.

Non-print material currently published could be divided into four broad classes: (1) microform material and (2) texts in hand-held electronic form (sometimes collectively styled 'glass-books', i.e. read from a glass screen as opposed to the printed page); (3) sound and video recordings; and (4) online databases. It was the last category that posed the most intractable problems for libraries with respect to publication, to archiving and to drawing up viable regulations governing legal deposit.

> The new legislation should be broad enough in principle to permit databases published online to be brought within its ambit in due course. But the immediate extension of the legal deposit system should cover only microforms, CD-ROMs and other hand-held electronic texts and sound and film recordings. As soon as the primary legislation is in place these media should be brought within the system by regulations to take immediate effect. At a later time, when the publication of electronic journals, for instance, has reached a stable state, regulations for their legal deposit should be issued by the Secretary of State after consultation with both producers and consumers.

To placate the non-print producers and publishers and to keep them on board, the British Library had extensively consulted these rights-holders before completing its proposals and had concluded that the most acceptable form of deposit for electronic texts was that which most closely resembled the existing regulations.

> In the case of CD-ROMs, for instance, one copy should be deposited gratis in each of the copyright libraries for consultation at a single stand-alone workstation. Any networking should be permitted only by agreement with the rights holders and any charges made by libraries for such consultations must include royalty payments to be passed on.

Should these proposals not be acted upon, it would be impossible for the national library to continue to maintain the public archive. In fact a large amount of non-print material had already eluded deposit.

> Reform here is urgent and the Library hopes fervently that new legislation can be introduced before the end of the present parliament. It will also be important to plug the gaps which already exist in the national published archive because of the inadequacy of the 1911 Act. This could not be done by retrospective legislation, but funding for the clearance of this backlog could be a suitable object of funding from the Millennium

Commission or some other arm of the National Lottery' ('Increased deposits on the next century', *THES*, **1218**, 8 Mar. 1996, Multimedia Supplement, p. vii; reprinted as 'Beyond the printed word', *Library Association Record*, **98** (4), Apr. 1996, p. 201).

Further details of the proposals and of the British Library's position, emerged in Paul Gibson's 'Preserving a digital heritage', *Library Manager*, no. 18, May 1996, pp. 6, 8, which included a number of observations from the British Library's Ann Clarke. Reinforcing her Chairman's views on a staged application of the legal deposit laws to non-print materials, she argued that online was not a great problem area, just an unknown one. 'We aren't yet sure of all the issues and we would need a few trials to ensure that there weren't any serious errors in our approach.' As for frequently updated CD-ROMs, she advocated an annual 'time-slice' cull. Neither did she foresee problems in deciding the location of where deposited materials should be held. The six UK copyright libraries possessed the skills, experience and facilities to store them as part of the national archive. But differing from Sir Anthony Kenny slightly in approach, she attempted to draw a line between the copyright and legal deposit issues in the short term: 'the copyright issue is one of the reasons we are not immediately tackling online databases'.

Ann Clarke had no doubt that if the British Library's proposals were adopted 'gaps in collections will start to disappear. It would also mean that we have a national published archive which will be of significant importance to the nation's researchers.' She was convinced that the proposals had been developed on behalf of all UK libraries: 'legal deposit is fundamental as a last resort for research and it will be of major future importance to all libraries and all their users'.

So persuasive were the British Library's proposals that they formed the basis for the section on 'Extending legal deposit to new publication media' in *Legal Deposit of Publications*, a 63-page consultation paper unveiled by the Department of National Heritage, 12 February 1997. Accepting the argument that the development of digital media had progressively eroded the all-embracing clutch of the existing legal deposit legislation, the Government expressed the view that 'some means must be found of ensuring the continuing comprehensiveness of the national published archive and that legislation is likely to be required to extend the legal deposit system to publications in new forms' but, as if recoiling from this startling radicalism, it stressed that 'retrospection would be neither practicable nor desirable and that any gaps in collections which have emerged before new arrangements take effect would have to be filled by purchase' (para. 3.4, p. 19). And, reverting to type, the Government expected 'that any additional costs to the repositories arising from the extension of legal deposit to non-print publication media will be absorbed by those repositories within existing levels of resources. The Government will not be providing additional public funds for this purpose' (para. 5.14, p. 43).

Despite this blinkered decision, the consultation paper examined the general issues to be addressed: drawing the line between publications and private communications and defining the person on whom the duty to deposit lies; deciding on the appropriate destination of deposited material; the procedure for deposit; defining each medium precisely; deciding the categories of material in each medium which require deposit and the possibility of introducing a mechanism for prescribing exceptions to the general rule; conditions attaching to the use which may be made of material deposited; and the possibility of establishing a framework for extending legal deposit to further publication media without the need for primary legislation.

Making it clear that it intended to follow the procedures for the deposit of print publications, that is an automatic requirement to deposit with the British Library and a system of deposit on claim for the other copyright libraries (now termed agency libraries), it nevertheless foresaw that some categories of material, for example sound recordings with a specific Scottish or Welsh content, should be deposited with the National Library of Scotland and the National Library of Wales.

> The possibility that legal deposit will be extended to new types of published material, the proliferation of published information sources and the ease and speed with which information can now be communicated emphasise the urgency of work on selectivity and co-operation. No single institution or group of institutions can now expect to have resources to be able to preserve *all* information which is provided to the public in the future (para. 2.26, p. 17).

For its part, the Government was prepared to take the selectivity principle into uncharted areas, questioning whether statutory powers on the disposal of material received under legal deposit needed to be enacted.

> The Government seeks views on establishing clear legal powers for the legal deposit libraries to dispose of material received under legal deposit

as they see fit, subject to safeguards to ensure that copies of material which publishers might be in a position to sell are not donated or sold by the libraries to institutions or individuals who might otherwise purchase them from publishers or distributors (para. 2.30, p. 18) [and, further,] whether specific statutory powers should be enacted in respect of legal deposit libraries withholding from users commercially sensitive or other confidential information (para. 2.31, p. 18).

With the general principles outlined the consultation paper proceeds to specify the media to be examined for immediate extension of legal deposit, electronic publications in tangible format, namely CD-ROMs, sound recordings, film and video recordings and microform publications, conforming exactly to those the British Library had identified. In the case of CD-ROMs the Library had proposed that in addition to the CD, information about its content, rights, data structure, format and chemical composition, should also be deposited. This, too, the Government was prepared to take on board:

> The Government believes that the deposit . . . requirement should require deposit of electronic publications in the form in which they are made available to the public, together with any associated software, manuals and materials which are also made available to the public in order to enable the publications to be used. [Moreover,] longer-term preservation issues, including information about data structures and the chemical makeup of the publication should be the subject of discussion between publishers and the libraries (para. 3.22, p. 27).

There were three options: deposit under voluntary arrangements with one or more of the legal deposit libraries; deposit of a single copy, or two copies (one for use and one for back-up) with a single repository; or deposit of one copy as of right to the British Library and of one copy, on request, with each of the agency libraries. In each instance access at the library of deposit would be confined to a single user at a time working at a stand-alone workstation.

Sound recordings were already being deposited, the major UK record producers depositing either one or two recordings in LP, tape and CD format with the National Sound Archive, which also received both BBC and independent sound broadcasts, concentrating on original material such as live concerts. What needed to be resolved in this context was whether the existing voluntary system should continue or whether deposit should be prescribed. Films and video recordings were the province of the British Film Institute's National and TV Archive. For microform publications the British Library proposed the deposit of negative copies of archival quality with access arrangements matching those for printed publications. The Government was contemplating safeguards in terms of exceptions for low production run and high-cost microform material. But, like all the points raised in this document, the Government was seeking views on the best way forward.

As the Library had foreseen, the most intractable problems concerned online communications, material supplied from a central database direct, on request, to a customer's database, or made available at any site on a publicly available network. A number of complex issues first had to be resolved before any system of legal deposit could be introduced. The enormity of the task is illustrated by the five most salient points cited: defining those responsible for publication and for depositing the material published; the volume of data available in this form and the ability of the libraries to process, store and provide access to it; dealing possibly on a 'snapshot' basis with the databases being constantly updated; and distinguishing between data published in this form and data which had been communicated privately. Again following the British Library line, the Government was prepared to allow for 'fine-tuning of definitions in the light of technical developments' in subsequent subordinate legislation.

The consultation exercise ended 11 April 1997. Subsequently, a working party was appointed, under the chairmanship of Sir Anthony Kenny, to advise on how a national archive of non-print material might be achieved; to draw up a voluntary code of practice to achieve deposits of electronic and microform publications; and to ensure that such measures are compatible with existing arrangements for voluntary deposit of films and sound recordings. It reports back at the end of July 1998.

THE SMETHURST REVIEW

Prompted by the growing needs of users and researchers, the constraints of available funding, the continued expansion and variety of publications inundating the Legal Deposit Office and continuing the internal review of its acquisition and retention policies commissioned as part of its ongoing planning processes in 1987 (reported in *Selection for Survival* (1989) and no doubt encouraged by that document's advice that it would be 'prudent for the Library to identify and assess crucial problems

rather than be subjected to the arbitrary imposition of unsuitable reme-
dies from outside, with external or governmental agencies setting the
agenda for reshaping the Library and its future'), the British Library
Board invited J.M. Smethurst, formerly Deputy Chief Executive, to
undertake a new review.

His terms of reference were 'to review the acquisition and retention
policies of the British Library in respect of British printed materials
received under the legal deposit privilege in the context of the Library's
duty to meet efficiently and effectively the needs of scholarship and
research both now and in the future'. Specifically, the Review was to

> consider the scope and range of materials to be acquired and retained by
> the Library with particular reference to its responsibilities for the cre-
> ation and maintenance of the national archive of printed material, tak-
> ing into account the National Libraries of Scotland and Wales and the
> Universities of Oxford, Cambridge and Trinity College Dublin as
> libraries of legal deposit; consider the effect of technological changes on
> information provision and publishing and upon the needs of scholarship
> and research in the development of the national printed archive; con-
> sider issues relating to access, storage and the maintenance of the
> printed material received under the legal deposit privilege; consider the
> feasibility of and potential for, agreeing clear responsibilities among the
> legal deposit libraries; and report to the Board of the British Library.

After several months' work the Review's conclusions were presented to
the Board in the summer of 1996 and were printed in *A Review of the
Policy and Arrangements for the Legal Deposit of Printed Material in the
British Library*, an eight-page document circulated in March 1997.
Although not strictly speaking a consultation paper, comments and
queries were invited. Allowing that legal deposit, which places a requirement on publishers to deposit their works free of charge in designated
institutions, underpins the collections of the great national libraries, the
Review concluded that 'it is no longer possible for any single library to
acquire, maintain and preserve the total output of British publishers
given the continual growth of publishing and the limited resources for
the development and maintenance of published collections'.

Against that stark and uncompromising background the Review rec-
ommended a reinforced sharing of responsibility for the National
Published Archive among the six legal deposit and other major libraries.
Each of these libraries would bear the additional responsibility of main-

taining access to and preserving its contribution to, the Archive, which would be achieved by the creation of a National Bibliographic Resource consisting of the records of accession and their locations. It is stated, at this point, that the concept of such a resource had already been discussed among the Consortium of University Research Libraries (CURL) and the United Kingdom national libraries. Despite apparently conceding that the British Library could no longer collect and maintain the National Printed Archive unaided, the Review nevertheless recommended that it should hold on to its right of automatic deposit (as opposed to the other legal deposit libraries which must claim whatever material they require) on the grounds that claiming would impose additional staff and data processing costs. To balance this the Review advocated greater selectivity at the point of receipt in the Library's Legal Deposit Office. The Library is encouraged to prepare detailed guidelines for selection at this point, to publish its collection development policies and to develop an agreed disposal policy with the publishers for unwanted items.

To augment initiatives set in place following *Selection for Survival* the Library is advised

> to review its collecting policy regarding new editions in paperback for the text of standard authors (i.e. those who are published in many editions and reprints), to consider further sampling techniques for the retention of reprints; and to review its intake of mass-market leisure journal titles of low use. It is suggested that such materials be collected on a sample basis and/or through more collaborative framework of distributed responsibility within the National Published Archive; to cease to collect newspapers which are primarily advertising journals, or to sample these selectively; and to cease to exercise responsibility for acquiring materials purely of local or regional interest which are likely to be held in well-managed local collections

and, because newspapers make a heavy demand on storage space, the Library 'should seek the deposit of either microform copies or electronic forms of British and Irish national newspapers instead of print on paper, where adequate substitutes exist'. If retention in paper form be considered essential the National Libraries of Scotland and Wales should participate in their archival storage. In addition the Library should develop a National Reports Centre for reports and grey literature building on DSC's existing national reports collection.

The Board accepted many of the Review's recommendations *in toto*, particularly those relating to internal British Library activities, but recognized that consultations would be needed with the other legal deposit libraries. Accordingly the British Library set up a programme at senior level to implement the Review's recommendations and to advance discussions with all the interested parties, including the regional and local library systems and with specialized libraries, if responsibility for some categories of publications is to be devolved among a range of libraries within the National Published Archive under the leadership of the legal deposit libraries through the Standing Committee on Legal Deposit (SCOLD).

Of course the British Library can propose but only government action or voluntary agreements at the local level can dispose, and it remains to be seen whether either of these will be forthcoming, although initial government reaction would seem to be favourable. Certainly this commendably succinct document contains some startling statements and sobering conclusions, notably that the British Library can no longer go it alone. It is true that one or two of the Review's recommendations could legitimately be challenged. For example valid arguments could be made against collection on a sample basis of mass-market leisure journals. At best this can only be an informed hit and miss measure and who is to know which particular journals will be required by future researchers, the constituency the Chief Executive invokes on suitable occasions? To cease the acquisition of material purely of local or regional interest which could be expected to be collected at local level undoubtedly makes sound professional sense, but will it be so explicable to a researcher not based in that particular region? No doubt, the Review's Advisory Group were aware of this kind of argument but at least the nettle of the sheer physical and financial impossibility of an all-embracing inclusive acquisition policy has been grasped.

A two-year implementation programme, led by Andrew Phillips, former Director of Humanities and Social Sciences, was set in motion to refine the Review's recommendations and to take forward the implementation of its proposals, in partnership with the other legal deposit libraries, publishers and other interested parties.

BRITISH LIBRARY READER SURVEY

At its summer 1992 meeting the British Library Board re-affirmed its policy of not charging an admission fee to the Library's reading rooms, although it was stated that this policy would be reviewed once the St Pancras building was opened. Shortly after the Board's November 1996 meeting – when it again endorsed the policy of no charges for admission – it became apparent that the government's grant-in-aid for 1997–98 and following years, would fall short of the previously agreed planning figures, leaving a sizeable hole in the Library's finances. One obvious option to offset the loss was to introduce admission charges, thus breaking a 250-year tradition of free access. In order that it might have the fullest possible information about reading room use and readers' attitudes should a policy review be required, the Board requested the Library management to investigate and analyse its findings before the first reading room opened at St Pancras.

First, the Library collated all the survey data it had assembled over the previous five years, breaking it down into types of readers, types and frequency of use and research or business interest. In the second phase the Library asked the Henley Centre to undertake research in to the current and future use of the Library's reading rooms. Consequently, 12-page questionnaires were distributed to readers, Wednesday, 30 April – Thursday, 1 May 1997, in all the Bloomsbury reading rooms, the SRIS reading room at Holborn and Aldwych, the OIOC reading room in Blackfriars Road and in the Newspaper Library at Colindale. Thirty-three questions were included in the survey, only four of which related directly to possible admission charges.

Respondents were asked to categorize themselves by occupation (36 were on offer), to describe the type of organization they worked for, how many employees their organization had, how many of these ever visited the Library and where respondents lived (in or out of the United Kingdom, within the European Union, or elsewhere in the world). Then came the serious business: what was the main purpose of their research, was it their first visit; how often had they visited in the last month, the last twelve months; which months of the year did they typically visit the Library, which days, what times; how long did they spend in the Library; did they intend to visit the Library again? What was missing here was a follow-up question in the event of a 'no' answer to elicit why not. Which of the Library's remote services were they aware of and/or used, which other libraries did they use for research purposes? Next, their opinions on various aspects of the Library's services were solicited on a 1 to 5 scale.

At this point, respondents were informed of the possibility of admission charges to the reading rooms and invited to consider two possible methods. One was to charge a flat fee for issuing a pass to each reader; the other would be a variable charge for maintaining and staffing the reading rooms and providing book delivery and enquiry services according to the level of use. For this second method a distinction was made between short-term access (up to five days access to the reading rooms) and longer-term access (i.e. regular access throughout the year). A range of charges was presented and respondents were asked to indicate how reasonable, or otherwise, these appeared. As if to reward their assiduity in completing the questionnaire, next came acres of tempting blank white space on which they were implored to register comments. Finally, they were asked to indicate in which reading room and on which day they completed the survey.

On Saturday, 3 May, a letter from Dr Clive Coen, Biomedical Sciences Division, King's College London, was printed in *The Times*. He, for one, was alarmed by the survey:

> From a range of possible fees I was expected to select the three that fit the following categories: 'reasonable', 'expensive' and 'I would no longer visit the library'. The absence of a box marked 'unreasonable in principle' seems likely to skew the results. Furthermore I was asked to classify possible charges for a 'flat fee per reader pass' without being informed whether this pass would apply to one visit or one year. To add infelicity to inadequacy the questionnaire also tried to establish how strongly I agree with various unintelligible statements such as 'Visiting the British Library is a uniquely different experience'; it certainly was yesterday. ('Pay per view?', *The Times*, 65880, 3 May 1997, p. 21).

One reader, at least, was not best pleased.

By that time a battery of heavy literary guns had already been wheeled out. Despite, or perhaps because of, the Chief Executive's protestations that there was no current plan to introduce charges in the short or long term, their reaction was immediate. Lady Antonia Fraser, a reader for over forty years, was of the opinion that citizens of this country 'should unquestionably have their rights to visit freely, great collections which have been built up for them', while Malcolm Bradbury expressed the view that the Library 'should be available to scholars on the principle of their research'. Brian Lake, secretary of the Regular Readers Group reported that there had been no consultation with them before putting out the questionnaire (David Lister, 'Literati read riot act over admission fees', *The Independent*, 3285, 1 May 1997, p. 5).

A number of questionnaires were also posted to a representative group of Library users who may not necessarily have been frequent visitors, with an additional survey of overseas readers. Corporate users were contacted by telephone. The results of the survey were presented to the Board at its July meeting.

Whether or not the survey was a timely reminder to the incoming New Labour government that without additional funding the Library could not sustain its services at the current level is a moot point. The Library dismissed any such Machiavellian intent but Vincent Brome, a member of the British Library Advisory Committee, 1975–82, suggested in *The Times* correspondence columns that

> Tony Blair or the new Heritage Secretary has a splendid opportunity to defend the principle of free access to books and information . . . it would be a wonderful gesture for the new Heritage Secretary to increase the Library's grant to the point where the sordid fumbling for fees from readers would become unnecessary. The sum is negligible: the principle profound. ('British Library fees', *The Times*, no. 65886, 10 May 1997, p. 23).

Future adherents to the conspiracy theory of history will have a field day on this.

In the mean time speculation started about what the Library might do with its increased revenue although fears were expressed that the Government might correspondingly reduce the Library's annual grant-in-aid. Formidable arguments against charges remained. The abolition of free access to academic researchers would doubtless lose the Library immense goodwill which it could ill afford. There was a strong argument, too, that the taxpayer was already contributing huge sums of money for the Library without charges being imposed for its use, also lowering goodwill. For the moment the *status quo* has been maintained. At its meeting, 18 July 1997, the Board reaffirmed its long-standing position that users should be able to access the Library's collections in its reading rooms without charge. However, the Board also decided that further work suggested by a report of the findings of the Library's survey of reader attitudes towards charging would go ahead.

5

INITIATIVES FOR ACCESS

The British Library's Initiatives for Access (IfA) was an extensive programme designed to investigate digital and networking technologies to improve access to its immense collections and to further its strategic objectives of becoming a major holder and supplier of digital data by the beginning of the next century. The longer term implications in terms of staffing, financial resources, data security and copyright questions are quite staggering. But revolutionary though IfA might have been, 'it is only a beginning for the British Library in its long-term strategy of offering services to its users based on electronic material and the use of networks' (Neil Smith, 'The British Library: Initiatives For Access', *Managing Information*, 1 (6), June 1994, pp. 39–40). To keep Library users and other interested parties up-to-date, an occasional illustrated newsletter, *Initiatives for Access News*, was published, providing information on the hardware and software platforms used in the different projects, on development strategies, and on demonstration sites and completion dates.

Other authoritative overview articles include Jonathan Purday's 'The British Library's Initiatives for Access', *Information Technology and Public Policy*, 13 (1), Winter 1994, pp. 37–9 and Michael Alexander's 'The British Library Initiatives for Access Seminar', *Information Services and Use*, 16 (3/4), 1996, pp. 165–73.

Edited by Leona Carpenter, Andrew Prescott and Simon Shaw, *Towards the Digital Library* (The British Library, 1998) gives a detailed account of the individual projects that comprised the Initiatives for Access programme with introductory and linking text that converges images, technical standards and service issues. Published whilst this present book was in the press, it also looks ahead to a future information environment in which digital technology is expected to play an essential role. (See Appendix 2.)

ELECTRONIC *BEOWULF*

One of the first fruits of the IfA programme was the launching of *Beowulf*, the 1000-years-old literary masterpiece, into cyberspace in February 1994. Test images from the Library's unique manuscript of the Old English epic poem were made available over international computer networks. Researchers from all over the world can now access pictures from the manuscript instantly through the Internet. Each page was photographed at high resolution under white light, ultra-violet light and with fibre-optic cable, which allows researchers to see letters formerly obscured by fire damage in 1731 and restoration of the manuscript in the nineteenth century. Eventually, the complete manuscript will be available in a variety of formats, including CD-ROM and network access.

Andrew Prescott's superbly illustrated 'Beowulf on the Super-highway', *Information for Access News*, no.1, May 1994, pp. 4–5, is an authoritative summary article while Tom Standage's highly technical 'On the horizon', *British Journal of Photography*, no. 6998, 2 November 1994, pp. 14–15, sets the project within the context of other digital photography developments. But the most detailed description of Electronic Beowulf is a paper by Kevin Kiernan printed in *Scholarly Publishing on the Electronic Networks: Proceedings of the Third Symposium*, edited by A. Okerson (Washington, Association of Research Libraries, Office of Scientific and Academic Publishing, 1994).

The Beowulf project won the 1994 Library Association/Mecklermedia award for innovation through information technology.

PIX PROJECT

Developed between September 1993 and March 1994, the electronic photoviewing system, PIX, is designed to speed up and simplify research for illustrative material in the Library's collection of books, manuscripts, music, original photographs and philatelic items. A representative sample of the millions of images held in the Library enables users to browse and view a tiny fraction of this immense resource.

The photo viewing system allows searches to be made on keygroups and keywords, including a subject index and incorporates traditional shelf-marks and useful data in up to twenty-two fields. For picture researchers and others seeking illustrative material the system opens up pictorial material which was formerly inaccessible ('Electronic photos delight readers', *IfA News*, no.1, May 1994, p. 1). [But,] apart from allowing the public to browse and view some of the Library's spectacular collection of pictures it was felt that the project could fulfil other important functions. Providing an electronic surrogate, for example, would help to protect the collections by reducing the need to handle the original material. It would provide the curatorial staff with a practical and efficient means of cataloguing and indexing the images and it had the potential of earning revenue for the Library by providing hard copy prints from the images held on the database. (John Fletcher, 'British Library's Electronic Photo Viewing System', *Online and CD Notes*, June 1996, pp. 5–6).

This article, reproduced virtually unaltered in *Audio Visual Librarian*, **22** (3), August 1996, pp. 179–81, examines the development of PIX, its use, quality and future as a component part of the Library's photographic section and in the new Picture Library. Ben Bergonzi's 'Electronic Photo Viewing System in the British Library', *The BAPLA Journal*, **31** (2), 1994, pp. 66–7 gives details of the content of PIX, how the system was created and of its potential use.

PIXTEX

Although building digital document stores from scanned images proved a relatively simple process, the effective retrieval of digitized data after its capture posed problems. In seeking to overcome these problems, the British Library encountered an American company, Excalibur Technologies Inc., whose main product PixTex/EFS (Electronic Filing System) was already successfully employed in a Library of Congress project. PixTex makes use of Adaptive Pattern Recognition Technology 'to recognise the occurrence and interlinking of patterns' by examining 'the way information is stored at its fundamental level – as binary numbers – and identifies patterns in these numbers . . . which are the basis of its indexing method' (Michael Alexander, 'Digital data retrieval: testing Excalibur', *Information for Access News*, no.2, December 1994, pp. 6–7). The full story is outlined in Alexander's 'Retrieving digital data with fuzzy matching', *Library Association Record*, **96** (9), September 1994, Technology Supplement, pp. 21–2 and reproduced in a slightly amended version in *New Library World*, **97** (1131), 1996, pp. 26–8 and in *Managing Information*, **4** (1/2), January–February 1997, pp. 34–5, 37.

PORTICO

When first launched on the Internet Portico was a pilot online information service providing from a single source information on the British Library's reading rooms, collections and services. The original gopher server is now upgraded with sound, vision, interactivity and hypertext links added to the original text files. Current features include: (1) World Wide Web pages describing British Library events, services and holdings, including full information on DSC, SRIS, NBS and OIOC accompanied by graphics and fine images from the Library's collection. Also available is the Portico Gopher, a guide in plain-text format to other Library services and collecting departments; (2) a guide to British Library catalogues and databases; (3) information on the Library's activities in Europe, with links to Web servers offered by national libraries on the continent; (4) text, images and sound from temporary Library exhibitions, plus images of treasures on permanent display and images of recent major acquisitions; (5) the most recent issue of *Initiatives for Access News* and sample images from several Initiatives for Access projects; (6) an interactive 'virtual tour' of the Library's St Pancras building; (7) a search engine to help users to find what they want on the system; and (8) links to a hundred other major World Wide Web resources.

Further details may be found in 'Portico opens: enquire within', *Information for Access News*, no. 2, December 1994, p. 1; 'The Wonderful Web', no. 3, Autumn 1995, p. 10; and 'What's New on Portico?', no. 4, Autumn 1996, pp. 10–11.

TURNING THE PAGES

The 'Turning the Pages' Digitization programme not only provides archival storage but, more dramatically, enhances access to the internationally renowned masterpieces on display in St Pancras' purpose-built John Ritblatt Gallery: Treasures of the British Library. These include, for first opening of the Gallery, the *Diamond Sutra*, the world's first recorded printed document, produced in eighth-century AD China; the Anglo-Saxon *Lindisfarne Gospels*; the *Book of Hours* of Bona Sforza; and Leonardo da Vinci's *Notebooks*. The aim is that visitors to the galleries might be given the opportunity to view the screen images, via browser kiosks and be able to magnify details and compare items. A brainchild of Jane Carr, Director of Public Affairs, and of Clive Izard, Head of Audio-

Visual Services, Turning the Pages, a system using computer animation, high-quality digitized images and touch-screen technology, permitting user-selected page-turning and zooming, and designed for use alongside the original items in the exhibition galleries, adds a whole new dimension. Describing how her idea was put into practice, Carr confided that

> The great challenge with exhibiting books or manuscripts is to explain the significance or beauty of each when only a single opening from the original can be displayed. As we began to plan for the exhibition galleries in the Library's new building at St. Pancras, we developed the very simple concept of allowing the visitor to turn a surrogate but facsimile page. Digital technology combined with animation and televisual techniques provide the perfect medium since neither the original nor the facsimile is damaged or degraded by the process and yet the visitor can have a real sense of what it might be like to turn the pages of the real thing.'

'A turn up for the Treasures', *Information for Access News*, no. 4, Autumn 1996, pp. 1–2 fills in the background.

OTHER PROJECTS

Other IfA projects, the Network OPAC, Project Digitize, Project Incipit, the Patent Express Jukebox, the Image Demonstrator Project, the Digitization of Microfilm Project, and Electronic Asia, are discussed elsewhere in this present book.

6

MANAGEMENT STRUCTURE

HUMANITIES AND SOCIAL SCIENCES

Recognizing that its relocation to St Pancras would lead to procedural and physical changes to its working environment, influencing the pattern of its reader and behind the scenes services, Humanities and Social Sciences resolved as early as 1992 to engage in an organizational development programme to ensure that it would be in good shape to cope with new methods of accessing and disseminating information and with the rising expectations of its users. Following the recommendations of a number of task groups, two redesignated services were created. The Early Collection Service comprises the Incunabula Short-Title Catalogue and the Eighteenth Century Short-Title Catalogue projects, together with the pre-1850 British and European collections, while a new Modern Collections Service was made responsible for post-1850 collections in English and other European languages. Greater prominence was given to reader services, with an increased involvement of curators and the development of public service expertise for all professional staff.

Thus, as was the intention, H&SS was fully prepared when a root and branch reform of the British Library's management structure was announced in May 1995 following an Efficiency Review undertaken in 1994 at the request of the Department of National Heritage. The objective was to bring together under more unified management those Library directorates responsible for maintaining and building the Library's collection of books and ensuring the most effective services to readers. Findings of the four Peterborough initiatives on collection development, collection management, access improvement and user satisfaction also contributed to the restructure.

1995

The first stage rearranged the management of the existing directorates under two Director-Generals. One, with a new title of Deputy Chief Executive, was to manage all collection and service based directorates, Humanities and Social Sciences, SRIS, Document Supply Centre, Special Collections and Public Services. The other would be responsible for all support directorates: Computing and Telecommunications; Collections and Preservation; Acquisitions, Processing and Cataloguing; and the National Bibliographic Service. This signified the dismantling of a largely location based, two-site management structure, in favour of a unified structure specially designed to prepare the Library for the move to St Pancras. The objectives were to unite the Library geographically and to eliminate the duplication of services and responsibilities deriving from the Library's origins in the disparate bodies and institutions corralled into the British Library in 1973, thereby operating as a single unit by taking advantage of the opportunities offered by the new networking technologies, to reduce distinctions between sites. A revised *Structure and Functions* brochure was issued outlining the various directorates' responsibilities.

1996

Plans for the second stage were presented to the British Library Board in June 1996. Based on a strategy to provide more focused services from fewer directorates, thus increasing efficiency and reducing bureaucracy, the aim was to achieve a more homogenous corporate culture and, more tangibly, to put in place effective lines of management which would rationalize and integrate the Library's services at St Pancras. It was a defining moment for the British Library as it corporately distanced itself from the separate and disparate institutions in which it had its origins and moved forward to a more modern two-site operation designed to fully exploit the new technologies. The 13 existing directorates were reduced to 11 for the interim period prior to the relocation to St Pancras and two more would be amalgamated with others once the St Pancras move was completed. This fundamental reorganization undoubtedly reflected more closely the Library's relationship with its three main client groups, academic researchers, industrial researchers and remote users.

With effect from 1 August 1996 the Director-General Collections and

Services assumed responsibility for four directorates. An enhanced Bibliographic Services and Document Supply directorate (BSDS) formed from the National Bibliographic Service and Document Supply Centre, to take charge of all the British Library's interlending and remote document supply services, including the London-based Patent Express service transferred from SRIS and for all bibliographic publishing including BLAISE and the network OPAC. The new structure enables users to gain access, make orders and process transactions through a single service point.

> A major strength of the new directorate is that it will integrate the process of research delivery and information retrieval with that of document supply. Already BLAISE provides a means for registered users to search the Library's holdings and order the documents traced. *Inside*, the integrated current awareness and document supply service, is another example of how bibliographic services and document supply are moving closer together as new technology develops. ('A United Service: Bibliographic Services and Document Supply', *Select*, **19**, Spring 1997, pp. 3–4).

Reader Services and Collection Development directorate (RS&CD) absorbed the former Humanities and Social Sciences directorate and is responsible for Early Collections, Modern Collections (English language, Western European and Slavonic collections), the Newspaper Library and the British Library Information Science Services. After its relocation at St Pancras in 1999, Science Reference and Information Service (SRIS) will also form part of RS&CD. Not everyone is too pleased at this. For example, Sandra Ward, Chairman of the SRIS Advisory Committee:

> We are concerned that the strategic planning of the BL's services in science, technology, industry and business is being delegated to too low a level. This is likely to affect the BL's ability to influence international developments and its relationship with the customer population it seeks to serve within the UK (quoted in Tim Owen's 'Management shake-out as BL prepares to move', *Information World Review*, no. 119, November 1996, pp. 14–15).

Book delivery services, user satisfaction, access, readers' admission and 'phone service, also come within RS&CD's remit. It works closely with Special Collections (Western Manuscripts, Map Library, Music Library,

Philatelic Collections, Oriental and India Office Collections and the National Sound Archive).

Support directorates reporting to the Deputy Chief Executive include Acquisitions Processing and Cataloguing (AP&C) which will merge with Collections and Preservation (C&P) to form a new directorate, Collection Management, in the third stage of reconstructing; St Pancras Occupation and Estate (SPOE); Information Systems (IS); and Research and Innovation Centre (RIC). Reporting direct to the Chief Executive are Public Affairs (PA), a new directorate with a remit to extend the Library's programme of exhibitions, education and public events in the UK and overseas, publishing, the book shop, media resources, corporate communication, design and development functions, a wider communication with the general public through its visitor services operations and Planning and Resources (P&R).

In the Chief Executive's words, the new structure

> will allow the Library to exploit cross-market opportunities and to ratio-nalise overlaps in services. We have also identified a senior focus for our vital digital library developments, set up a new directorate for public affairs and corporate marketing, prepared for our future estate responsi-bilities, brought research and innovation into the core of the Library's activities and strengthened our planning, finance and human resources functions.

Expressed differently, the Library has at last successfully disengaged itself from the constraints of its historical heritage and transformed itself into a coherent, forward-looking, function based and businesslike corpora-tion. If staff, suddenly bereft of a long-accustomed culture, had suffered from a certain disorientation while the restructuring was in progress, they now emerged into a logical and reinvigorated management system. (See Figure 6.1 on facing page.)

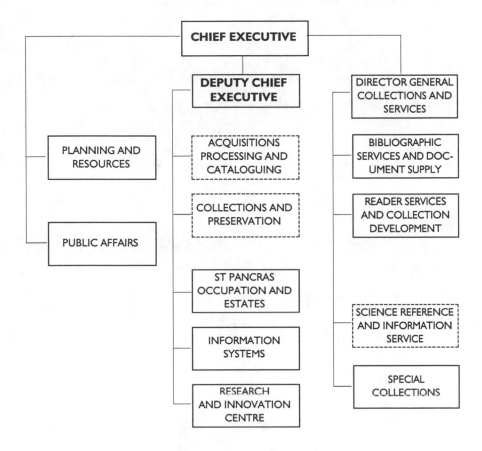

Acquisitions Processing and Cataloguing and Collections and Preservations will merge to form a new directorate, Collection Management, in the final phase of restructuring. The Science Reference and Information Service will become part of Reader Services and Collection Development when it moves to St Pancras

Fig. 6.1 *The British Library 31 March 1997*

PART II

COLLECTIONS AND SERVICES

7

BIBLIOGRAPHIC SERVICES AND DOCUMENT SUPPLY

National Bibliographic Service

One of three directorates carved out from the former Bibliographic Services Division in 1989 – the others being Acquisitions, Processing and Cataloguing (AP&C) and Computing and Telecommunications (C&T) – the National Bibliographic Service was charged with the responsibility of providing UK libraries with a bibliographic agency giving them access to details of the national current imprint and to the British Library's catalogues and bibliographic databases. To mark its first five years, a six-page brochure, *Fifth Anniversary Facts and Figures*, outlining its principal activities and service developments, was circulated in 1994. A summary article, 'Britain's National Bibliographic Service', was printed in *Information Retrieval and Library Automation*, 30 (6), November 1994, pp. 1–2. Christopher Easingwood's 'Five Years of NBS', *Select*, no. 13, Autumn 1994, pp. 2–3 is a personal account of his work experience in the Directorate, which included developing and adapting *BNB on CD-ROM* in the light of customer feedback, testing software, writing specifications, providing technical support to customers and the relocation to Boston Spa.

In the August 1996 restructure NBS was merged with Document Supply Centre in a new enhanced Bibliographic Services and Document Supply (BSDS) directorate, thus integrating resource discovery, information retrieval and document supply. NBS' remit was extended to embrace a wider range of bibliographic publishing. BSDS claimed that the merger would enable it to develop key products and services more successfully by allowing for more effective service presentation and promotion, by addressing users' uncertainty on how to get the best out of its services and by ensuring users would receive better services. Evidence to support this well-intentioned optimism was meagre.

To assist NBS in developing strategies for the provision of bibliographic information which would meet the needs of all types of libraries and information units, its Marketing Research section organized a major survey into the extent of automation in UK libraries in July 1994, dispatching some 15,000 questionnaires to school, further education, university, government, business and public libraries. The response was overwhelming. John Lee's 'Automation in UK libraries', *Library Technology News*, no. 16, February 1995, pp. 1, 3–4 identifies some of the key trends, in particular the usage of electronic mail, online technology, CD-ROMs and their networking. Lee's 'Automation In Libraries Questionnaire: a brief summary of findings so far', *Select*, no. 14, Winter 1994/95, p. 9 covers much the same ground.

BRITISH NATIONAL BIBLIOGRAPHY

Produced from the BNBMARC files of NBS, the printed *British National Bibliography (BNB)* lists new and forthcoming titles published in the British Isles. Each Weekly List is in two sequences: Recently Received and Forthcoming Titles are arranged by subject according to the Dewey Decimal Classification. New books and serials received by the British Library under the Copyright Act, 1911 each have a full Dewey 20 classification number. They are catalogued according to the Anglo-American Cataloguing Rules (2nd edn, 1988 revision). Until January 1997 COMPASS subject headings appeared in italics at the end of each record but were then replaced by Library of Congress Subject Headings which have been applied to British Library MARC records since 1995. Records for forthcoming titles are prepared by Bibliographic Data Services (BDS) Limited and all have full Dewey 20 numbers. These records are prefixed by an asterisk (*). Name and title index entries are under authors, titles, series and names as subjects. Records in this latter category are marked with a dagger (†) for easy identification.

Following the demise of COMPASS headings in *BNB*, a new, enhanced level of indexing has been introduced to redress the imbalance between the levels of access provided for fiction and non-fiction, by adopting *The Guidelines on Subject Access to Individual Works of Fiction, Drama etc*, (GSAFD) devised by a subcommittee of the American Library Association. These *Guidelines* recommend four kinds of subject access to fiction: access by form/genre; access for characters, or groups of characters; access for setting; and access for topic.

Full application of GSAFD to British Library records will be in stages. The first phase includes their application to CIP records and future developments will extend coverage to other literary forms in *BNB* and coverage in other British Library catalogues. The implications for library catalogues of GSAFD, the enhanced *BNB* access, their use in the United States and Australia, their effect on the development of subject search capabilities in libraries' OPACs, and the quality of future electronic access to fiction are addressed in Andrew MacEwan's 'Where do you keep the dystopias?', *Library Association Record*, **99** (1), January 1997, pp. 40–1; in 'A Novel Form of Access to Fiction in the British National Bibliography', *Select*, no. 19, Spring 1997, pp. 15–16; and in his 'Electronic access to fiction', *Vine*, no. 105, 1997, pp. 41–4.

BNB's extension to CD-ROM is likely to prove the most significant of all the information transfer technologies in the long term. *BNB on CD-ROM Version 5*, probably the last major upgrade to the DOS version, was officially launched at the International Online/CD-ROM Exhibition in London in December 1994 and was dispatched to customers in January 1995. 'The software upgrade is the most substantial to date and offers valuable new features for all types of user. The software upgrade is free to all subscribers and single networking is free, giving important benefits at no extra cost.' Moreover, the new networking facility allows *BNB on CD-ROM* to be networked over all the major networks so that 'libraries can now make the networked *BNB on CD-ROM* available simultaneously throughout their operations: in the selection and acquisitions section, in the cataloguing department, in the reference library and out on public access terminals' ('BNB on CD-ROM: Version 5 Up and Away', *Select*, no. 14, Winter 1994/95, p. 3).

But the speed of electronic change never slackens and within 18 months a new best-ever *BNB on CD-ROM*, the Windows® version, was being introduced at LIBtech '96 at the University of Hertfordshire. This has

> all the functionality of the DOS version including Boolean searching in the search workspace, browseable indexes, output in catalogue card, detailed and MARC formats and batch searching with barcode input, with the addition of a Form Search screen in which the user will be able to enter search terms into an on-screen form. Both platforms offer advantages over the DOS version . . . a clear and easy to use graphical interface, a simplified method of creating a customised detailed format, more detailed and user-friendly help screens and much improved printing options. ('Test Sites Wanted for Windows and Mac', *Select*, no. 17, Spring 1996, p. 3).

The backfile, covering 1950–85 records, previously available on a two-disc set, is now compressed to one disc. In January 1997 the Macintosh® version became available. This included some extra features, notably the facility to add annotations or bookmarks to the records.

Following the deliberations of an internal Working Party on the Coverage of the National Bibliography, a thorough reassessment of *BNB*'s scope, purpose and function was initiated by the British Library at a seminar in June 1997 when representatives of all types of libraries and of other interested agencies, were invited to participate in the debate and to define the issues which needed to be addressed in order to develop the national bibliography. The papers presented by senior Library staff centred on five key propositions: (1) The case for national bibliographies is a strong one; a national bibliography is the primary record of a country's publishing output. (2) The British Library has a central role to play in the compilation and publication of the UK national bibliography. (3) The British Library regards this role as a key responsibility. (4) It is desirable that the British National Bibliography should continue to be made available in printed form. (5) The development of the British National Bibliography in terms of scope and content will depend in the future on a more cooperative and collaborative effort between the British Library and other national agencies (Arthur Cunningham's 'A New Direction for the National Bibliography', *Select*, no. 21, Winter 1997, pp. 1–2). One suspects that the first four were but a prelude to the fifth.

In the event the British Library was urged to cooperate even more closely with other national agencies to further develop the concept of 'a distributed national bibliography', involving a shared responsibility of editorial, resourcing and publishing responsibilities by a number of agencies working together to increase and enhance access to the material included in *BNB* – which would continue to be the main record of the national imprint – but which would be increasingly supported by electronic and printed supplementary listings not derived from the British Library's legal deposit accessions. The seminar papers and the subsequent discussions, were printed in *The Future of the National Bibliography. Proceedings of a Seminar held in June 1997*.

To move the discussion forward and to widen the consultative process, *The Future of the National Bibliography. A Consultation Paper from the British Library* was circulated so that the views of interested constituencies could be made known to the British Library no later than 1

April 1998. A statement of British Library policy on the national bibliography's further development will be made in the summer of 1998 once the submitted views are analysed.

The difficulty was to reconcile BNB's primary purpose of providing a bibliographic record of British publishing, with its responsibility for opening up the British Library's stock and services 'to the widest possible range of use by fully cataloguing its acquisitions and making that catalogue available in electronic and other formats.' Salient areas of concern included BNB's exclusion policy; its role in a distributed national bibliography; possible supplements; the content of its bibliographic records; and the different emphases on public responsibility and commercial viability.

Reviewing the many categories of material excluded from BNB, it was clear that some material, like large print publications and some reprints, could justifiably be included. But how is information on these items to be gathered? 'In some cases, as with reprint material, acquisitions processing routines within the British Library can be modified to allow catalogue records to be created before the material is disposed of or deposited elsewhere.' Responsibility for the bibliographical control of other material not within BNB's ambit, such as the Stationery Office's responsibility for government publications, rested with other bibliographic agencies. The point the British Library was striving to make here was that, if certain categories of material should be excluded from the national bibliography, this should not be determined by whether or not they are deposited with the British Library, but because a deliberate decision has been taken to exclude them.

Stemming from the concept of a distributed national bibliography, i.e. a scenario in which the British Library builds on existing links, more especially on the Copyright Libraries Shared Cataloguing Programme (CLSCP) and develops new ones with other national agencies, the consultation paper outlined a model on which the further development of the national bibliography might be based. It proposed the publication of BNB supplements, noting that as a first step British Reports, Translations and Theses would be renamed British National Bibliography for Report Literature with effect from January 1998, whilst the scope and contents of Serials in the British Library would be kept under review. If NBS's proposals were accepted, then the structure of a distributed national bibliography, the methods of obtaining and publishing bibliographic data, might conveniently slot into the NBS's proposed pattern (see Table 7.1).

Table 7.1

Coverage	Method of obtaining bibliographic data	National Bibliography supplements
Printed trade monographs (including advance information)	Legal deposit; CLSCP; Cataloguing-in-Publication; Outsourcing bibliographic record supply	Printed listing equivalent to the current *British National Bibliography*
Microforms	British Library acquisitions; Outsourcing bibliographic record supply; Change to legal deposit legislation	New printed listing: *Microforms in the British Library*, eventually with electronic versions
Printed serials	Legal deposit; CLSCP; Cataloguing-in-Publication; Outsourcing bibliographic record supply	Printed listing equivalent to revised *Serials in the British Library*
Electronic publications	Short-term: reliance on information from publishers or outsourcing of data; Longer-term: change to legal deposit legislation	New printed listing: *CD-ROMs in the British Library*, eventually with electronic versions
Non-trade literature	Legal deposit; Outsourcing bibliographic record supply	*British National Bibliography for Report Literature*
Film and video	Continuation of relationship with the British Film Institute	*British National Film and Video Guide*
Official publications	Cooperation between originating bodies and the Stationery Office	Catalogues of the Stationery Office and Chadwyck-Healey

(Reproduced by kind permission of the British Library's National Bibliographic Service)

As for the content of *BNB*'s bibliographic records, the core record could possibly be enhanced by value added data – contents data, reviews, or notes on availability in other formats – to be derived from other agencies. But 'the cost of doing this becomes part of the total cost of maintaining the national bibliography' which raises the whole question of commercial viability. At the moment the British Library requires *BNB* to cover all its costs, including overheads but not the cost of cataloguing, and to make a net contribution to its finances. Although the buoyant subscriptions to the *BNB on CD-ROM* are causing no concern, there is a worrying decline in the sale figures of the printed *BNB* and while the electronic version might justifiably subsidise the now venerable printed version, it could reasonably be argued that the latter, after 50 years of stalwart service, should now be withdrawn. Conceivably, the price for adding more comprehensive bibliographic data to the BNB record, which would inevitably either increase its already unwieldy size of the printed version, or else further reduce its type fount to microscopic illegibility, might be its total abandonment in favour of the electronic version.

A definitive and meticulously researched history of BNB's early years before it was incorporated into the British Library, Andy Stephens's *The British National Bibliography 1950–1973* (The British Library, 1994, 159 pp.) begins with its six original staff gathered inside a bomb-damaged house in Russell Square in London to start their first day's work in an enterprise established with a capital of just 15 shillings and accommodation borrowed from the British Museum. It then chronicles its rise from those humble origins to its integration into the newly formed British Library in 1974. As is evident in Stephens's list of 217 references, there was no lack of source material to be excavated from conference reports and papers, journal articles and personal correspondence, but he welds it into a coherent and readable narrative of a major achievement in postwar British librarianship.

SELECT

Select, NBS's occasional newsletter (i.e. two or three issues a year), first appeared in July 1990. A typical issue will contain news of the latest OPAC developments, online exhibition news, recent European library related projects, anecdotal peeps behind the scenes at NBS, articles on major decisions relating to MARC, news of MARC hit rates, new publications, user news and matters of topical interest in Acquisitions, Processing and Cataloguing. Following the NBS/DSC merger, a questionnaire and a joint letter from the editors of *Select* and *Document Supply News*, together with the most recent issue of each, was dispatched to regular recipients in April 1997, requesting their opinions on both newsletters' style and content, so that the topics of most interest and relevance to readers could be taken into account when designing future issues.

INTERFACE

Interface, NBS's technical bulletin, began publication in February 1994, on a two-monthly basis and runs in parallel with *Select*. It informs subscribers of developments to BLAISE-LINE and to NBS's CD-ROM products and cataloguing services, keeping them up-to-date with technical advances, suggesting additional uses for these services within the library environment and also publishing amendments to the UKMARC format. A complimentary spring-binder is supplied so that the cumulated issues may be conveniently consulted at the workstation.

BRITISH NATIONAL FILM AND VIDEO GUIDE

The successor to the British Film Institute's *British National Film and Video Catalogue* (1963–92), NBS's *The British National Film and Video Guide* was launched in 1995. This lists films, videos and multimedia programmes with a substantial moving-picture element offered for non-theatrical loan or purchase within the UK and covers educational and training films, independent productions, documentaries, TV programmes and feature films. Over 500 items are recorded in each quarterly issue. Entries for non-fictional productions are classified and arranged according to the published schedules of the *Universal Decimal Classification*. These are followed by a separate alphabetic sequence of fiction films. In addition, each issue contains a title index and address list of distributors. A separately published index of subject terms derived from the UDC schedules is sent to each subscriber as part of the subscription. The information is based on details gathered by staff in the Cataloguing Department of the National Film and Television Archive, a Division of the British Film Institute.

GENERAL CATALOGUE OF PRINTED BOOKS

Also within NBS' orbit is the *British Library General Catalogue of Printed Books to 1995 on CD-ROM* (1997), published on four CD-ROM discs on behalf of the BL by Saztec Europe and distributed by Chadwyck-Healey. This latest edition contains

> an extensively re-edited version of the original file to 1975 and adds 1,900,000 records. Many records have been expanded to include cross-references from the original printed editions, making navigation of the catalogue and its contents easier. This edition adds *The Humanities and Social Sciences File*, comprising over 1,700,000 records for items acquired since 1976 and with a publication date of 1971 or later and including acquisitions in Oriental languages since 1980, audio-visual items and some private press material. A second new file is *The Science Reference and Information Service* comprising nearly 300,000 records listing books catalogued since 1974, virtually all periodical holdings and many records of conference proceedings published in periodicals.'

It uses Chadwyck-Healey's CARAVAN software running under Microsoft Windows. Records are first displayed in a summary of matches, after which they may be displayed in catalogue card, detailed or UKMARC format. Records up to 1975 may display and print Greek, Hebrew and Cyrillic scripts; the HSS and SRIS files contain transliterated titles (from an announcement printed in *Reference Reviews*, **11** (7), 1997, p. 51).

BLAISE-LINE

BLAISE-LINE, the British Library's Automated Information Service, launched in 1977, provides access to 22 retrospective and current bibliographic databases, including a group of files covering the comprehensive collections of its London-based collections and DSC's online holdings and serials file. Containing over 17 million bibliographic records, BLAISE-LINE offers an online retrieval service 20 hours a day, six days a week, via either traditional command language or a user-friendly graphical interface on the World Wide Web. A direct online link to DSC allows registered customers to transmit requests for individual items quickly and conveniently.

A refreshing, almost iconoclastic, approach to BLAISE-LINE is evident in David Nicholas and Louise Boydell's 'BLAISE-LINE: enigma, anomaly or anachronism', *Aslib Proceedings*, 48(3), March 1996, pp. 55–9, which views it as the odd man out of online hosts, deplores the lack of research and comment on it in recent years, and presents the results of a questionnaire survey of BLAISE-LINE users conducted with BLAISE cooperation at the price of including a few questions BLAISE itself wanted answers to. For reasons of customer confidentiality BLAISE distributed the questionnaires to just 70 subscribers. Nicholas and Boydell nursed reservations about the sample: it was not wholly representative since BLAISE selected those they believed most likely to respond and overseas subscribers were, in their view, slightly over represented.

BLAISE's oddity is perceived as deriving from four factors:

1   'it is one of the few government owned hosts in a sea of commercial services';
2   it is probably the smallest of them all in terms of users, database and record numbers;
3   'bucking the full-text trend, it is strictly bibliographical'; and
4

'it is plain old fashioned – redolent of times gone by. The screen layout, the online messages, the record structure and the indexing (Library of Congress, Dewey and PRECIS – though the latter is no longer used) are all located firmly in the days when librarianship was dominated by cataloguing and classification. BLAISE is an intermediaries tool *par excellence*; further removed from Netscape and the World Wide Web you cannot be.'

By unfortunate timing and circumstance, this appeared in the same month as NBS announced the imminent arrival of a new service BLAISE Web providing quick and easy Internet access to British Library's catalogues and bibliographic databases.

Not that the two pundits were unduly perturbed by BLAISE-LINE's apparent anachronous status: 'it offers probably the best controlled language searching around' and, not least, 'the system provides you with the confidence of knowing that if it says nothing is there, it is genuinely not there – it is not simply a case of you having failed to spot and adopt all the variant forms'. Analysis of the 37 returned questionnaires encompassed BLAISE-LINE's uses and users, its frequency and ease of use, the problems in using the system, cost issues, training and support. Essentially,

the survey paints a picture of a small, content and very active user group . . . wholly professional in character . . . This is a service tied into daily work routines [But,] despite its happy band of users and the intention of a good proportion of them to increase their use of the system, it can be by no means certain that BLAISE, with its small number of files and highly processed and expensive-to-produce data, will survive the economic rigours of the market place [However,] there are good grounds for believing that an online search facility combined with a full-text fax or postal document delivery service might prove to be the most economic/effective information system model. After all not everybody needs their information straightaway.

Unfortunately BLAISE-LINE's appeal to many users, NBS now admitted, was limited by its lack of an attractive user interface which often made searching cumbersome and time consuming. Exploiting the development of the Internet and the World Wide Web, NBS launched Blaise Web at the Internet World International Exhibition, Olympia, 21–23 May 1996. Based on BLAISE-LINE and complementing British Library's Network OPAC, soon to be replaced by OPAC 97, Blaise Web was marketed with a strong emphasis on its improved access to BLAISE: Blaise Web, it was claimed, 'enables quick and easy searching of the databases by users unfamiliar with the complexities of command language'. 'BLAISE World Wide Web Access', *Interface*, no. 15, June 1996, pp. 1–3 provides instructions on how to search Blaise Web, outlines the search options available and describes step-by-step how to order items online from DSC. 'A New Initiative for Blaise', *Information for Access News*, no. 4, Autumn 1996, p. 9 expresses the hope that the number of subscribers to the new service will continue to grow and reassures existing BLAISE-LINE users that their user-ids and passwords can be used to access the new interface without any further requirement to register. John Lowery's 'New Online User Guide for Blaise Web Makes Searching Even Simpler', *Select*, no. 18, Winter 1996, p. 9 reports that Blaise has introduced a new pricing structure to help users choose how to spend their online time. 'This enables purchase of blocks of hours and/or record citations depending on whether you are a daily, occasional or infrequent user.' When OPAC 97 was introduced in May 1997 it was made clear that while it is an ideal service for end-users, readers, scholars and students, BLAISE, either as BLAISE-LINE, or as BLAISE Web, continues to be indispensable for the information professional. John Lowery's commemorative article, 'Blaise of glory – twenty years of service to the online community', *Select*, no. 21, Winter 1997, pp. 3–4, indicates that replacements for both BLAISE and OPAC 97 will be unveiled early in 1999.

BLAISE 1997 Online Databases, a striking eight-page brochure, is an authoritative guide to its databases and an all-embracing compendium of what BLAISE-LINE and Blaise Web offers to librarians, information specialists and other professional groups. Full details of the support offered by way of printed manuals and training and a list of subscription options, are also included in this very useful document.

BNBMARC

BNBMARC, available in print, on magnetic tape for downloading onto libraries' own automatic systems, online and on CD-ROM, contains detailed bibliographic records for all books and serials received at the Legal Deposit Office under the requirements of the 1911 Copyright Act. Indexed by subject and other cataloguing data, BNBMARC is thus an essential source for information on all UK publications, provided always that the records are available when required for libraries' cataloguing or ordering processes. What is known as the BNB Hit Rate measures the effectiveness with which a changing selection of academic and public libraries is able to find records for new acquisitions on the BNBMARC database. Timeliness is regarded as a key factor.

Conducted since 1980 by UKOLN, the United Kingdom Office for Library and Information Networking, the Hit Rate survey is now published in *Select* on a six-monthly basis. The most recent figures to hand are included in Jonathan Purdey's 'The Hit Rate', *Select*, no. 20, Summer 1997, pp. 8–9 where two tables present the cataloguing and ordering survey hit rates, January 1983 to April 1997. Every month a rolling selection of public and academic libraries each select at random ten titles in process of ordering and ten titles about to be catalogued and provide UKOLN with the details. *BNB* is then searched and the number of 'hits' recorded.

> It is at cataloguing stage that the Library is most concerned to provide a quality record, because the majority of our customers use our services for derived cataloguing – downloading *BNB* records onto their own automated catalogues from the BNB-file on Blaise, Catalogue Bridge, CD-ROM or from a database supplier . . . The Library is responsible for supplying the majority of the main UK and international libraries with authoritative MARC-format AACR2 records with LCSH and Dewey. Hence the importance which the Library sets upon the 'headline rate', the combined libraries hit-rate at time of cataloguing, which it seeks to maintain at 80%.

Failure to aim at a higher rate is attributed to publishers forgetting to send in copies of their new titles to the Legal Deposit Office at the time of publication. Both the Legal Deposit Office and the Copyright Agent pick up some of this material and, in addition, UKOLN sends lists of all misses to the Legal Deposit Office who then claim the missing titles. 'When the hit rate is measured again, six months after the original sample date, it is on average 5% higher.' In September and October 1996 the cataloguing hit-rate six months after sample date climbed to 92% for public libraries and 90% for academic libraries.

Anne Chapman's 'National Library Bibliographic Record Availability: A Long-Term Survey', *Library Resources and Technical Services*, **39** (4), October 1995, pp. 345–57 provides an authoritative summary of UKOLN's involvement; the survey's key objectives (to establish what proportion of UK titles have a BNBMARC record available when it is most needed and is this proportion increasing or decreasing in the long term); the survey methodology; the overall hit-rate; the effect of the British Library's four-page consultative paper, *Currency with Coverage* (1987); NBS relocation to Boston Spa; CIP records purchase and the CIP element of the hit rate; and the implementation of the Copyright Libraries Shared Cataloguing Project in 1990. An objective overview of BNBMARC's overall performance is also provided.

On a different tack, Chapman's '1994 Revisited: A Year in the Life of the BNBMARC Currency Survey', *International Cataloguing and Bibliographic Control*, **26** (2), April/June 1997, pp. 41–5, focuses not on the hit rate, or how and why it changes, but on what further information can be obtained from the data collected. The most startling fact to emerge was that up to 10% of books published in the UK were never received at the Legal Deposit Office.

R.W. Hill's *Setting the Record Straight. A Guide to the MARC Format*, NBS's free non-technical booklet, containing sections on what MARC is; the UKMARC format; its role; the anatomy of a BNBMARC record; UKMARC and the book industry; the international format UNIMARC; a short bibliography; and a glossary of MARC-related terminology, first published in 1993, was issued in a second edition in 1994. It is difficult to overestimate the value of this introductory guide, especially to those in the library and information community who are not always absolutely sure whether MARC is a catalogue, a method of cataloguing or a catalogue record. Its text has been mounted on Portico and it is intended that future amendments and updates will be made to this online version.

CATALOGUE BRIDGE

Launched in 1994, Catalogue Bridge is a customized service linking NBS electronically to bibliographic library departments, offering access to 10 million records from the BNBMARC and LCMARC files for selection, acquisition, current cataloguing and retrospective conversion purposes. File Transfer Protocol and Dial-in enable files to be transferred between computer networks.

> During 1996 a stream of customers migrated to FIT via the Internet and Dial-in via the Catalogue Bridge Bulletin Board for delivery of their BNB MARC Weekly File. FTP costs less, is more timely and not subject to postal delays. The Dial-in process (which uses a modem to the Catalogue Bridge Bulletin Board) takes just over five minutes before files are ready for use; FTP is even quicker ('National Bibliographic Service', *Library Technology*, 1 (5), November 1996, p. 95).

In his 'Catalogue Bridge in Birmingham', *Select*, no. 17, Spring 1996, pp. 6–7, Brian R. Gambles reports his experiences in installing, testing and using the new system. Although the exclusion of HMSO, non-UK publications, printed sheet music, non-book materials, books in community languages and sheet maps and atlases is seen as a shortcoming (these categories of course are mostly not within BNB's ambit) Gambles is generally satisfied: 'overall we believe Catalogue Bridge is a quick and easy route to quality record supply, offering good value for money'.

CATALOGUING-IN-PUBLICATION

Not all librarians have been too impressed with NBS's Cataloguing-In-Publication programme (CIP). At length NBS conducted a detailed questionnaire survey to find out what the problems were, how seriously they were viewed and how many organizations were experiencing them. The survey covered the overall satisfaction rate with CIP records by their physical format in stock selection, acquisitions and cataloguing; their timeliness; their content and accuracy; their timeliness according to use; users' own upgrading and record replacing practices; the use of printed CIP blocks; the required fields in CIP data; and the question of value for money. As so often happens, the fire and passion of criticism withered when reduced to statistical analysis. Even so, 'the results of the survey have been endorsed by NBS in that we are establishing an editing team to enhance certain elements of the CIP records to bring them into line with BNBMARC practice' (James Elliot 'The British Library CIP programme: the 1993 survey results', *Select*, no. 12, Spring 1994, pp. 10–12).

Elliot also recorded the signing of a new contract with Bibliographic Data Services of Dumfries for the supply of bibliographic records for the CIP programme in June 1995. The new records were to be catalogued according to AACR2 with headings created according to the British Library's Name Authority file. In addition full Dewey Decimal Classification 20th edition numbers and Library of Congress Subject Headings would be assigned.

> The change in supplier has resulted from the increased importance to the Library of subject access to its collection. The development of the British Library OPAC together with the reinstatement of LCSH and their adoption as the core subject retrieval system for the Library has highlighted the value to users of subject access to the collection ('Cataloguing-In-Publication Contract Moves', *Select*, no. 16, Autumn 1995, p. 3).

Quite so, but why persist in designating it a cataloguing-in-publication programme when the only information printed is a bald statement that 'a catalogue entry for this book is available from the British Library'? It surely cannot be an income generation mechanism.

NATIONAL BIBLIOGRAPHIC RESOURCE

In 1996 the British Library/Consortium of University Research Libraries Working Party on Bibliographic Services proposed

> the establishment of a record and access resource to be known as the National Bibliographic Resource comprising the linked catalogue databases of the national libraries and the eleven CURL libraries and a common on-line search interface through which users, including individual academics, would be able to access the CURL and national library databases as though they are one. The National Bibliographic Resource would provide an unparalleled research resource comprising the major academic 'holdings libraries', the British Library, the National Libraries of Scotland and Wales plus other databases that would be of benefit to the communities served; provide academic and other end users with improved access to the combined range of research materials held by the constituent libraries; support interlending and document supply to make the most effective use

of the collections; improve the supply and exchange of records, thus further contributing to the efficient operation of libraries; and assist the coordination of collection development, preservation and collection management policies.

NETWORK OPAC

It was always the intention that automation would play a large part in providing speedy and efficient reader services at St Pancras, but when the handover of the new building to the British Library was delayed, the systems were at an advanced stage and it was decided to go ahead with an online catalogue in the existing buildings. Accordingly, a new prototype OPAC system was installed in SRIS's Aldwych and Holborn reading rooms and H&SS's reading room at Bloomsbury, September to November 1993, replacing an interim system that had been operating since 1991. This served the dual purpose of allowing readers an enhanced access to the Library's collections and giving staff experience in operating this type of catalogue before the upheaval of relocation to St Pancras.

The principal design requirement of the new OPAC was that it should be able to handle a large number of different catalogues, diverging in their rules, subject content, and record structure within the same system. In addition it must be user-friendly as many readers would likely be unfamiliar with computer systems, with some betraying an inborn aversion to such systems. Other basic requirements were that the system should offer scope for significant enhancement without needing rebuilding and that it should give a wide range of searching. In the event, search types included name, titles, subject, publisher, place and date of publication, language, a control number and type of publication, although not all of these options were available on all catalogue files. Files available initially included the Science, Technology and Business catalogues, the current and retrospective catalogues of printed books relating to the humanities and social sciences and the current music catalogue. Later the retrospective music catalogue and the DSC Monographs catalogue were added.

Designed and built to operate not only within the St Pancras building, but also to remote users, the OPAC was made available to UK academic and research institutions on JANET for a year's free trial as from April 1994 following tests at the universities of Bath, Newcastle and Westminster. Details of the procedure were given in 'Open Access to the

Network OPAC', *Select*, no. 12, Spring 1994, pp. 1–2:

> the British Library will provide client software to run on a PC which will set up a Network OPAC icon running under Windows. Clicking on the icon will take the user into the OPAC itself. This gives remote users access to the system without losing the attractive user interface based on good use of colour and graphics which has proved so popular with readers using the Online Catalogue in the reading rooms in London. Users will not hold the bibliographic data on their PC but will be connecting to a data server at the British Library which holds the catalogue information.

This development turned into reality one of the Library's strategic objectives for the year 2000, outlined in *For Scholarship, Research and Innovation* (1993): to 'provide a simple means of access to the Library's collection and its services via electronic networks' (para. 7, pp. 15–16).

A progress report, Jan Ashton's 'The British Library Network OPAC', *Select*, no. 13, Autumn 1994, pp. 6–7, noted that 125 sites within the UK had registered for trial service. Twelve months later it was announced that the trial of the Network OPAC had been extended for a further year (still free of charge in the UK), 'partly as a result of the quality of the feedback that we have been receiving from the participating sites' ('Extending the Network OPAC', *Select*, no. 15, Spring 1995, pp. 1–2). Doubts as to whether the Network OPAC would remain free of charge, or not, should have been settled by the publication of *Information Systems Strategy* (1995) which declared unequivocally that 'consultation of the Library's online catalogue over JANET, Super-JANET and the Internet, will be provided, extending the current availability at pilot sites in university libraries'. 'Use of the catalogue', it was stressed, 'will be free within the United Kingdom' (para. 44, p. 20).

Roger Butcher's 'Development of the British Library Online Catalogue', *Managing Information*, 1 (2), February 1994, pp. 41–3 expounds on the current position of the Online Catalogue, its basic requirements, the catalogue files available, character sets, links to other British Library systems, the technical details of the Online Catalogue's design, and links to external users. For a full technical overview encompassing the prototype system, why a full-text retrieval system was chosen rather than the more conventional relational database management system, what OPAC does, the OPAC's architecture, and the OPAC software development, refer to Dick Pountain's 'The British Library's Catalog Is On-Line', *Byte*, 20 (5), May 1995, pp. 62–3, 65–6, 68 and 70.

OPAC 97

Replacing the prototype NETWORK OPAC, OPAC 97 was launched at Internet World, Olympia, in May 1997, to provide free world-wide electronic access to British Library catalogues, containing 8.5 million records for books and other materials dating from 1450 to the present day.

> The development of OPAC 97 means that anyone, with an Internet con-nection and any standard Web browser (Netscape Navigator or Internet Explorer for example) can have access to the Library's unique collections. An added advantage for DSC customers is that, for the first time, they are now able to search its holdings and send orders for the material they require through a simple user interface.

Search options include any one or combination of personal or corporate author, words or phrases from book titles, subject words, publisher, date of publication and from ISBN or ISSN. Although allowing users to check holdings, at the moment OPAC 97 offers no facility for placing advance orders for material held on closed access in the London reading rooms for which the time-honoured advance ordering procedures have still to be followed.

> The launch of OPAC 97 is a major development for the British Library and forms an important part of the plan to create a digital library to com-plement the traditional hard-copy collections. Although most British Library catalogue records are now automated, there are still parts of our collections that do not yet have automated records and we will add these as resources allow. The Library is also working on the integration of records into a single database to facilitate searching across collections. (John Lowery, 'The British Library's OPAC 97 Service', *Friends of the British Library Newsletter*, no. 25, Autumn 1997, pp. 3–4).

Spontaneous approval of OPAC 97, stemming from user experience was expressed in *Library Review*:

> having used this service in its first couple of days, we can confidently pre-dict that it will become one of the major free research tools available to scholars, as well as to any interested party, world-wide. The search screens themselves are simple enough to use and follow and the results impressive. In the longer term the British Library will be working closely over the

next few years with major UK university libraries, as well as the national libraries of Scotland and Wales, to develop a sophisticated system providing joint web access to the catalogues of most major British research library collections. The immediate power of this research tool is impressive, its medium- to long-term implications are dramatic. With free electronic access to an enormous database of bibliographic information, followed by broadening electronic access to documents themselves, or to the means of ordering documents, the question of access to physical reading rooms in Central London almost pales into insignificance. ('Editorial', *Library Review*, **46** (6), 1997, pp. 376–7).

NBS IN EUROPE

A group of eight European national libraries designated CoBRA (Computerized Bibliographic Record Actions) was established after the European Commission asked the British Library to lead a forum to stimulate cooperative research projects with other national libraries to deal with the exchange of electronic records between all sections of the information industry across Europe. One of the first projects to obtain funding from the European Commission's Libraries Programme was to study the implications for libraries of the exponential increase in electronic publications. Concern was growing in two areas: the cost of providing correct hardware for the diverse formats produced and the general lack of provision for their legal deposit. It was hoped that the study would contribute to policy-making in this area. Full details of this and other projects, are included in Stuart Ede's 'Libraries and Technology in the European Union: Soldering the Connections', *Information Technology and Libraries*, **15** (2), June 1996, pp. 117–22. Funding for CoBRA ceased in 1996 but a new contract was awarded later in the year for an extension, CoBRA+, whose aim is again to foster initiatives in the area of bibliographic services and also to be concerned with all types of electronic publications and related services developments in national libraries. To this end it has established two appropriate task groups. Its secretariat is based at Boston Spa within NBS (See Ross Bourne's 'CoBRA+', *Select*, no. 20, Summer 1997, p. 6).

Devolving from CoBRA, Project BIBLINK, which was launched in April 1996, with funding from the European Commission's Telematics Application Programme, aims to establish a link between bibliographic agencies and publishers of electronic material in order to create authoritative bibliographic information for their mutual benefit. Led by the British Library, BIBLINK will address three main issues:

1   the lack of an agreed standard of bibliographic description for electronic publications;
2   the absence of direct bibliographic links between publishers and national bibliographic agencies;
3   bibliographic control over electronic publications (especially those published via networks) is not adequate despite the continuous growth in the amount of material being published chiefly or solely in electronic form.

Its declared objectives to address these deficiencies are to further the development and improvement of national bibliographic services by establishing a link between the parties concerned. It is intended to deliver an interactive prototype/demonstration system which will enable publishers of electronic documents to input and transmit an agreed minimum level of data describing the documents to national bibliographic services, allowing those services to enrich the data by the application of authority control for proper names or the addition of subject information and retransmit it to the publishers. The prototype demonstrator will employ an agreed standard format for transmission and will convert as necessary to library-based MARC formats for use by the national libraries.

Operationally BIBLINK was divided into two distinct phases each lasting 18 months:

1   April 1996–September 1997, during which time basic information is being collected about data formats, numbering systems, encryption, authentication and format conversion; consensus about these will be sought with a representative group of publishers; and
2   October 1997–March 1999 when the prototype demonstration system will be developed and installed at the sites of the project partners and the participating publishers for trials.

Robina Clayphan's 'The BIBLINK Project: Linking Publishers and National Bibliographic Services', *Select*, no. 19, Spring 1997, pp. 13–14 outlines the project and names the project partners.

Managed and coordinated by Ifigenia Plus, the Spanish software developers, Project Delicat (Data Enhancement of Library Catalogues) was launched in May 1996 to promote the greater and more efficient exchange of bibliographic information between European libraries. Part-funded by the European Commission's Telematics Applications Programme, the full partners of the Project Delicat consortium comprise several national libraries, including the British Library and the German applied research organization, Fraunhofer Gesellschaft.

Using leading-edge artificial intelligence technology, Project DELI-CAT aims to create an expert system capable of automatically detecting errors in library catalogues; the development and testing of the system is expected to take two years. However, while delivering significant savings in time and effort and increasing the range of information available to users, such shared cataloguing initiatives can lead to the duplication and sharing of defective records. The Project's objectives in addressing these problems are outlined in Neil Wilson's 'Project Delicat', *Select*, no. 19, Spring 1997, p. 13: (1) to reduce the number of inconsistencies and errors found in library databases and improve the quality of information circulating on library networks; (2) to reduce the costs of controlling database errors for library and information services; (3) to improve quality control of information by creating software designed to examine source records and indicate those potentially requiring correction; and (4) to develop proposals for a new service based on this software so that libraries producing or importing records can easily check data for inaccuracies.

Brian Lang's 'The Exchange of Bibliographic Data Across Europe', a paper given to the EFLC Conference, Brussels, in October 1994, printed in *Select*, no. 14, Winter 1994/95, pp. 10–12, illustrates the value of collaboration and resource sharing by giving examples of projects and initiatives which have technologically paved the way for bibliographic resource sharing and exchange. Among the topics discussed are cooperation through harmony and diversity, bibliographic building blocks, OPAC sharing, and the collaborative nature of the CD-BIB project.

OPAC NETWORK IN EUROPE

Starting in February 1995 and ending mid-1997, the European project OPAC Network in Europe (ONE) involved 15 partners in eight countries and was funded by the EU Libraries Plan to the tune of 2.4 million ECU (about £1.7 million). Its main aim was an operational service based on access to the partners' OPACs for all types of library users. The key building block was Z39.50 and the major objectives were to link library users in partner institutions to the information resources available in each others' catalogues; to establish a service infrastructure for searching in Europe which can be extended to include resources worldwide through the Internet; link together and enhance existing Z39.50 implementations in the participating institutions; to develop a toolkit – MARC conversion; to develop a Neutral Entry Point; and to develop a stand-alone windows client.

Achievements of the project to date and future plans are sketched out in 'The British Library and Project ONE', *Initiatives for Access News*, no. 4, Autumn 1996, pp. 4–5. Two potential benefits to the British Library are discerned: the provision of services based on Z39.50 will allow the Library to improve access to its catalogues by remote users and will make it possible to provide access to the catalogues of other European national libraries for users of the library's reading rooms. Neil Smith's 'The British Library and Z39.50', *Vine*, no. 97, December 1994, pp. 25–7 is a technical paper investigating the possible future development and application of Z39.50 and SR standards. His 'Z39.50 and the OPAC Network in Europe (ONE) Project', *Information Services and Use*, **16** (3/4), 1996, pp. 189–97 outlines how the Z39.50 protocol will offer seamless access to the EC's major databases.

Document Supply Centre

According to Bibliographic Services and Document Supply's eight-page document, *Facts and Figures, April 1997*, DSC's collections occupy 95 miles (152 km) of shelving. Figures of holdings and annual acquisitions are tabulated (see Table 7.2).

Table 7.2

	Holdings	Annual intake
Journals	259,841	63,070*
Books	3,074,691	36,710
Reports in microform	4,100,000	140,000
Other reports	555,000	30,000
Doctoral theses (US)	462,000	5,000
Doctoral theses (UK)	127,840	9,840
Conference proceedings	368,590	17,590
Translations	569,645	5,645
Music	133,325	825
Cyrillic science & technology books	221,660	660
Microform:		
Roll microfilm over 2000 miles	(3226km)	
Microfiche (other than reports)	4,250,000	50,000

includes titles held at SRIS.

Additionally, we are told that

> the main criterion for acquisition is that items are likely to be requested by customers in higher education, research, business and industry. Journals are collected irrespective of subject and language. English language books are acquired wherever published, subject to the current selection policy. Other categories taken are British official publications. European Community material, unrestricted report literature, theses, conference proceedings, Oriental and Slavonic material, translations into English and music scores.

Constantly attempting to obtain full value for its scarce and diminishing resources, DSC decided, towards the end of 1993, that the acquisition of American journals would be more efficient by adopting the use of consolidation services, thus making the latest issues available to its customers very much sooner. Consequently, in January 1994, the supply of almost 3000 American science, technology and medical journals was transferred to consolidation through one of its existing subscription agents who already handled considerable British Library business and who was familiar both with its accounts system and the range of American titles for which the Library was the only overseas subscriber. By 1996, when the number of consolidation journal subscriptions had risen to 5500, acquisition spending on American titles totalled £699,000 at the US domestic rate; the equivalent cost to post-direct overseas subscribers would have been £781,000, a saving of 11.73%. Although DSC's primary objective in transferring to consolidated supply was to improve delivery times, the savings on costs were manifestly more than incidental.

Andrew Davis' 'Consolidation Services: The British Library Experience', *Serials*, **10** (4), March 1997, pp. 45–7 first examines the entire consolidation operation, with 500 journal issues air-freighted into East Midlands Airport every week for onward transit to Boston Spa by road. Davis then compares DSC's consolidated supply with SRIS's continuing post-direct method; relates the results of detailed analyses of receipt patterns at the two locations; summarises the financial benefits; and concludes

> in our experience consolidation has shown itself to be successful in the speedy provision of US journals with swift resolution of any problems. In the light of these findings, the BL is considering increasing the number of titles that it receives through consolidation services.

A package of spending cuts, forced on the British Library's £30 million funding shortfall during the period 1996/97–1998/99 included DSC having to reduce its overall acquisitions budget severely in the 1996/97 financial year. Consequently it ceased purchasing one-off copies of market reports and all foreign language monographs and imposed strict selection criteria for non-UK English language monographs. Additionally, monographs costing more than £300 were no longer considered for purchase as from 1 April 1996. However, foreign language monographs acquired in the London directorates would be made available to remote users through the normal interlibrary loan and document delivery system. Spraying a fine gloss on the situation, the Library claimed

> changes in the provision of foreign language monographs have been made, not only to assist the Library in coping with financial stringencies

by reducing unnecessary duplication of stock, but are also part of a move to develop the concept of a single collections accessible both by visitors to our reading rooms and through interlibrary loan ('Foreign Language Monographs', *Document Supply News*, no. 52, December 1996, p. 3).

Despite DSC's confirmed market leadership, a continuing sense of being assailed on all sides by new technology seems to pervade the professional literature. DSC has always aimed to be at the leading edge of information technology in the capture, storage and transmission of documents to remote users and it may be that this preoccupation displays nothing more than a determination to keep ahead of the field. For example, Stephen Vickers's 'Recent developments at The British Library Document Supply Centre', *Vine*, 95, June 1996, pp. 7–11 proclaims: 'What is clear is that the Centre has taken and will continue to take, an innovative approach to the development of products and services and will take full advantage of new technological possibilities as they arise.' Specifically, Vickers has in mind *Inside Information* and *Inside Conferences*, both available either as CD-ROMs or as tapes. He also underlines the various interlibrary loan packages existing to help in the creation, transmission and management of requests, especially the introduction of requesting items via email, being used on a trial basis by a number of customers. 'The system is intended to provide the functionality of ARTTel 2 but is based on a store and forward email system as opposed to interactive session.'

Further integrated developments will, however, cause problems. Optimistically, a brave new technological world may be contemplated whereby,

> a user sits at a terminal and accesses *Inside Information*, identifies a needed document, sends the request to the Centre through automated channels, where it is sorted using Automatch and directed to the electronic store holding the item, which in turn would be sent electronically either directly back to the user's terminal or through an intermediary such as the library: payment would be debited automatically from a deposit account.

But 'we are seeing the development of hybrid systems, of amalgamations and joint ventures that bring together the complementary expertise (and cash) of different organisations.' This will require 'considerable investment and the associated risks of misjudging the nature and timing of that investment'. Nevertheless Vickers ends on a positive note, even if it has a slight air of whistling in the dark:

> The future of the Document Supply Centre will not be determined by technology alone, but by a range of legal, social, cultural and financial factors . . . What is clear is that the Centre will continue to adopt and adapt the possibilities offered by technological change to ensure that it offers appropriate services in ways which meet customers' needs.

Variations on the automation theme are played in Bernard Williams's 'Automated document delivery at the British Library Document Supply Centre', *Information Management and Technology*, **27** (4), January 1994, pp. 36–7, 40. His starting point is the experimental IBM/Martec document imaging system, recently installed at DSC, which might conceivably supersede the present manual photocopying operation and therefore have a significant impact not only on DSC's document delivery service, but also on the future of journal publishing. Sensing potential competition from publishers, or large subscription agencies, encroaching on its traditional market, and conscious of the time lag between user request and receipt, at least a week despite its 24-hour turnaround, DSC's intention is to speed up its internal processing by scanning incoming periodicals as they arrive, thereby cutting out the time-consuming tramp to the shelves, selecting the required journals, photocopying the requested articles and posting them off, thus expediting the majority of its 15,000 daily requests.

Accessing articles from disks would be much less labour-intensive than traditional methods but 'before this could be achieved the volume of storage required would necessitate a shift from magnetic to optical disk storage and beyond that to the automatic accessing of disks via a jukebox or multiple drive array'. In addition, the delivery of electronic images would pose problems out of DSC's control. Many of its customers are simply not equipped to print out such images.

> These difficulties could potentially be solved by supplying articles in electronic form direct to requesting individuals. However, the issues involved in supplying electronic copy direct to individuals are even bigger and would cause a lot of heart-searching among publishers even given that they would receive a royalty payment for each item.

At this point the larger question of whether specialist, high-price low-circulation journals would survive is raised, 'if document delivery on demand replaced the printing of periodicals, the results might prove devastating to publishers and authors'. Moreover, if DSC 'lost is predominant position in document delivery there could be a "cherry picking" problem with commercial services offering document delivery from recent popular periodical titles while the BLDSC was left with the servicing unprofitable requests for old and low demand titles'. In the mean time, 'how quickly and indeed whether, the BLDSC switches to image based document delivery will be watched with interest worldwide'.

PUBLICATIONS

For the benefit of personnel in libraries and information units engaged in interlibrary loan and request services, DSC distributed in 1994 a new style *UK Customers' Handbook* (7th ed.) in A5 ring-binder format. Containing more information than previous editions, signifying DSC's broadening range of services, the *Handbook* outlines all standard request procedures, documentation, services and information on using automated equipment.

Primarily geared to its role as a source supplier of documents, in paper or electronic format, to intermediate users, academic, public and company libraries worldwide, DSC's eyeball contacts with flesh and blood users are comparatively few, being mainly restricted to visitors either in the reading room, those arriving to tour the library, or on user courses which may be either onsite or offsite. A *Guide to Visitor Services* provides background information on the British Library's functions, purpose and history and gives details of the reading room services, restaurant facilities, the gift shop, travel to Boston Spa by road, rail and air, nearby hotel accommodation, together with a local map. For use in the reading room only, a 34-page, spiral bound *Document Supply Centre – Reading Room Guide to Abstracting and Indexing Periodical Titles Held in the Reading Room from 1989 to Present Day* (3rd ed., 1995) is in two parts, a subject index and an alphabetical listing of journals (inclusive of shelfmark and reading room holdings).

New editions of two of DSC's directories were published in 1997. *Directory of Acronyms* (3rd ed.) expands to some 10,000 abbreviations present in the Conference Index database of over 335,000 records relating to societies, organizations, conference titles and scientific and medical terms. Because each acronym is used as a key-term in the *Index of Conference Proceedings*, this directory is invaluable when searching the printed, CD-ROM, or online versions. *Alphanumeric Reports Publications Index* (4th ed.), originally devised for staff use to trace individual series through the maze of primary and secondary report numbers in dispersed locations at Boston Spa, now allows easy access to over 4 million reports held in some 12,000 series. Published annually since 1978, *Current Serials Received*, listing all titles held either at DSC or SRIS, is now online from the British Library's World Wide Web pages at < http://www.bl.uk./ serials/ >. Details of all DSC published serials, monographs and electronic publications may be found in two annual brochures, *Document Supply Centre Publications* and *CD-ROM Catalogue*.

Document Supply News, first printed in March 1985, reached its 50th issue in June 1996. The opportunity was taken to look back at the contents of that first issue and to relate them to developments in the intervening period, including administrative restructuring, funding problems, services, overseas demand, new technology, electronic networks and customer relations. A regular Spotlight feature continues on selected DSC activities, services or processes, invariably accompanied by a photograph of bright, cheerful staff, beaming at the camera and replete with first names, nevertheless presents useful information on DSC's services and internal organization. The most recent examples include Customer Services (March 1997); Patent Express (June 1997); and Premium Services (September 1997).

Bibliographic Services and Document Supply Facts and Figures, April 1997 is an 8 page conspectus of DSC charts and statistics (demand, source of requests, satisfaction rate, collections, current awareness services, Patent Express) and the National Bibliographic Service (BNB hit-rate, BLAISE, online access, publications). Code of Service results for 1996/97 are also printed.

NATIONAL REPORTS COLLECTION

According to its own description, the National Reports Collection is 'an invaluable resource for the information professional working on up to the minute reviews of topical issues for policy makers, or on detailed analyses for practitioners and the academic community'. Often, 'grey literature is the only source of information (not everyone publishes in peer reviewed journals) and it invariably provides the most up to date view of developments in policy, practice and research. If currency and comprehensiveness are important in a review, the National Reports Collection is a must.' It was not always so.

As can sometimes be the danger with a large organization, comprising many disparate semi-autonymous divisions, each responsible for its own operations and not always completely *au fait* with what is happening elsewhere, so the British Library discovered in the early 1990s that its report literature collections were in some disarray. Even more serious, 'there was no single access point through which the user could identify all the Library's holdings and it was not always possible to identify what these holdings comprised'. Despite having collected, in the years since 1986, 113,000 British reports in the field of science, technology and medicine; over 75,000 in the subject of business, economics, management and public administration, and a further 30,000 in other social sciences and arts and humanities, the Library found that many key documents were not available in any of its collections. Conversely, there was considerable overlap between DSC, H&SS and SRIS.

This chaotic state in the British Library's reports acquisition policies was graphically revealed in an interview with Alan Gomersall, Director of SRIS:

> We at SRIS were collecting reports from companies and research institutes which included material like a report into probation activities in Cleveland, research into childcare, papers on family problems or the rich/poor divide. Bloomsbury was receiving these on legal deposit. The Document Supply Centre at Boston Spa was buying them all to lend as part of the document supply service. On occasion we were also buying them if they were relevant to science, so the library was acquiring three or four copies of some reports.

In addition the cataloguing was 'rather impenetrable'.

> Reports which were part of a series were logged only as a series number, giving no idea of the content of the document. So researchers were unable to access what might have proved to be valuable material unless they were armed with the full bibliographical reference. (Don Watson, 'New report collection founded', *Library Association Record*, **98** (3), March 1995, p. 118)

To remedy this frightening situation, the management committee accepted three major recommendations:

(1) The creation of a single, rationalized report literature collection in the DSC to be the repository for all UK reports entering the BL through legal deposit and other routes. The collection will be developed and exploited as a corporate resource for the Library as a whole and will be known as the National Reports Collection.

(2) The improvement of existing methods of exploiting report literature and the creation of new methods, to raise its profile, boost demand and generate revenue.

(3) The establishment of a small working party to consider the detailed implications of the creation of the National Reports Collections and the development of measures to exploit it.

('British National Reports Collection', *Interlending and Document Supply*, **23** (4), 1995, p. 32).

A working party, set up in 1994, initiated a number of programmes to resolve possible areas of dispute and uncertainty. Guidelines were agreed between directorates for reports received under deposit which were largely routed to DSC where they are made available for loan through the document supply service. All items added to the Collection are indexed on the SIGLE (System For Information On Grey Literature In Europe) database, which can be accessed online through BLAISE. A CD-ROM version is available in the London reading rooms, enabling subject and key term access to the Collection. Acquisitions Processing and Cataloguing directorate assumed responsibility for an alerting service to remind institutions and organizations of the need to deposit reports. All material received is listed in DSC's *British National Bibliography for Report Literature*.

A special information pack, *National Reports Collection*, was dispatched to over 2000 academics, commercial organisations and specialist groups, to encourage researchers to deposit their results in the Collection and was also distributed to 700 journalists. This contained various printed information sheets like *National Reports Collection: Grey Literature at the British Library Document Supply Centre*; *SIGLE on SilverPlatter*; *Serials Information*; *Index of Conference Proceedings*; *Stock Alert Service*; and samples of current awareness services.

To publicize the advantages of the Collection, the British Library enlisted the support of 'sectoral champions who encourage the participation of organisations within their professional ambit'. For example, Cranfield University's Information and Library Service, in cooperation with DSC, has prepared a proposal for the management of information within the UK aerospace industry including an enhanced request and document supply service based on the National Reports Collection.

SLAVONIC COLLECTION

One of the prime reasons for establishing the National Lending Library of Science and Technology in 1962 was to provide a Russian Literature Centre in order 'to build up as far as possible a comprehensive collection of Russian scientific literature . . . to obtain by purchase or exchange the current parts of all the Russian periodicals covered in their abstracts' (D.J. Urquhart, *Mr Boston Spa*, 1990, p. 80) so that British scientific and technical research centres could be supplied with the Russian language material they needed from a conveniently accessible central source. The material acquired forms the core of DSC's Slavonic Sections.

A close insight into DSC's Slavonic acquisitions and collections is available in Kathleen Ladizesky and Ron Hogg's 'Slavonic Publications at the British Library Document Supply Centre', *Serials Review*, **21** (2), 1995, pp. 65–70:

> Two sections in the library – Slavonic acquisitions, with a staff of three; and Slavonic, with a staff of six – are responsible for dealing with Slavonic materials. Publications acquired are mainly in Cyrillic script, of which the largest part is the Russian-language material . . . The collections in Cyrillic script and non-Russian script from the former Soviet Union are housed in a store by themselves due to the often inaccessible nature of the material for people who do not read the language... Slavonic acquisitions obtains 2,000 Cyrillic serials and 250 cover-to-cover translations with over 1,750 non-Cyrillic script serial publications. There are more than 200,000 Cyrillic monographs. Ninety percent of the stock is of a scientific nature.

This paper also ranges over DSC's acquisition methods, the sources of supply and the inherent difficulties of obtaining Slavonic language material.

A major microfilm research collection now being acquired is The Archives of the Soviet Communist Party and Soviet State, jointly produced by the Russian State Archives of the Government of the Russian Federation and the Hoover Institution on War, Revolution and Peace. By December 1995 over 2000 reels had been received in a long-term programme involving several years of filming. Acquisition of this particular collection, distributed by Chadwyck-Healey, presents no problems, apart from financial pressures, but this is by no means standard in acquiring material from Eastern Europe. Ladizesky and Hogg's 'Some Changes in the Work of Acquiring Slavonic Serial Publications – A Review of Experiences at the British Library Document Supply Centre (BLDSC) between 1900–1995', *International Journal of Information and Library Research*, **6** (3), 1994, pp. 147–58 examines all aspects of what this involves in the wake of the disintegration of the Communist states in Eastern Europe, exploring the pros and cons of library exchange agreements, the use of country agents, direct purchase from publishers, technological advances in modern communications, intermediary agents or distributors with exclusive rights, and the problems caused by changes in titles.

Hogg and Ladizesky also compiled the *East-West Links Directory of Information Providers in the Former Soviet Union and Central-Eastern Europe* (1996). First published in 1994 as *Directory of Libraries and Book Agents in the Former Soviet Union and Eastern Europe*, this completely revised and updated edition, based on DSC's Slavonic, Central & East European Acquisitions Department, includes address records and lists 1593 libraries and agents in 39 countries.

ORIENTAL COLLECTION

DSC's Oriental Collection receives 3392 serials published in Japan, China, Taiwan, Hong Kong and Korea, printed either in English or the native language. Science, technology and medicine are the strongest subjects although law, business and finance are being actively developed. Titles currently received are listed in *Current Oriental Serials* (Oriental Section, BLDSC, 1996) which also includes serials held in RSCD and SRIS, revealing 'an information source of extraordinary variety, little appreciated and rarely used as thoroughly as it might be' (H.G.A. Hughes, *Reference Reviews*, **10** (3), 1996, p. 6).

Supporting DSC's loan service, all the collections at Boston Spa are subject to much hard wear and tear. New-style binding operations, including substantially reduced turnaround times, are outlined in 'Preservation at the BLDSC – The Way Forward', *Document Supply News*, no. 50, June 1996, p. 5.

CONFERENCE PROFILING SERVICE

Building on its renowned collection of conference proceedings and on its acknowledged expertise in dealing with this form of material, DSC announced a Conference Profiling Service in March 1994. Profiles or bibliographies can be constructed according to customer specifications. Any item held in stock can be supplied either as a photocopy or as a loan.

BRITISH DOCTORAL THESIS SERVICE

This service is based on DSC's incomparable thesis collection, currently standing at 100,000+ theses, acquired at a rate of 5000 annually as universities release them on awarding their doctorates. They are available for loan or purchase either in bound photocopy, microfilm or microfiche format and are listed monthly in *British National Bibliography for Report Literature* and in four subject bulletins.

MUSIC SERVICE

The Music Service at Boston Spa, a folded A4 brochure, gives details of DSC's unique collection of printed music scores dedicated to interlibrary loan, comprising some 130,000 items, ranging from individual piano sonatas to parts of a chamber ensemble, from facsimile reprints of medieval illuminated manuscripts to anthologies of popular music of recent years. The emphasis is on new publications, composers' collected editions and other monumental series. Every item in the collection is available for use 'at home' provided always that the requirements of the Performing Rights Society are respected. Although DSC does not publish catalogues, and although all requests are necessarily of a speculative nature, over 85% of requests are satisfied from DSC stock. The normal loan period is three weeks from the date of issue with an automatic extension period of up to 12 weeks provided the item is not required by another customer.

In 1994 DSC produced a supplement to the *British Union Catalogue Of Orchestral Sets* (2nd ed., 1989) which included information on nearly 10,000 orchestral sets held in 66 UK libraries arranged A–Z by composer and titles. Containing 500 new entries and a further 2000 locations and with 150 deletions, the *Supplement* also includes updates on the lending policies of contributing libraries.

ARTTel

Primarily intended for heavy users who prefer a large number of requests to accumulate in advance of transmission from their own terminals directly into DSC's computers, ARTTel (Automated Request Transmission by Telecommunications) was originally developed in 1981. ARTTel 2, 'a totally redesigned, modern, sophisticated yet user-friendly version', which came into operational use in April 1993, has a more effective logging-on procedure, a status facility enabling users to check the numbers of requests received, an informative online screen and a message exchange scheme between DSC and its users. By June 1994 over 700 UK and overseas customers had switched to the new version.

Because it allows DSC to process requests more quickly and efficiently, the British Library encourages users to move towards automated methods, but it also perceives advantages for customers: savings in postal times; confirmation of receipt of requests; a lower percentage of check references; automatic matching of requests against stock; the ability to access replies to requests online; access to previously transmitted files and alternative document delivery addresses.

Two alternative services were introduced in July 1995. ARTEmail by which automated request transmission to DSC is sent via electronic mail for which an electronic system with access to the Internet or JANET is required; and ARTTel via the Internet. At this point the *ARTTel Version 2 User Guide* (1993), containing general information, log-on instructions and technical information, was replaced by *Automated Requesting User Guide*. In December DSC reported that the last remaining customer still using ARTTel Version 1 had moved to ARTTel 2. As automated requests increased in number, with a corresponding decline in postal customers, DSC arranged workshops for postal customers interested in changing their systems. By June 1997 automated requests accounted for over 80% of all requests received at Boston Spa.

A new Microsoft Windows application programme, WinForm, produced for the British Library by Venefica Systems to facilitate access to DSC's services

> provides an alternative to using text editor and modern communications programs to construct and send files to ARTTel. Instead, it provides a simple on-screen form to enter requests. Once the requests have been entered off-line the program can be instructed to call up the BLDSC via your modem and phone line, automatically log on to ARTTel, send the

request file and then disconnect. The program also tracks the request numbers used for each item and provides printed reports . . . (WinForm, *Document Supply News*, no. 52, December 1996, p. 2).

Sharon Pegg's 'BL document supply made simpler', *Information World Review*, no. 126, June 1997, p. 29, dilates on its installation and ease of use, concluding that:

> Winform greatly simplifies the process of preparing and sending document requests to the British Library at a cost that even the smallest organisations will be able to afford. It allows the user to take full advantage of the fast turnaround that an online ordering system can provide, while sparing them from the technical difficulties of file formats and communications packages.

ARTICLES IN COLOUR

Allowing customers to specify a full colour copy of illustrated journal articles, this service was initiated in 1994. Where the original article contains colour photographs the appropriate pages can be supplied as high-quality colour photographs with the remaining pages of text in standard black and white copy. If required, Lexicon staff can check in advance for any colour plates.

STOCK ALERT SERVICE

Part of DSC's Current Awareness Services portfolio, the Stock Alert Service was introduced in June 1995 to operate for a six-month trial period. Its aim was to open up DSC's collections to those not enjoying ready access to detailed information about the collections through key-term searching, using terms supplied by researchers, in order to identify journal articles, conference papers, books, British theses, grey literature, UK government publications, and scientific reports. All the items identified are available from DSC's own collections so that subscribers can be certain that all material listed can be supplied. In effect DSC is searching its own stock to maximize its exploitation while simultaneously promoting a useful service.

So successful, in fact, was the trial period, with dozens of customers requesting tailored searches, that the service became a permanent feature of DSC's alerting services, *Journal Contents Page Service*, *Forthcoming Conferences Events*, and *New Titles Alert*. The Journal Contents Page Service provides customers with copies of contents pages of any of the 47,000 journal titles currently received at Boston Spa, allowing access to titles, either too expensive for libraries and document services to order, or to which a subscription has been cancelled because of budget restraints. Forthcoming Conference Events provides subscribers with profiles of specific forthcoming conferences, detailing the event, with contact information, either as a one-off search or with regular updates. The New Titles Alert service is intended to provide information on the most relevant new journal titles in science, medicine and technology, appearing on any subject, in any language and from all parts of the globe. For an annual subscription, customers receive a weekly listing of new journals added to DSC's holdings. Colour-coded sheets on all four alerting services are included in an *Alerting Services* information pack.

BOOKNET

The British Library's BookNet department, which operates a recirculation service for previously used books for libraries wishing to dispose of material surplus to requirements, and perhaps acquire wanted items, started an online service to customers in September 1994. Those with compatible systems can log into DSC's databases and view the material available on current and past lists and order wanted items. To keep costs to a minimum, the online service has been priced at the same level as BookNet's Telephone Order Priority Service. At first only available to UK libraries, from April 1995 the service was extended to European Union countries, the first step in an ambitious programme to offer BookNet's services worldwide.

Following a reappraisal of BookNet in 1996, it was decided

> to invest in an upgraded automated system, to offer new and improved services to customers and to widen the customer base. The new automated system will allow BookNet to process material quicker, produce listings in a fraction of the previous time and to offer the listings both in the form of e-mail files and on the World Wide Web. As both of these files will be searchable, customers will be able to find material they require more quickly and will also be able to make access more readily available to others within their organisations. Ordering will be via e-mail or via a

direct order facility on the web version. Priority orders will still be accepted on the special telephone number as before. ('Booknet', *Document Supply News*, no. 54, June 1997, p. 4)

DiSCovery

Building on two years work by British Library and Mercury Communications on Service 21, a little publicized project, discontinued in January 1995, following Mercury's restructuring, a Library team from DSC and SRIS began investigating a commercially viable service combining current awareness and document ordering and supply, both key areas of development if the British Library were to achieve its strategic objectives. The plan was that the new service, known internally as DiSCovery, should be based on the Library's unsurpassed scientific journal and conference proceedings holdings and, eventually, on SRIS's 36 million patents. A trial service was already in progress at York University, ICI Wilton, Unilever Bedford, ERA Technology and BOC Gases, all DSC customers, and at SRIS, to establish whether the system was genuinely user-friendly and whether DSC could supply material on time.

During the trial a weekly CD was issued containing the latest six months of the *Inside Information* database.

A brand new searching interface has been developed which is designed with novice users in mind. It makes full use of the latest standard Windows features and hides the complexities of traditional Boolean searching. When a researcher finds an article of interest, a few additional keynotes send an order to our ARTTel 2 service and the requested article is returned by fax to the nearest fax machine at the user's site within two hours . . . All documents are supplied royalty paid and this together with the new agreement with the CLA . . . sets the stage for a useful dialogue with publishers on electronic storage, retrieval and delivery. ('DiSCovery', *Document Supply News*, no. 46, June 1995, p. 2).

A prime motive in DiSCovery was to maintain DSC's status as document delivery market leader and to strengthen its revenue income. Frank Oliver, who was responsible for managing the production and testing of the trial version, commented,

This is the kind of service the BL needs to offer if it is to continue to be a major player in the world of document supply. With growing computer literacy and the emergence of the Internet, end-users are increasingly searching for information themselves without recourse to libraries and increasingly expecting to get what they want in electronic form. Meanwhile their librarians are recognising this trend as being cost-effective as it reduces the number of journals they need to subscribe to and the staff resources they require. If the BL doesn't meet users' growing demand for computer-based information delivery, someone else will. Many potential competitors, ranging from publishers to library utilities, are already moving into the marketplace.

In 'Great Expectations: The Impact of New Technology on Information Access and Delivery', pp. 5–20, *Electronic Documents and Information: From Preservation to Access*, edited by Ahmed H. Helal and Joachim W. Weiss (Universitätsbibliothek Essen, 1996), Oliver examines DiSCovery's key components and features; why the British Library and other organizations are investing in this type of product; the trial service; its index, ordering and communications, retrieving and document delivery processes and their management; the key technologies used in the trial; future developments; and the impact on publishers, end-users and intermediaries, and libraries.

INSIDE INFORMATION

Launched in 1993, *Inside Information*, is based on a file covering DSC's most heavily requested 10,000 journals, backed by its document delivery services. Available monthly on CD-ROM, online, or via licensing arrangements by which organizations either take all, or sections of the file, for mounting with their own software, about one million articles are added annually. Andrew Everest's 'Inside Information On CD-ROM', *Managing Information*, **1** (2), February 1994, pp. 52–3 is a highly technical review which ends with the forecast that 'Inside Information will find its way into the CD resource base of many an academic institution and other high volume suppliers of journal information.' From 1993 *Inside Information* became available on CitaDel, the Research Libraries Group document delivery service and from March 1995 it has been possible to search records over BIDS and OCLC using Dewey Decimal Classification numbers.

A similar service, *Inside Conferences*, appeared in October 1993 containing paper level information from the 17,000 conference proceedings received at DSC annually. This, too, is available as tape, file transfer or on CD-ROM.

The first results of the DiSCovery project, and based on *Inside Information*, but with major enhancements, *Inside Science Plus* and *Inside Social Sciences and Humanities Plus* made their debuts at the Computer in Libraries Exhibition in February 1996. After further public appearances they were made available to UK customers in April and subsequently phased in across Europe. Combining comprehensive current awareness with end-user ordering and document delivery, these CD-ROMs possess search and browse options, searchable abstracts, a hypertext searching facility, a save search capability and detailed references to two million articles from 20,000 journals (Science: 1.3 million from 13,000; Social Sciences and Humanities: 700,000 from 7000). Button press document ordering, with automatic connection and uploading of orders to ARTTel, enables end-users to select references, transmit requests to DSC and receive documents within two hours. Disks appear monthly with six-month accumulations in June and December for archival purposes.

R. Roman's 'INSIDE – an integrated searching, ordering and delivery service from the British Library', *Information Services and Use*, **16** (3/4), 1996, pp. 179–83 describes its database, its searching and ordering facilities and speculates on its future: 'tests have been run in developing a virtual library and discussions are being held with a number of potential partners to add further value . . . to continue to be at the forefront of the digitisation of knowledge to the worldwide research community.' Roman returned to this theme in 'Inside', *Online and CD Notes*, **10** (3), April 1997, pp. 3–4.

While *Inside Science Plus* and *Inside Social Sciences and Humanities Plus* were being launched, work was progressing on the online and Web server products. *Inside* online, including enhanced diary search features, which allow preselective searches to be run at regular intervals, was available to subscribers using Microsoft Windows™ software by May 1997. Details of DSC products with Microsoft Windows™ interfaces, the equipment needed, communications packages and contact information are included in 'Windows™ On Boston Spa', *Document Supply News*, no. 53, March 1997, p. 2.

The British Library, and Dataware Technologies, hosted a technical preview of Inside Web at Online 96, at Olympia, 3–5 December 1996.

Inside Web offers subscribers, via the Internet, end-user access to a database listing 10 million journal articles, conference proceedings and serial holdings held by the British Library. Articles on the database can be ordered directly from the Library for delivery by fax, courier or mail. The service has been designed as a copyright fee paid service and aims to open up the British Library's holdings to be searched remotely by anybody in the world. Initially, the service will be made available on an annual subscription charge. The Library's Chief Executive described the new service as

> an exciting development for the British Library and researchers worldwide. The World Wide Web is a major communications force being used by thousands of organisations for exchange of information. Now researchers in those organisations will be able to use the British Library's Inside on the Web to find the document they need, order it at the press of a button and then choose the most appropriate method of delivery.'

The British Library is currently exploring ways of making Inside even more comprehensive than the contents of the 20,000 serial titles it already holds. DSC is a member of

> an experimental project to develop a document searching, ordering and delivery system which will be able to search multiple databases. The project, called UNIverse, has been selected by the European Commission for support under the Telematics for Libraries 4th Framework Programme to run for 30 months from October 1996 to March 1999. The UNIverse consortium involves 17 organisations from seven member states. ('UNIverse', *Document Supply News*, no. 52, December 1996, p. 2).

The significance of the Inside service will not be lost on librarians and information specialists.

> A major design innovation . . . makes it much easier for non-information specialists to undertake their own searches, thus allowing it to be networked around an organisation. The librarian or nominated staff member retains management control over who has access to the service and who can establish ordering facilities with the British Library. ('Inside Keeps Growing', *Document Supply News*, no. 51, September 1996, p. 1).

Librarians will take what scant comfort they can from that.

PATENT EXPRESS

A significant development in the Patent Express document delivery service came in May 1994 when, as part of the Initiative For Access programme, the British Library launched its Patent Express Jukebox, a mammoth digital store of patent documents that will allow the Library to provide information about advanced technology to inventors, researchers and business, faster than ever before. Holding a million current British, European, Patent Cooperation Treaty and United States patents, stored on 1,000 CD-ROMs in twelve linked jukeboxes, within which it searches for known patent items in less than two minutes, the Jukebox then produces high-quality laser-printed copies of the required patent for dispatch by post, courier or fax.

Dr David Newton, Head of Patent Services, was quoted on future plans for this major advance in customer service.

> Our long term intention is to give customers the option of using a fully automated ordering and delivery system for current patents. Using this system customers will be able to dial up the jukebox from their own PC using telecommunications networks, order copies of the documents needed and have them sent via a fax gateway. This service should be available within the next few years. ('The Patent Express Jukebox: Quicker hits on disc', *Initiatives for Access News*, no. 1, May 1994, p. 3).

This is a big step forwards for the Patent Express service; remote users represent two-thirds of its total revenue.

Although remaining physically within the SRIS ambit, management control of the service was transferred to BSDS in the second stage of the British Library's administrative restructure. It was announced that customers would not notice major short-term changes, but the Library claimed that 'the service will be able to operate more efficiently and to exploit new technology more effectively in the future' although chapter and verse on how exactly was not stated. From the service point of view this internal change was just one element in the ongoing Patent Express Change Programme incorporating 'streamlining existing processing systems to cut delivery times; introducing electronic document ordering and delivery; developing electronic gateways to other British Library automated services; and improving order processing, tracking and billing procedures' ('All Change and No Change at Patent Express', *SRIS Newsletter*, no. 27, Winter 1996, p. 4).

Fulfilling one item in this ambitious programme, the Patent Express service with On Demand Information brings an individually tailored electronic library of patents within the reach of customers equipped with a desktop PC and an ISDN connection, allowing customers to download and display documents from their own personalized patent library at high speed. An A4 page of text and line drawings can be downloaded in less than four seconds, with the quality indistinguishable from the printed original. David Newton remarked:

> Any patent user is faced with two issues as their library of paper-based document grows: can they locate the information they need quickly and can they manage the distribution of this information around their organisation? Our new On Demand service addresses both these concerns – efficiently, quickly and with remarkable cost-efficiency.

IMAGE DEMONSTRATOR PROJECT

Devised to evaluate the feasibility of establishing an electronic document store, an essential prerequisite for an electronic library, to be used as the basis for electronic document delivery, the Image Demonstrator Project was set up in cooperation with the publishers of 50 major journals which were scanned to create an electrostore. Handling input, processing and output, in three connected subsystems, the Image Demonstrator scanned the journals cover to cover, indexing each page separately, stored the images on four separate magnetic disks and produced hard-copy documents which were retrieved and ready to print within five seconds on a high-speed laser printer via a DOS server. 'Quality of output from the system is excellent for text and diagrams, certainly comparable to a photocopier. Output for grey-scale and colour images is acceptable, though not as good as we would have hoped for.' Although largely satisfactory, the system required fine-tuning in that the images were initially very large after compression, affecting the speed of printing and storage requirements. Optical and manual storage were used necessitating a seamless search interface between the different media. Besides which its print speed is an obstacle to rapid document delivery.

Future developments envisaged include the possibility of using the Excalibur PixTex/EFS software to allow the optical character recognition to operate as the page is scanned; automated use of the retrieved information; and automated fax delivery.

The Image Demonstrator Project has proved to be a valuable experiment in the practical implementation of new technologies required for the building of the electronic library. Such a concept can be implemented but it is more difficult than many coming to the topic from a theoretical point of view might imagine. Nonetheless, the Library is pleased with the project and will continue to refine the system. (Phil Barden, 'The electronic library: theory into practice', *Initiatives for Access News*, no. 2, December 1994, p. 8).

This is an abridged version; the full text is available on Portico in the electronic version of the newsletter. Barden's 'The British Library Image Demonstrator Project', *Information Management and Technology*, **27** (5), September 1994 provides technical detail on input, processing, output, system problems and future developments.

TRIAL ELECTRONIC DOCUMENT STORE

Because many publishers now produce electronic versions of their printed journals, with some titles no longer existing in print form – DSC initiated a Trial Electronic Document Store (TEDS) whose aim is to store electronic journal articles and their associated bibliographic data, in a computer database for use as an optional source for document requests received by its Automated Request Processing (ARP) system. An experimental system to print articles on demand from requests passed to it became fully operational at the end of July 1997. In its first month of operation it satisfied 60 requests. The next stage of the project, expected to be completed within 12 months, involves upgrading the equipment to improve performance, modifying the system to accommodate material direct from journal publishers, integrating TEDS with BSDS' Scanning Integrated Delivery System for electronic delivery of articles, and using other remote electronic document stores for automatic on demand access for printing and delivery.

COPYRIGHT

The background to the British Library's endeavour to reach an accommodation with the Copyright Licensing Agency (CLA) and various groups of publishers over the vexed and fundamental question of reconciling photocopying and document supply with what constitutes fair dealing, exacerbated by the latest developments in information technology, is authoritatively outlined in Gordon Graham's 'How the U.K.'s publishers and librarians have grown (a little) closer: one publisher's experience', *Learned Publishing*, **7** (4), October 1994, pp. 219–22. Graham, who spent six years on the British Library Board, recalls a 1986 colloquium at a secluded hotel in Kent, when the chairmen and chief executives of the British Library, the Library Association, SCONUL, Aslib, the Society of Authors and the Publishers' Association, three copyright experts and a university vice-chancellor, discussed licensing fees for photocopying, strictly off the record.

At that time publishers were of the firm opinion that

> the sophistication and omnipresence of the photocopier and latterly electrocopying, whatever the law says, have made fair dealing (by which they mean payment for every copy made) impractical. The making of single copies for private study is conceded, but the service offered by the BLDSC remains, in the eyes of the publishing community, systematic copying, which by-passes the moral rights of copyright holders.

Following these informal talks, the atmosphere improved and in 1990 the Library and the Copyright Licensing Agency came to an agreement whereby DSC offered a range of copyright cleared services by which it could offer customers multiple copies of articles and papers, copies of more than one article from a journal, copies of complete journal issues, or even whole books if out of print, with a flat rate royalty fee per copy and full legal protection. Fees would be collected by DSC and passed on to the Copyright Licensing Agency for distribution to publishers.

Ending in April 1994, the CITED (Copyright in Transmitting Electronic Documents) project, carried out under the ESPRIT programme, produced a model of protection for digital data, equally applicable to text, images and sound, which ensured protection for electronic information and guaranteed appropriate royalty payments to rights holders, thus modifying the reluctance of publishers to make their material available in digital format because of the difficulties in tracking it. The model is also sufficiently flexible not to transgress worldwide copyright regulations.

In April 1995 the British Library and the CLA signed a two-year agreement covering the reproduction of work subject to copyright, regarded as a significant step towards further discussion on the more difficult issue of electronic storage and transmission of copyright material by the Library. Through the new licence, the British Library, when supplying photocopies from books and other documents under its copyright paid services, paid copyright fees at the individual rates set by authors and publishers. The new agreement succeeds an earlier licence that came into force in 1990 and covers copies sent out from the British Library by post and fax. Initially the Library continued to pass this charge on to its users at a flat rate to cover the copyright fee but it would in the future move to a system of charging the user the exact rate set by the author or publisher. Nicolas Thompson, Chairman of CLA, stated:

> CLA's new agreement with the British Library is a considerable achievement. The national library has accepted the principle that rightsholders should set the individual rates for the reproduction of their work, which is an important step towards securing the financial recognition they deserve . . . What rightsholders want is a just reward for the reproduction of their work and a fair return on their investment – this agreement creates a new standard in the UK and sets the stage for more useful dialogue to explore issues like electronic storage, retrieval and delivery of copyright material.

For the British Library, the Chief Executive commented:

> The British Library's central concern is to ensure that information is available without unnecessary impediment to those who need it, while recognising the intellectual and financial investments made in the creation and distribution of that information by authors and publishers. The new agreement meets this concern. It also allows the library community to continue its dialogue with publishers over how best to ensure that the benefits of new electronic information technology will be enjoyed by all parties, now and in the future.

In pursuit of its strategies and in the light of both national and European legislation, the British Library, from 1 October 1995, extended its policy of requiring certain groups of overseas customers to use the copyright fee paid service for satisfaction of all their requests. UK users and some users in certain EU countries, continue to have the right, under the Library's privilege of the Copyright, Designs and Patents Act 1988, to order a single copy for research or private study from the Library without paying a copyright fee, provided the strict provisions of the Copyright Act are met. For the time being at least the Library, whose main concern was to ensure the unhindered flow of information, although acknowledging the intellectual and financial input of the authors and publishers, was able to reach a *modus vivendi* with the Copyright Licensing Agency. A platform of cooperation had been established although the issues of the electronic storage and transmission of copyright material had not been settled.

DSC promptly replaced its Copyright Cleared Service by a Copyright Fee Paid Service whereby full legal protection was provided for the supply of multiple copies of articles and papers, for copies of more than one article from the same journal issue and also for copies of complete journal issues. In the mean time the CLA will explore new mechanisms for granting electronic storage and transmission rights with the rightsholders. By virtue of its interest in the long-term cost-efficiencies of electronic delivery over information superhighways, the British Library volunteered to play a consultative role in this process. At the end of June 1996, DSC announced that substantial publication specific fees had been paid to the CLA although customers had been charged an averaged flat-rate fee. From the Autumn onwards variable copyright fees were charged.

> We have a responsibility to ensure that the amount we collect from our customers is of an appropriate level to enable us to pass on to the CLA the full amount required. Collecting variable copyright fees will ensure that our customers pay the fee set by rights holders for each publication . . . The Library is continuing its commitment to respecting copyright. Feedback from customers suggests that they are reassured by and supportive of this stance. ('Copyright changes in fees', *Document Supply News*, no. 51, September 1996, p. 4).

In January 1997, the British Library and Elsevier Science reached agreement on the use of electronic versions of scientific, technical and medical material to improve the availability of information to researchers and students. The agreement allows the British Library to incorporate bibliographic data of over 1200 journals produced by Elsevier Science directly into the Library's current awareness products and, on an experimental basis, to use the electronic full text of some of these journals as a source for satisfying document delivery requests. The bibliographic information is made available on the same day as the journals are received in the British Library through the Library's *Inside* service. Customers are able to request copies of these articles and, if the fax delivery option is chosen, have them delivered within two hours – or faster if the titles are held in electronic format. All copies are delivered in paper format or by fax methods, but not by other electronic means. The British Library pays copyright fees directly to Elsevier Science.

Frans Visscher, Director of Elsevier Science said, 'Key to our participation has been the willingness of the British Library not only to act responsibly in purchasing the underlying paper and electronic subscriptions, but also to provide some compensation for the provision of statutory copies.' Both parties are committed to developing services further and will review and further develop the present agreements over the next two years.

The Elsevier agreement served as a prototype for a much-expanded agreement with nine mainstream publishers of scientific, technical and medical journal literature, announced in July 1997, with the aim of improving the availability of information to researchers and students by allowing the British Library to deliver copies of articles from the journals produced by the publishers by facsimile and other controlled methods of electronic transmission as well as conventional document delivery. Some of the publishers involved have also agreed in principle for the provision of electronic bibliographic data and access to full text in electronic format. The agreements will play a key role in the British Library's *Inside* service, but will also apply to all requests processed by the Library's Copyright Fee Paid service.

The publishers involved are responsible for over 10% of the items supplied by the British Library to remote users. 'These are important agreements for the research community, many members of which rely upon the British Library for access to a very wide range of the world's published literature,' said Malcolm Smith, Director of Bibliographic Services and Document Supply, 'These agreements will allow the British Library to offer an improved service to its customers. We look forward to a long-term working relationship with these publishers and hope that others will agree to similar arrangements in future.'

Building on the results of CITED, COPYSMART, a project partly funded by the European Commission, due to be completed by the end of 1997, investigated copyright protection and usage monitoring in electronic material by using smart-card technology to monitor access and control payments. The British Library's role was to run user trials testing the software in a networked CD-ROM environment.

8

READER SERVICES AND
COLLECTION DEVELOPMENT
Reader Services

EARLY COLLECTIONS

Two items of wide public interest have been acquired in recent years, the *Mercator Atlas of Europe* and what was thought to be the only surviving complete first edition of William Tyndale's New Testament (1526), the first English translation of any part of The Bible ever to be printed. For this a down payment of £200,000 was made initially and a Tyndale Bible Appeal was launched to meet the purchase cost of over £1 million. The Library was indebted to the National Heritage Memorial Fund which agreed to match donations to the sum of £500,000. Described by the Chief Executive as 'one of our most important acquisitions in our 240 year history', the New Testament formed the centrepiece of a special exhibition commemorating the 500th anniversary of Tyndale's birth which traced his life and work through a display of fifty books and documents, 'many of them extremely rare works and landmark publications of the Protestant Reformation'. David Daniell's *Let There Be Light: William Tyndale and the Making of the English Bible* (The British Library, 1994) sets Tyndale in his historical background, depicts the academic and theological world he inhabited, investigates his thwarted attempts to publish the *New Testament* in Cologne and examines the significance of the 1526 edition, before following Tyndale's subsequent publishing career which ended in imprisonment and execution. 'Tyndale's New Testament', *Friends of The British Newsletter*, no. 16, September 1994, pp. 1–2 traces its provenance from the first half of the eighteenth century when it entered the Harleian Library.

A previously unknown copy of the 1526 New Testament, which retained its original binding and title page, came to light in 1996 in a Stuttgart library where it had been mislabelled and overlooked for centuries. Mervyn Janetta, curator of English antiquarian books, travelled to Germany to confirm its identification.

ISTC

Although available on BLAISE and other online systems, the British Library's Incunabula Short-Title Catalogue (ISTC), a comprehensive bibliographic database of fifteenth-century books and other material printed from moveable type, had never been published before early 1997 when it became available on CD-ROM from Primary Source Media (PSM). The disc holds some 28,000 records from libraries worldwide, along with over 10,000 high-quality images associated with 2000 bibliographical records of original incunabule editions. Approximately 10,000 additional images will be added annually until the project's goal of illustrating all extant incunabula is realized.

Digitization of ISTC began as Project Incipit (1994–96) which was partly funded by the European Commission Libraries Programme DG XIII (LIB-INCIPIT/4 – 2031). Acting in partnership with PSM were the British Library; the Koninlijke Bibliotheek (The Hague); the Bibliothèque Royale/Koninlijke Bibliotheek (Brussels); the Instituto da Biblioteca Nacional e do Livro (Lisbon); the Biblioteca Nazionale Centrale and the Consiglio Nazionale della Ricerche (Rome). The partner libraries filmed their incunabula using microfilm, slides or black and white photographs, which were sent to the British Library for scanning and then digitally linked to the corresponding catalogue entry on the CD-ROM.

By scanning photographs of books rather than the books themselves Project Incipit avoided undue damage to the 500-year-old books, while it also permitted enormous leeway in selecting the source material.

> Rather than taking rare and precious books to a scanner in a single location, the project can gather pictures of incunabula from all six of the partner libraries, as well as from smaller, more specialised collections around the world. In some cases, the project has located, filmed and scanned the only known copy of a particular book . . . it is expected that every one of the 27,000 incunabula documented in the ISTC will eventually be illustrated with digital images, making the Incipit CD-ROM the first and only complete repertory of fifteenth-century printing history, literature and graphic design and bringing the incunabula treasures of the British Library and other libraries around the world to a far wider audience of scholars and connoisseurs. ('Incipit – Scanning the Incunabula', *Initatives for Access News*, no. 3, Autumn 1995, pp. 6–7).

Edited by Dr Martin Davies, Head of ISTC, *The Illustrated ISTC on CD-ROM* (IISTC) provides unprecedented access to the incunabula holdings of 3000 libraries, enabling researchers to locate and access in seconds early printed books in libraries around the globe. The disc also gives access to PSM's *Incunabula: The Printing Revolution in Europe 1455–1500* microfiche collection.

By far the most comprehensive summary of ISTC and IISTC is Davies's *The Illustrated ISTC on CD-ROM*, a ten-page prospectus issued by Primary Source Media, in which he reviews ISTC's development in the 1980s, its format and contents, the global nature of its records, its naming conventions, instructions for its use, and notes on its origins, progress and technical team:

> the images of incunabula assembled for each record are intended to document the edition in much the same way as a transcription in a traditional printed catalogue by showing the start and end of a text and by indicating the presence of any other printed matter such as preliminary material, table of contents, colophon or printer's device. IISTC is not a full-text database and does not provide images of every page in an edition. Nor is it designed as an art-historical tool . . . The principle behind selection of pages is first, to present all pages necessary for identification of the edition and second, to present all pages necessary to indicate the basic structure and contents of the book.

MODERN COLLECTIONS

As one of the world's foremost research libraries the British Library's collections encompass the languages of Eastern and Central Europe. RS&CD's Slavonic and East European Collections are pivotal to scholars and researchers since its holdings are often more complete than in the country of origin because of damage sustained in the Second World War and the subsequent social and political upheaval. Moreover, acquisitions have increasingly included underground material in addition to mainstream publications, thus allowing the collections to keep in touch with current developments. Unfortunately, economic changes in the former Communist countries have compounded the difficulties of ensuring adequate coverage and cooperation and the exchange of materials between the large national research libraries is assuming a key role.

The British Library's holdings of Polish material, believed to be the largest collection in Western Europe, range from incunabula printed in Krakow to nineteenth- and twentieth-century material published by Polish émigrés, notably in Paris and to the 'Solidarity' collection of clandestine books and periodicals by the political opposition to the Communist régime in the 1970s and 1980s. The Czech and Slovak collection contains similar material. Janet Zmroczek and Devana Pavlik's 'Polish, Czech and Slovak Acquisitions', *London Services - Bloomsbury Newsletter (LSBN)*, no. 10, Summer 1994, p. 5 describes important works recently acquired including five new titles from Correspondence des Arts, the Lodz fine printers; facsimile editions of heritage manuscripts; new reference works, notably *Polskie Archiwum Biograficzy* and the Polish Who's Who, *Kto jest kim w Polsce*; and significant additions to the Czech Art Collection including several works representing the Czech avant garde of the 1920s and 1930s. Christine Thomas's exhaustive study, 'Russian Printing to 1700, as Reflected in the Collections of the British Library', *Bulletin du Bibliophile*, v.1, 1995, pp. 16–42 underscores the wealth of RS&CD's collection of early Russian printed books.

Denis Reidy's 'Acquisition News', *LSBN*, no. 12, Spring 1995, p. 3 draws attention to significant items held in the Italian section, including some important recent acquisitions. These latter include two CD-ROMs, *Thomae Aquinatis opera omnia* edited by Roberto Busa, making consultation of St Thomas Aquinas' complete works readily accessible and *LIZ Letterature Italiana Zanichelli*, edited by Pasquale Stoppelli and Eugenio Picchi, containing the basic texts of some of the classics of Italian literature. Both CD-ROMs have extensive and very informative accompanying manuals.

RS&CDs Hispanic Section is responsible for collecting material from the 28 countries in which Spanish, Portuguese and other Hispanic languages are spoken. It aims to acquire all significant publications in the humanities and social sciences. 'Acquisition News', *LSBN*, no. 13, Summer 1995, 3 provides a microcosmic representation of its range of acquisitions: modern first editions from Argentina; a proclamation issued by the British forces in Uruguay in 1807, possibly the first ever Uruguayan imprint; early Brazilian works; examples of Catalan fine printing; hand-made books, using offcuts and waste paper produced in Cuba in 1985; and two CD-ROMs.

Under the Republic of Ireland's legal deposit legislation, Irish publishers are required to send copies of each item published to the British Library in return for Trinity College Dublin's right to claim material from UK publishers. Mary Doran's 'The British Library's Modern Irish Collection', *LSBN*, no. 15, Winter/Spring 1997, p. 2 reviews, with examples, the type of material held: works on all periods of Irish history published during the present century; modern literary material; the published output of literary, historical and cultural societies; research publications covering contemporary Irish communities in Great Britain; and cultural, political and social issues in Northern Ireland and in the Republic of Ireland; and Irish language material.

Similar in content and arrangement, Gillian Ridgley's 'International Organizations Publications In The British Library', *LSBN*, no. 14, Summer 1996, p. 3 examines not only publications currently received from international organizations, obtaining hundreds of publications issued annually in a variety of formats, but also some of the publications of organizations which flourished in the second half of the nineteenth century many of which other libraries have discarded.

NEWSPAPER LIBRARY

Space and preservation problems

With public and professional attention focused on the high-profile transfer of the British Library's main central London reference collections to St Pancras, the Newspaper Library at Colindale is facing the same challenges and pressures without enjoying the relocation escape route. The ever increasing demand for access to its collections was underlined in the Summer of 1996 when it was reported that, for the fifth successive year, use of the Reading Room had increased. Already there were signs that on some days readers faced the possibility of queuing for entry and for access to a microfilm reader. Acute storage problems also confront the Library as its unused shelving reduces year by year. Comparatively minor short-term shifts do little more than delay the dispersal to remote stores of original newspapers which have been microfilmed. In times when thinking the unthinkable is becoming politically fashionable, now is seen to be the right moment to consider discarding rather than dispersal however irrevocable such a decision would be. And so the British Library has revived and accelerated a policy which operated between 1964 and 1976, of replacing originals of overseas newspapers by purchasing microfilm copies. The intention is to dispose of all original newspapers held on microfilm of acceptable quality, except for all material printed before 1850, material received under colonial copyright and material which had previously been agreed should be retained because of its special nature. Titles will be offered to the national library of the country of origin and, if not required, the library will be asked to suggest an alternative home in that country. Material for which no home can be found will be offered to dealers for sale or, as a last resort, sent for pulping. By whatever means the Newspaper Library expects to dispose of some 60,000 bound volumes of broadsheet newspapers occupying 3750 linear metres of shelf space. But legislation to amend the legal deposit requirements would be necessary.

Preserving its collections to keep them available to generations of future readers remained a constant problem, highlighted in a letter to *The Times* from Mr W.C.F. Butler. He reported that on a recent visit to the Newspaper Library seven out of ten of the South London and Thanet newspapers he wished to consult for the period June to October 1893 could not be produced because they were unfit for use; they were on the shelves but were in such poor condition that they could not be read without unacceptable risk of damage. Staff had advised him that the Library contained thousands of volumes in similar condition. Mr Butler suggested a substantial lottery grant to speed up microfilming ('Damage to newspapers', *The Times*, no. 65864, 15 April 1997, p. 19). A reply from the British Library's Chief Executive followed six days later informing readers that the Newspaper Library's microfilming programme was underfunded and a bid for additional funds had been made to the Department of National Heritage. 'If the bid is successful we shall be able to microfilm (at a cost of £1.8 million) some eleven million pages of newsprint' ('Damage to newspapers', *The Times*, no. 65869, 21 April 1997, p. 23).

Responding with commendable alacrity, *The Times* printed the same day a feature of its own.

A national archive of great importance is gradually turning to dust in a wholly unsuitable building in an obscure corner of north London. The British Library newspaper library is the repository of the nation's press. More than 600,000 bound volumes fill 18 miles of shelving and each year some 40,000 researchers dig in the library's boundless mine of instant history . . . Colindale is the poor relation of the British Library and its annual budget of around £1.25 million is loose change when compared with the £500,000 million cost of building the British

Library's state-of-the-art headquarters at St Pancras. (Alan Hamilton, 'History in danger of crumbling away to dust', *The Times*, no. 65869, 21 April 1997, p. 6).

Long-standing pressure on reading space in the Newspaper Library at Colindale was alleviated by a new reading room opened in September 1996 which accommodated a further 29 reader places, made up of 18 microfilm readers, bringing the total up to 52, four extra microfilm reader printers and seven computer work stations, six of which will be linked to existing facilities to provide networked access to newspapers on CD-ROM and later, it is hoped, to newspaper sources accessible via the Internet ('New Reading Room at Colindale', *Newspaper Library Newsletter*, no. 21, Summer 1996, p. 1). Ingeniously created by utilizing space previously occupied by the Library's ground floor meeting room to erect a two-storey prefabricated building, the new reading room is on the first floor linked to the main building by a short corridor, while the ground floor provides extra space for meetings, visitors reception and extended staff accommodation. Additional shelf space for reading room reference material has also been procured.

An earlier improvement was the clearing of an entire floor of the Library's 'new wing' (i.e. dating from the 1950s) and the installation of mobile racking for microfilm storage in 1995. Before then nearly 300,000 reels of microfilm were scattered all over the library, some at a considerable distance from the reading room. With a rack capacity for 380,000 reels of microfilm, the new store can house the whole of the existing stock with room for another six to seven years' accessions. But such measures could only ease the problems, not solve them. In 1996 preliminary work was set in train to construct a new building at Colindale under the Conservative government's Private Finance Initiative which would have involved the Library going into partnership with a private-sector company to carry the financial risk. Eventually the plan was shelved on the grounds of expense although the commitment to develop the Colindale site remains.

NEWSPLAN

An important milestone was reached in the history of NEWSPLAN, the cooperative microfilming project to preserve local newspapers published throughout the British Isles, maintained by the British Library, in conjunction with public library authorities, record offices, local newspapers and the regional library bureaux. The publication early in 1996 of the *Report of the NEWSPLAN project in the London and South Eastern Library Region (LASER)* completed the identification programme which began with the report of the pilot project in the South-West region ten years earlier. Taken *en masse* the series provides comprehensive listing of the principal surviving files of UK and Irish local newspapers, with information on their extent, gaps and physical condition. The reports also identify what preservation microfilming had already been achieved besides recommending priorities for the microfilming which still needed to be done. Each project started with research to draw up a survey and inspection of newspaper files held, storage conditions and restrictions on access were noted and the quality of existing microfilming programmes assessed. The cost of this research was shared between libraries in the regions and the British Library. Much of the microfilming was undertaken at Colindale and it is estimated that since the late 1980s over 12,000 reels of microfilm, each corresponding to a bound volume of historic local newspapers, was filmed for NEWSPLAN participants, in addition to a similar number of current local newspapers filmed on standing order. From 1992 onwards the Newspaper Library offered concessionary rates for NEWSPLAN microfilming in recognition not only of its intrinsic importance but also of the contribution NEWSPLAN makes to the preservation of its own collections.

Jennifer MacDougall's *NEWSPLAN: Guidelines for the Microfilming of Newspapers*, covering the preparation of material, microfilming procedures and quality control, bibliographic targets, boxing and labelling, storage, transportation and security, was published jointly by the National Library of Ireland and the British Library Newspaper Library in 1994.

Future plans were announced in 'Newsplan News', *Newspaper Library News*, no. 23, Summer 1997, p. 5. At its April meeting the LINC NEWSPLAN Panel decided to apply for Heritage Lottery Funds to support a feasibility study into the establishment of a national coordinated programme of preservation microfilming of local newspapers and the preparation of a full-scale lottery application for its funding. A coordinated national bid would be preferable to individual local authorities going it alone with each making a separate bid for their own collections. Progress would be more consistent and priorities could be established to microfilm those newspapers most at risk.

Three authoritative articles offer an insight into NEWSPLAN's origins, aims, value and operations. Selwyn Eagle and Geoffrey Hamilton's 'Preserving the perishing papers: NEWSPLAN and your local newspaper' (*Local History Magazine*, no. 37, January–February 1993, pp. 8–11) underlines the value of local newspapers for historical research, reminds readers of their ephemeral and fragile nature and insists that public demand for access to historical files remains constant.

> At the British Library Newspaper Library in Colindale, the 112 seats are fully occupied, on average, one day in every three on which the Library is open. These users come equipped with their own lap-tops, make extensive use of the copying services and whisper into tape recorders.

Fortunately, librarians and archivists, hoarders by training and inclination, collected and retained local newspapers although not always in ideal conditions.

> Any use and consultation of old newspapers and the conditions in which they are stored, will tend to have an effect on how long they will survive. If you have ever tried unfolding one which has been exposed to light and is more than a few years old, you may know the chances of anyone else consulting it at a later date are minimal.

In this context Eagle and Hamilton explain how, where and why NEWSPLAN came into existence and speedily evolved into a nation-wide project.

Geoff Smith's 'Involved with past and future' (*Library Association Record*, **98** (5), May 1996, pp. 252–3) reports on NEWSPLAN's ten years of achievement, the British Library and other national libraries working together with public libraries and the newspaper industry for the preservation of a print medium recording 200 years of life in Britain, but he is still worried about the impact of public library funding pressures and of local government reorganization. 'New approaches to the funding of newspaper preservation need to be identified and addressed, including the feasibility of obtaining lottery funding for the preservation of this very important aspect of the national printed heritage.'

In contrast, Selwyn Eagle's 'The LASER NEWSPLAN Project: reflections on four years before the masthead' (*Newspaper Library Newsletter*, no. 22, Winter 1996/1998, pp. 4–7) tells how he came to be appointed a two days a week part-time Coordinator of the London and South East Region NEWSPLAN report, as opposed to full-time Project Officers elsewhere, the problems he faced, how the estimated period of the project inexorably stretched from two years to almost five and how he and a student helper transferred all entries by hand to the US MARC format. At the end

> recommendations were one of the final problems to be addressed. In other regions the Project Officer had been able to make these, title by title, on the basis of personal examination of files. In my case this was not possible and so recommendations are on a broad brush basis, stemming partly from BLNL's needs and practices but also leaving it open to the Implementation Committee to draw in local authorities where particular problems of heavy use, deterioration etc, demand action.

Not only historical files of local newspapers urgently needed preservation microfilming. The proliferation of local free newspapers added further difficulties, so much so that in 1990 the Library commissioned an investigation of the problems encountered by libraries attempting to collect and preserve this type of material. A report from the consultant, Selwyn Eagle, a year later

> identified the growth in publication of free newspapers during the 1980s, the difficulties experienced by libraries (including BLNL) in acquiring them systematically, the high level of advertising content in relation to editorial mater, the duplication of content in multiple variant editions and the problems of bibliographical control because of title changes and variant editions.

Eagle recommended that

> certain responsibilities in relation to Scottish and Welsh newspapers should be delegated to the National Libraries of Scotland and Wales, that surveys and regular reviews of the collecting of free newspapers by public libraries should be carried out within the framework of NEWS-PLAN, that there should be liaison on microfilming arrangements, including the purchase by BLNL of locally produced microfilm where this was of suitable quality, that the possibility of the deposit of sets for microfilming of main edition and changed pages only be explored and that further efforts should be made by BLNL to develop contacts and cooperation with the newspaper industry.

These proposals were adopted by the Newspaper Library and were included in a draft national policy statement which was discussed by the

NEWSPLAN regional committees, the LINC NEWSPLAN Panel and by the British Library's Consultative Group on Newspapers before a revised policy statement was issued:

1   Each free newspaper which regularly contains news and editorial features and is not merely a local variant edition, will be permanently retained by a library which has national archival responsibilities (the British Library, the National Libraries of Ireland, Scotland and Wales). Changed pages in local variant editions also should be permanently retained.

2   The British Library will not collect or preserve free newspapers which contain advertising matter only. Such titles should be held locally and the British Library may be able to help local libraries with their acquisition. However, the National Libraries of Ireland, Scotland and Wales aim to collect **all** free newspapers published in their respective countries.

3   The British Library will negotiate with the National Libraries of Scotland, Wales and Ireland arrangements which recognise their responsibility for maintaining the national archive of free newspapers published or circulating in their respective countries. The aim of each national library should be to acquire all free newspapers required for the national printed archive through enforcement of legal deposit. The Newspaper Library will continue to retain Irish, Scottish and Welsh free newspapers selectively and with local advice. There will be coordination of preservation microfilming between the national libraries.

4   The British Library will encourage local libraries to formulate and implement their own policies for collecting and preserving free newspapers and to do so with regional needs and interests in mind.

5   Legal deposit items, not required for the national printed archive, may be disposed of. The Newspaper Library will not dispose of free newspapers already in its collections, other than any which consist solely of advertising. Any items that are to be disposed of will first be offered to a local library.

6   The Newspaper Library's preservation treatment for free newspapers will be the same as for paid-for titles. Each title will be microfilmed and a master negative will be produced which meets standards required for the Register of Preservation Microforms. Original copies of filmed newspapers will be wrapped in acid-free paper and stored at

Colindale or elsewhere.

7 Where there are variant editions the aim should be to produce composite microfilm of the main edition and front and changed pages only from variant editions. However this can only be done by BLNL if the publishers can provide the necessary information or composite sets for microfilming. In other cases BLNL will microfilm each edition in full unless changes are confined to the masthead or front and back pages only. For these the main edition in full plus front and back pages only of the variant editions will be filmed.

(Extracted from Geoff Smith's 'Free Newspapers: A National Policy For Their Collection and Preservation', *Local Studies Librarian*, **14** (1), Summer 1995, pp. 13–14. See also 'A Free Newspapers Policy', *Newspaper Library Newsletter*, no. 17. Summer 1994, p. 9).

NEWSPAPER LIBRARY CATALOGUES

Work started in October 1994 on the retrospective conversion of the Newspaper Library catalogues to machine-readable form after a feasibility study had investigated whether the catalogue records were suitable for conversion and eventual mounting on the British Library online public access catalogue. The conversion method, the technical operations involved, the order in which catalogue records were to be converted and the merger of records from the Library's printed and card records with the computer printout used since 1988, are described in 'Automation of the Newspaper Library Catalogue' (*Newspaper Library Newsletter*, no. 18, Winter 1994/95, p. 4). At the time of writing the updated progress reports that were promised have not yet appeared. Microfilm series not fully listed in the Newspaper Library's catalogue are described in 'Microfilm Series in the Newspaper Library' (*Newspaper Library Newsletter*, no. 21, Summer 1996, pp. 10–12). Probably the most well-known is *Early English Newspapers*, a microfilm set of the Burney Collection (1603–1818) held in their original form in RS&CD Collections.

READ ALL ABOUT IT

Although the *Newspaper Library Newsletter* continues to print a regular feature on individual newspapers and journals – David Reed's 'Radio

Times: High or Low?' (no. 17, Spring 1994); 'The Life and Times of Time and Tide' (no. 18, Winter 1994/95); Dennis Griffith's 'Plant Here the Standard' (no. 19, Summer 1995); and 'The Daily Mail 1896–1996' (no. 21, Summer 1996) are some recent examples – articles on the Newspaper Library's collections as a whole are not so thick on the ground. *United States and Canadian Holdings at the British Library Newspaper Library*, published by the Eccles Centre for American Studies in 1996, lists nearly 1400 United States titles of newspapers, trade union, church, ethnic and political associations publications and fashion and arts magazines. Omitting the 780 single issues of American titles published in the spring of 1858 and obtained by Henry Stevens on a book-buying expedition to the United States in that year for the British Museum Library, the list is arranged in two separate sections for the two countries, each followed by an index covering state or province and town. 'United States Material at the Newspaper Library', *Newspaper Library Newsletter*, no. 22, Winter 1996/1997, pp. 10–11 and *Newspaper Library News*, no. 23, Summer 1997, pp. 3–5 outlines the Library's collection of early US newspapers, either in the original form or in facsimile and indicates the range of other types of material held, black newspapers, the native American press, magazines and various bibliographies and directories.

'The Newspaper Library: Read All About It' (*SRIS Newsletter*, no. 26, Autumn 1996, pp. 4–5) is a brief overview of its collections, its use of new technology, its readers and reader access. Celebrating the 90th anniversary of the opening of the original British Museum Newspaper Repository, '90 Years of Colindale' (*Newspaper Library Newsletter*, no. 20, Winter 1995/96, pp. 9–11) complements earlier historical articles and confirms that Colindale was not always 'an obscure corner of north London'. Together with a change in design, although not in content or arrangement, the *Newspaper Library Newsletter* became *Newspaper Library News* with effect from issue no. 23, Summer 1997.

BLISS

As the date for the transfer of the British Library Information Sciences Service (BLISS) from the Library Association headquarters in Ridgmount Street, to the St Pancras building, drew nearer, so the concern of Library Association members as to the future provision of professional literature for continuing personal development became more focused. At the Association's AGM in October 1994, a motion to canvass the general membership for views, possibly by a questionnaire, or by a consultative document, was approved. In the event a consultative document was published in the *Library Association Record*, 97(8), August 1995, pp. 440–1 and copies sent with a covering letter to all Branches and Groups of The Library Association, asking for responses on behalf of their constituencies by the end of the year.

Contributions to the *Library Association Record*'s correspondence columns moved the debate forward. L.J. Taylor's 'Replica LA library not the answer', *Record*, **97** (9), September 1995 asked the crucial question, 'will the collection retain its integrity in the new BL and is that important?' His own oblique answer was 'Much of the LAL stock was always very lightly used – especially foreign-language material – and space constraints in the new BL may relegate this and historical items to a storage area away from the LA members' easy access, a process I fancy already happening in the LA building.' As for a loan service, 'it seems the only solution is to rely on *Lisa* and the BL's Document Supply Centre, hard though that decision might be'. Taylor, whose views carried weight as a former LAL Librarian (1964–78), ended on a pragmatic note: 'After all, the last 20 or so years have seen the LA riding high on the altruism of the BL for its library service. That happy state had to end some time.'

Maurice B. Line's 'My idea of Bliss, by an active professional' (*Record*, November 1995) unequivocally listed nine requirements:

> (1) a strong and broad current collection in a convenient place, for browsing and serendipity – with titles not easily accessible elsewhere . . . ; (2) a good collection of older (1970–) material that is likely to be wanted; (3) a basic collection of ordinary reference material; (4) access to selected general management literature (with a sprinkling of computer literature); (5) frequent lists of current accessions, including journal issues; (6) a photocopying service; (7) rapid access to bibliographic databases of LIS, both electronic and printed (much easier for browsing); (8) basic (not expert) assistance on the spot; and (9) rapid and guaranteed access to older material, for consultation, photocopying and loan.

The loan service requirement, he thought probable, could be supplied by DSC. 'All other needs should be met in the same place, including bibliographic access (for convenience) and management literature, which is available elsewhere but not easily accessible.' After considering various possibilities and dismissing them, he was of the opinion that

> A British Library collection, with its own space in the new building, open to LA members, has many things in its favour. The BL should have a good LIS collection for the use of its own staff anyway; it has material that can be used for exchange for foreign journals' it has (or should have) all British materials, though some duplication would be needed; the location is convenient; and the additional money required to supplement the collection is small in relation to the BL's budget . . .

A former Director-General, Science Technology and Industry, the British Library, and LA President (1990), Line's views demanded respect even if they were unpalatable to some LA members.

Antony Croghan's 'Plans for Bliss material' (*Record*, June 1997) posed three pertinent questions: (1) What is its future identity – if any – within the British Library? (2) What in general is the nature of the materials to be taken by the BL Foreign Serials? American monographs? Only English language materials? and (3) What will be disposed of and where will it go? In reply, Christine Burden, Head of BLISS, reported that

> The focus for LIS in St Pancras will be on the second floor of the General Humanities Reading Area. Bliss staff are, at present, selecting material to form an up-to-date, professional open access collection. Readers will also have access to the full range of humanities open access material as well as to the collections held in the St Pancras basements, ordered through the online catalogue. From May 1998 when the Rare Books and Music Reading Room opens, there will be access to pre-1850 material and from 1999 the stock and services of the Science Reference Information Service will be available on the same site.
>
> All stock from Bliss not held elsewhere in the London collections will be transferred to St Pancras (both monographs and serials). The exercise to identify the monographs to be transferred has already taken place and work on the serials is well advanced. Bliss is bidding for funding to maintain the LIS stock (although it will benefit enormously from access to copyright deposit material). Bliss staff will work closely with colleagues in the collection areas to ensure continuity of supply. There will continue to be professional staff with specific responsibilities for services in the LIS field. The BL will shortly take a decision on the future of the stock not going into St Pancras, after seeking advice from the Bliss Consultative Group.

No doubt Croghan took what comfort he could from that. One positive step was that, although a reader's pass will be required to use the St Pancras reading rooms, members of The Library Association and of the Institute of Information Scientists, are *ipso facto* entitled to a pass.

A profile of the BLISS database, which covers all aspects of library and information science, together with material on the book trade, book production and archives and records management, appeared in *Interface*, no. 16, August 1996, p. 6.

READER SERVICES

In St Pancras' transition period, November 1997 to May 1999, Reader Services will play a key role as the British Library's scattered London reference collections are relocated in the new building. Re-educating established and welcoming new readers and users simultaneously will be crucial for a successful culmination to the Library's major upheaval. A good start was made on the opening day of the two Humanities Reading Rooms, 24 November 1997, when each reader was handed an information pack containing a colour illustrated brochure, *Using the Reading Rooms*, providing general information on the staggered opening dates of the various reading rooms, what the British Library could offer readers, admission requirements, access to the collections and services, general services and facilities at St Pancras, its location, a map, hours of opening, how to register comments on the services and contact information. Also enclosed were two colour-coded floor plans of Humanities 1 and Humanities 2, locating the reference and issue enquiry desks, the OPACs, the open access shelves and microform readers. Detailed notes on the use of personal computers are printed on their reverse sides. Two other information sheets completed the information pack, one giving details of the new Reader Education Service, the other an annotated list of the Library's reading room regulations designed to ensure a pleasant and orderly environment as well as to protect the collections.

A few months before the St Pancras opening, a new Reader Education Service was set up to ensure that established and new readers alike received sufficient information to enable them to make the most effective use of the Library's collections and services. The problem is especially acute in that the Reader Admissions Office has predicted that within 18 months the British Library might expect 200 new readers daily. And, to exacerbate the problem, large numbers of established readers will have to be introduced to the OPACs before they can call up the material they require. To make headway on this potentially crippling problem, induction sessions on how to use the Automated Book Request System will be held thrice daily in the St Pancras opening period. How long this will be necessary is uncertain but it will be a heavy drain on staff resources. Eventually RES programmes will advance beyond this first basic strategy and evolve into a wider range of courses developed in conjunction with reading room managers. Tailored sessions for specific groups are being advocated.

The Reader Satisfaction Service produces a *Readers' Bulletin* designed to inform readers about changes to services at St Pancras as they occur. The first issue, dated 24 November 1997, which concentrated on responding to some of the questions and concerns previously raised about services, policies and facilities in the new building, was deposited on all readers' desks on the opening day of the Humanities reading rooms.

CENTRE FOR THE BOOK

Founded by the British Library in 1990 'to promote the significance of the book, in all its forms, as a vital part of the cultural, academic, scientific and commercial life of the country', the Centre for the Book has developed its major activities along three main routes. Its lecturing programme includes the annual Winter lecture series in which eminent writers share the book-related experiences with their audience. The 1998 series consisted of three lectures by historians concentrating on periods when the idea of one epoch ending and another beginning was a central theme in the writings of the time. An ambitious one-off series of lectures, in 1997, hosted by the University of St Andrews and the Centre for the Book, celebrated the bicentenary of Robert Burns. Intended to encourage a wider appreciation of Burns' poems, to demonstrate his sophistication in poetic form and thinking, and to place him in his eighteenth-century context, the programme was so arranged that nine distinguished authorities, including Seamus Heaney, the Nobel laureate, addressed different facets of Burns's life and work, either at the University or in Edinburgh one day and in London the next.

A whole faculty of Fellowships represents the Centre's second major activity. Judged to be the most prestigious is the Visiting Fellowship, designed to honour a distinguished scholar 'in the book based subject area within the focus of the Centre's activities' which allows what is called 'privileged access' to the Library's staff and collections. This was first awarded to Henri-Jean Martin, eminent historian of the book in France. If the British Library has a weakness, it has to be its uncontrollable urge to alter its nomenclature, sometimes to the confusion of readers, scholars and commentators. A minor example of this is the redesignation of what were initially called Non-Stipendiary Fellowships (not an inspired choice by any means) to Research Fellowships awarded each year in open competition. These, too, offer privileged access and a reserved desk space as perquisites and also the opportunity to give public lectures. Recent examples include Dr Maureen Perkins's 'Visions of the Futures: Almanacs, Time and Cultural Change 1775–1870' and Professor Joseph M. Levine's 'John Evelyn: Between the Ancients and the Moderns'.

A new Fellowship for Non-Fiction, designed to recognize research conducted outside the academic establishment, was initiated in the spring of 1997, with the generous support of the American arts organization, the Gladys Kriebe Delmas Foundation. An annual award of £2,000 is made to the successful candidate who, typically, may be a biographer, travel writer or a scientific author, unsupported by an academic institution. The first recipient was Nicholas Murray, biographer of Bruce Chatwin and Matthew Arnold.

In 1994 the British Library Penguin Writers Fellowship was created with funding from Penguin Books Ltd to support and encourage the use of the British Library by creative writers. The Fellowship carried an honorarium of £2,000 and lasted for six months, giving access to the specialist skills and the knowledge of the collections possessed by the Library's curators. Preference is given to proposals setting out projects particularly dependent on the British Library's collections. The *Times Literary Supplement* took over sponsorship in 1997 when the award was increased to £3000. Fellows are expected to give a public reading from their works and a public lecture on a literary theme. The Centre also hosts an occasional series of lectures on the Art of Translation.

To promote a greater knowledge and use of new technology in the book world, the third string to the Centre's bow is the New Technology Seminars held annually since 1991. This series is especially intent on exploring social and political issues of the new technology which may be obscured in the surrounding hubbub as the next technological innovation overtakes the last. From 1994 to 1996 the Centre was involved with the University of Hertfordshire's LibTech Conference and Exhibition, hosting a discussion concerning new technology's effects on the book world. The 1996 topic was 'Text and the Internet', introducing its information potential, but also looking at the possibilities for its regulation.

Issued three times a year, in single-sheet format, the *Centre for the Book Newsletter* was first circulated in Summer 1994. Its contents include the names of speakers in the lecture series, Fellowship awards and programmes, lectures published and diary dates. Mike Crump's 'The Centre for the Book', *Friends of the British Library Newsletter*, no. 4, December 1993, p. 3 is a general background article whilst Richard Price's 'The Centre for the Book', *London Services Bloomsbury Newsletter*, no. 15, Winter/Spring 1997, p. 5 is a résumé of the Centre's programme and activities to date.

READING EXPERIENCE DATABASE

In conjunction with the Open University, the Centre set up the Reading Experience Database (RED), formally launched in September 1994, the first systematic project to collect data about the experience of reading 1450–1914. The project will try to establish how, when, where and what people read. Given the scale of the project it is currently limited to recording the reading experience within the British Isles and among those born there although it is hoped that the project will be taken up elsewhere. Simon Eliot's 'What Are We To Do about the History of Reading?', *The Author*, **105** (2), Summer 1994, pp. 69–70, reprinted in *Rare Books Newsletter*, no. 48, November 1994, pp. 30–35, expands on RED's chronological and geographical scope, the design of the record form, and the Steering Committee's drafting of a list of standard works, diaries, journals, autobiographies, to be scanned; Crump's 'The Reading Experience Database', *Library Review*, **44** (6), 1995, pp. 28–29 amplifies why the project was started; and Eliot's 'The Reading Experience Database: Problems and Possibilities', *Publishing History*, no. 39, 1996, pp. 87–100 discusses the latest draft of the RED record form, explains the reason for offering a World Wide Web version and explores how the project might develop if it is to provide the scholarly resource needed by researchers into the history of reading.

ECCLES CENTRE FOR AMERICAN STUDIES

One of the world's most important resources for the study of North America, its heritage, people, geography and power, the British Library's links with North America do not solely relate to its extensive collections which contain an impressive range of North American material in the form of manuscripts, maps, books and newspapers. Moreover many organizations and institutions in North America make regular use of the British Library's up-to-the-minute information and document supply services. (The British Library Document Centre has just under 1900 customers in the US). Currently some 1200 customers in the United States and Canada subscribe to the Library's Patent Express Service.

The David and Mary Eccles Centre for American Studies at the British Library was established in 1991 following a generous gift of £1million from Viscount Eccles, first Chairman of the British Library Board and his wife Mary Hyde. Its purpose is to develop and promote the British Library's collections of North America as a means of increasing understanding and knowledge of North America and strengthening the bonds of friendship with Great Britain. To that end it publishes a number of subject guides listing studies of American interest to be found in the Library's collections. Titles include *American Slavery Pre-1866 Imprints; United States Government Policies Toward Native Americans 1787–1900;* and *The Harlem Renaissance.*

Set to become the outstanding reference source to academic American Studies courses in both the United Kingdom and Europe, the Centre publishes an annual guide, *American Studies in the United Kingdom: Undergraduate and Postgraduate Programmes* and, on behalf of the European Association for American Studies, a bi-annual newsletter, *American Studies in Europe.*

THE AMERICAN TRUST FOR THE BRITISH LIBRARY

Formed in 1979, by Douglas W. Bryant, former University Librarian at Harvard, the American Trust for the British Library's primary objective is to purchase American material, selected by the Library's curatorial staff, to fill gaps in the collections caused mainly by cutbacks in acquisition funding in the nineteenth century, or by enemy action in the Second World War. Most of the missing books have been supplied in microform produced by University Microfilms International.

FRIENDS OF THE BRITISH LIBRARY

Fully aware of the advantages offered by organized public support enjoyed by a number of comparable institutions, and sensitive to the subscription income that accumulates, an influential group of directors backed a paper submitted to the British Library Board in May 1987 proposing the formation of an organization to be known as the Friends of the British Library. After six months serious planning the Board gave the scheme their approval but expressed the hope that within a short period the Friends would become self-sufficient in terms of staffing and finance. Richard Luce, Minister for the Arts, publicly launched the Friends as a registered charity in May 1989.

Officially the aims of the Friends are:

(1) to widen public understanding of the British Library through the provision of information on its collections and services; (2) to improve awareness of the Library's role as a cultural centre and guardian of the national heritage; (3) to provide a means of developing special relationships with the private sector for fund raising and joint venture activities; and (4) to establish itself as a self-financing and profile raising organization over a period of two to three years.

Less formally, in an early interview, Hugh Cobbe, the Friends Secretary, remarked that the Friends' main purposes were to give people a way to support the Library positively and say 'thank-you' for its services, to raise money for the Library, to contribute towards exhibition costs and to the purchase of individual items of collections. For example, during the year ending July 1996 the following grants were made: £2350 for an eight-page colour section in the forthcoming special Maps issue of *The British Library Journal*, in memory of Helen Wallis, Map Librarian from 1965 to 1986; £2000 towards the purchase of parts of the archive of the music publishers, Novello & Co., which were missing from the company's original gift to the Library; £1800 towards the purchase of Giovanni Bernardo Rastelli's dedication copy of his contribution to the Gregorian reform of the Julian calendar, *De ratione atque emendatione Anni, & Romani kalendarii Opusculum* (Perugia, 1579); and £1740 to purchase 3 pH meters for use in the Conservation Workshop in connection with the deacidification of paper. In all this the Friends membership list provides a ready-to-hand directory of sympathizers to whom appeals can be directed.

In 1996 a conscious effort was made to increase both income and capi-

tal funds. Since its inception the Association had set aside half its subscription income each year to build up an endowment fund. An
approach was made to members to contribute to this. At the time it was
hoped to take over from the Library full responsibility for the payment
of its Administrator's salary, thus attaining full financial independence
from the Library.

Benefits and privileges of membership include the use of an attractive
Friends' Room; a discount off the price of British Library publications;
the right to a reader's pass for individual members (subject to the normal
regulations of the Library); lectures and discussions on the work and collections of the Library, the development of the new building at St
Pancras and other relevant topics; in addition to the Library's normal
programme of public lectures; special visits 'behind the scenes'; special
private views of British Library exhibitions; priority booking for the
British Library Stefan Zweig Concerts and similar events; and a regular
Friends' newsletter which provides information about events in the
Library. A number of tours and visits are also arranged, perhaps the
most ambitious so far has been a Paris weekend for a private visit to the
Bibliothèque Nationale and other cultural places of interest in
September 1997. A scheme to expand its membership in the north of
England by providing a northern programme based on Boston Spa was
announced in March 1996. Successful meetings and visits to York and
elsewhere have already taken place.

One of the most felicitous events ever presented in the Friend's programme was the Celebration of the Bicentenary of the Birth of Sir
Anthony Panizzi, an afternoon and evening lecture programme in the
British Museum Lecture Theatre and in the Conference Centre at St
Pancras, 16 September 1997. Between the afternoon and evening sessions groups toured those parts of the British Museum Library most
closely associated with Panizzi. Lectures included 'The Young Panizzi'
(Prof. M.R.D. Foot); 'Consort and Cupola: Prince Albert, Panizzi and
the Reading Room' (Dr Christopher Wright); 'The Legacy of Panizzi: his
successors in the nineteenth century' (Dr Andrew Prescott); and 'Panizzi,
Grenville and the Grenville Library' (Denis Reidy). All four, along with
David Paisey's 'Adolphus Asher (1800–53): Berlin bookseller, Anglophile
and friend to Panizzi', Christine G. Thomas and Bob Henderson's
'Watts, Panizzi and Asher: the development of the Russian collections
1837–1869'; and Martin Spevack's 'James Orchard Halliwell-Phillipps
and the British Museum Library' appear in the *British Library Journal's*

Autumn 1997 issue.

The Friends of the British Library Newsletter was first issued in September 1989 and is published three times a year. Typical contents include the progress of the St Pancras building, profiles of individual Library departments and morale-boosting messages from the Chairman of the Board of the British Library. Regular features are notices of events and news of British Library exhibitions, details of new and forthcoming publications and details of grants from the Friends' funds. Commander Michael Saunders Watson's 'Broader Scope for the Friends of the British Library' (no. 13 Summer 1995, pp. 1–2) draws all the threads together.

Science Reference And Information Service (SRIS)

SRIS was constantly preoccupied in the three years run-up to relocation at St Pancras by the cuts in public spending as a result of the 1995 Autumn Budget which threatened to make substantial inroads into SRIS's journal acquisition funds. At one time there was talk of subscriptions to 8000 scientific and technical journals being cancelled to the detriment of its comprehensive coverage (Alison Motluk, 'Desperate (sic) library slashes science to pay for paint', *New Scientist*, **149** (2012), 13 January 1996, p. 11). Alan Gomersall's gloomy forecast after the first swathe of subscription cancellations six years earlier that 'the steady attrition of the national scientific/technical periodical collection could continue throughout the 1990s without any relief as periodical subscriptions increase and budgets remain fixed' (*Serials*, **4** (3), November 1991, pp. 13–18) was beginning to look positively benign now that increasing prices are outpacing not fixed budgets, but reducing budgets.

Having to split journals between the London reference collections and the lending stock at Boston Spa, exacerbated the problems. SRIS currently received 22,000 scientific, technical and business journals, a third of which arrived under legal deposit, the other two-thirds being either purchased or obtained by donation or exchange. DSC subscribed to 45,225 titles to support its loan and photocopying services, which generated £21 million annual revenue. Despite cuts elsewhere in the Library's overall budget, the duplicate subscriptions remained an easy target for savings; nearly £1.7 million could be saved simply by cancelling duplicate overseas journals. At best it seemed that the Library was being hurried towards a single copy journal collection to support both reference and document supply services.

But how to decide its location? 'Although DSC is able to monitor usage levels of a journal very easily by recording the number of requests received . . . it is much more difficult to obtain such data in an open access research library as SRIS.' Three possible unsatisfactory scenarios presented themselves: (1) 'SRIS to hold most single copy journals which would then support existing reference uses as well as document supply on behalf of DSC, although this would make reference access less easy and document supply more expensive'; (2) 'a greater use of shared run arrangements, with some parts of a journal held at SRIS and others at DSC'; and (3) 'some degree of subject specialisation held only at DSC or SRIS'. ('British Library to Reduce Journal Duplication', *SRIS Newsletter*, no. 26, Autumn 1996, pp. 1–2).

In the event it was decided that the most important scientific journals would continue to be available in SRIS and DSC. Duplicate subscriptions would be maintained at least during the 1997 subscription year although other non-British titles would be reduced to single copies to support onsite and remote use when 1996 subscriptions expired. These measures were calculated to save £1m in the financial year. This

> interim solution has been found by looking at the individual titles and ranking the 5,025 purchased scientific journals in terms of their importance to the Library's users. Tier 1 journals are those judged to be the most important, Tier 2 next important and Tier 3 the least important for both reference and remote services. Assessments were made on the basis of levels of known use and the specialist expertise of the Library's professional staff. In practical terms this means: 1,150 first tier journals will be held both at Boston Spa and SRIS, requiring funding of £625,000 for at least one further subscription year. 2,000 second tier journals will be reduced to single copy status. For the first six months after publication, when remote demand is heaviest, they will be held at Boston Spa. During this period, reference users will have access to contents lists and will be able to order photocopies of individual articles. After six months the issues will be transferred to SRIS, which will support document supply activity from the reference copies. 1,100 third tier journals, which are covered by the Library's Inside current awareness service, will be held at Boston Spa. After the first six months, reference users will be able to request specific issues for consultation in the reading rooms. 775 third tier journals not covered by Inside will be held in SRIS. In the humanities and social sciences, 1,450 titles will be reduced to single copies and held at Boston Spa. ('Update on Journals', *SRIS Newsletter*, no. 27, Winter 1996, pp. 1-2)

Around 4500 other titles, which are mainly donations or obtained through exchange arrangements, will remain duplicated in 1997. Reducing donations to one copy provides no acquisition savings, but does provide other savings which have to be compared to the extra costs of meeting demand from single copies. Duplication of exchange titles is planned to cease at the end of 1997. As a result of these decisions, the Library will reduce its expenditure on duplicated serials by £1 million in 1996–97, rather than by the £1.7 million originally planned. The Library believes this course of action achieves the best compromise between expenditure reduction and maintaining service and between reference provision and remote provision. In making the decision to reduce the duplication of and thus the cost of acquiring, these non-British journals, the Library was aware that the quality of its reference and lending services would be affected. The Library had already planned to reduce the duplication of journals but hoped to phase in the reduction more gradually.

By chance, use of SRIS's reading rooms had recently received a good deal of attention, notably in an issue of the *Newsletter* focused on reading room services. A year later and charges of special pleading might well have been levelled at the SRIS directorate. 'Why Come to the SRIS Reading Rooms?' noted that in the previous year 160,000 visitors had been recorded and that over three million items of stock had been consulted, indicating that its reading rooms were among the most heavily used within the British Library. This was attributed to SRIS' unique combination of subjects, physical, earth and life sciences and technologies and scientific material, business information and patents.

Information gathered in recent surveys identified five reasons why reading room use was so heavy: (1) extensive collections, both the depth of coverage in each subject and the broad range of subjects covered, giving a high probability of finding everything needed in one place; (2) good subject searching facilities for finding information when no previous references are to hand; (3) open access collections leading to high-use items available for consultation on the shelves; (4) items arranged on the shelf by subject, allowing related material to be found close by once the first item had been located; and (5) use of the reading rooms open to all, free of charge and with no reader's ticket required. (*SRIS Newsletter*, 23, January 1995, p. 2). 'Using SRIS Reading Rooms – Tips for the New User' (ibid., p. 3) answers six questions relating to admission procedures, subject searching, which catalogue to use, using the CD-ROM work stations; obtaining photocopies and obtaining outhoused material.

Andrea Reid and Beryl Leigh's 'The Science Reading Rooms of the British Library: the User Community and patterns of Use', *Alexandria*, 7 (1), 1995, pp. 61–70 reports on a survey carried out one day a week, 12 November to 6 December 1993, structured on the same lines as previous surveys over the previous 25 years so that the results could be compared and trends identified. Although one or two facts of interest emerged, advocates of the 'research doesn't tell you anything you don't know already' school would feel their position strengthened rather than weakened. Student use rose 12% in the period 1983–93 while patent community use fell 10 per cent in the same period which might, or might not, be explained by the overall increase in student numbers and the decline of the UK manufacturing industry. It is suggested that when planning reader admissions at St Pancras, a streamlined pass issuing system will be needed for readers accustomed to having immediate access to the SRIS reading rooms.

In summary:

> a picture of the overall user community has been obtained, as well as an indication of who the main types of users are on an average day and the trends that have been influencing this during recent years. Information on the way in which readers use the library has also been obtained: how often they come, how long they stay and what they use the library for while they are there. (p. 69)

SRIS's range of specialist information services encompasses science and technology, business, the social sciences and patent information. Staff are available to provide expert help to reading room users and also to remote users unable to visit SRIS in person. A number of free quick enquiry services are available to provide answers to brief enquiries and stockholding queries. Expert staff working on the reading room enquiry desks handle most reader enquiries, but specialist free enquiry services are available for environmental, health care, social policy and business information. In addition, SRIS offers a range of competitively priced research services for users with more complex enquiries. These offer online database and extended manual literature searches to survey the literature or obtain hard data.

Science, Technology and Innovation, formerly *Science and Technology Policy*, a bi-monthly journal, addresses the impact of government policy on industrial competitiveness and monitors the effects of national decisions on companies, on the science and technology community and on education. Other matters within its province are the public perception of science, research and development and developments overseas. Each issue contains a bibliography of recent publications.

History

SRIS does not often examine its own history but a series of illustrated articles, 'The History of the Patent Office Library', looking at the history

of the Southampton Buildings site from the twelfth century, the formation of the Patent Office and the development of its library up to the creation of the British Library, including some key dates 1969–96, appeared
in four consecutive issues of *SRIS Newsletter*, nos. 23–6, January 1995 to
Autumn 1996. If costs allow reprinting in pamphlet form would seem
desirable.

Classification Scheme

Jennie Grimshaw's 'The SRIS Classification Scheme', *Catalogue and
Index*, no. 112, Summer 1994, pp. 7–9 is an up-to-date guide, encompassing its history, a technical description, automation of the schedules and
the published volumes. These last include a detailed introduction to the
scheme and how it is applied at SRIS, the schedules and the index.
Offprints of individual schedules or other subsets can be produced to
order. Revision is by a rolling programme and new schedules have developed for Robotics, Automation of Manufacturing, Electronics,
Economics, Pathology and Diagnosis in Medicine, Field Theory of
Fundamental Particles, Chromatography and Computing.

A new edition of *Using the Catalogues*, including appendices delineat-
ing which classmarks are in which reading room and what the location
mark prefixes and suffixes mean, and where the items can be found, was
published in March 1994. SCICAT, the current catalogue of SRIS on
microfiche, which started in 1974, provides details of all serials, bibliographies and abstracts in the collection published before that date, plus
all the books published after 1968 held by SRIS. SCICAT allows the
reader to find appropriate references using an author's/corporate
author's name (including named conferences), the title of a work or a
subject. It can be used to compile specialist bibliographies; conduct current awareness searches; locate existing catalogue records; and answer
awkward queries. SCICAT is available online via IRS-Dialtech, the
British Library service which provides online access to ESA-IRS, the
European Space Agency's Information Retrieval Service. 'SCICAT On
ESA – Improving Access to the SRIS Collections', *SRIS Newsletter*, no.
25, November 1995, p. 6 has details of identifying and acquiring documents, costs and getting access.

SCICAT on CD-ROM was launched in the summer of 1997, featur-
ing

a Windows-style of searching, so users are in complete control and are not trapped within the confines of a menu. They can make searches as complex or as simple as they wish whilst the ability to mark, sort and print records enables users to print precisely what they need . . . Subscribers to the existing fiche product are being offered the chance to switch to the CD-ROM but we expect the fiche to continue to be available in 1998. ('What's New SCICAT?' *SRIS News*, no. 28, Autumn 1997, p. 15).

Publications

SRIS's publication programme includes a number of substantial Library Reference Guides including the longstanding *Guide to Libraries and Information Units in Government Departments and Other Organisations* (32e., 1996, 195pp.) edited by Peter Dale. Over 700 detailed A–Z numbered entries (840 including sub-entries) provide directory information including stock and subject coverage, services, availability, opening hours and publications. An increased coverage of e-mail addresses, World Wide Web addresses and 150 new entries are features of this latest edition.

Guide to Libraries in London (1995, 384pp.) edited by Valerie McBurney features over 690 libraries (1058 including sub-libraries) in 33 London boroughs. *Guide to Libraries in Western Europe* (2e., 1994.,160pp.) is divided into four sections: library entries A–Z by country; international organization libraries; and national libraries, library associations and British Council Libraries. *Guide to Libraries in Central and Eastern Europe* (1992, 96pp.), compiled by Maria Hughes, is similarly arranged.

SRIS Newsletter changed its title to *SRIS News* with the Autumn 1997 issue when, for no apparent good reason, apart from a vague hope that readers would be better able to find their way around, a new cover design and layout were introduced. An independent observer might suppose the new cover design was falling into line with *Select, Philatelic Collections Newsletter* and RIC's *Research Bulletin*.

STM Search

STM Search, covering science, technology and medicine, replacing the Science and Technology Information Service, was launched in September 1995. Expert searchers exploit a wide range of printed, online and CD-ROM information sources to produce the information required. If regular updates are needed, customer profiles can be stored for matching against new material. Besides detailed searches STM Search can undertake subject overviews to brief customers on significant recent developments, or to provide a current awareness service. Search results can be delivered or collected in a variety of ways. Further details are printed in 'STM Search Takes Off', *SRIS Newsletter*, no. 25, Nov.1995, pp. 2–3.

Anne Summers' *British Library Collections on the History and Culture of Science, Technology and Medicine* (British Library, 1996), published in SRIS's How To Find Information Series, is a guide to those Library departments holding important source material, including SRIS, DSC, Western Manuscripts, OIOC, the Map Library and the National Sound Archive, together with information on each department's facilities and opening hours.

Business Information Research Service

Holding the most comprehensive collection of business information literature in the UK, SRIS's Business Information Research Service is dedicated to providing information to UK business and industry, assisting its users to investigate new market sectors, to keep track of the activities of competing firms, and to identify products and suppliers. Broad categories of information most frequently demanded are listed in *Your Business Needs Our Information*, a four-page inventory of services available including company profiles, stockbroker reports, market overviews, data on market leaders, geo-political backgrounds, news items, statistics, supplier and manufacturer details, mailing lists and document supply. Following the success of the British Library–Lloyds Bank Business Line (*vide infra*), SRIS received additional sponsorship from Lloyds to offer a tailored service to the Bank's business managers, providing market and product information to aid understanding of the needs of innovation or technology firms and to assess their requests for loans.

A strong publishing programme includes guides to its own collections, a range of practical business guides and guides to sources of information. *Market Research: a Guide to British Library Collections* (8e., 1996, 324pp), edited by Michael Leydon and Leantha Lee, lists 3000+ current market research reports, including surveys and country profiles, published since 1990, available for free consultation in the British Library and a comprehensive directory of over 500 market research producers both private and public in the UK and overseas. In this 8th edition UK reports are listed by industry and product, with a separate subject index, non-UK reports are listed by geographic area, and reports from the top 10 market research journals, including *Mintels* and *Market Research UK-Europe*, are included for the first time. David Barrett and Val Peel's *Business Journals at SRIS* (1996) contains entries on over 2000 important business and trade journals, listed alphabetically under more than 1600 subject headings, showing the subject areas covered and the types of data included.

Compiled and completely revised by Business Information Research Service, *Sources of European Economic and Business Information* (London, Gower, 6e., 1995, 352p.), is a listing of the major sources of economic and business statistical information for 32 countries in Europe. Publications listed cover a wide range of topics, including economic conditions, socio-economic data, public finance, industry, business and commerce published by a variety of bodies – international organizations, national statistical offices, government departments, specialist publishers, banks and financial institutions, professional and trade associations, etc. For each publication information is given about title, date or frequency, language, cost, coverage and summary of contents. There are comprehensive indexes by title, subject and country and full information on all issuing organizations.

Ronald Clough's *Japanese Business Information: An Introduction* (1995, 116pp.) includes chapters on doing business in Japan; Japanese companies' activities abroad; Japanese economics; Marketing to Japan; Japanese products and technology; Organizations providing data on Japanese business; Trade and company directories; Standards, statistics and regulations; Japanese patents; Online information sources; Periodicals and newsletters; Japanese company reports; and Dictionaries.

British Library–Lloyds Bank Business Line

On a different level to the Business Information Research Service, the British Library–Lloyds Bank Business Line, launched in April 1994, offers a quick information telephone enquiry service limited to ten minutes to UK business.

> The Business Line is able to provide details of companies (e.g. address and telephone numbers, director's names and other basic details), search for manufacturers or suppliers of a product or service and identify useful

companies and organisations in Britain and abroad. The service will also give details of the holdings of the Business Information Service for clients wishing to visit the library to carry out their own research ('British Library–Lloyds Bank Business Line Launched', *SRIS Newsletter*, no. 22, August 1994, p. 1).

Within four months of starting the demand for the service was so high that a third dedicated telephone had to be installed and by June 1996 over 70,000 enquiries had been answered.

Social Policy Information Service

A strategic review of the British Library's social science information provision was commissioned by the Library's Management Committee and carried out by Lesley Grayson, an external consultant, in 1994. Her report proposed

> to create a Social Policy Information Service (SPIS) within SRIS, retaining most of the current responsibilities of OP&SS and sited in the former OP&SS reading room in Bloomsbury; to offer dynamic information services on social issues such as the family, law and order, community care, national and local administration, quality of life, employment and social change; to call upon collections at the Document Supply Centre for the bulk of enquiry answering rather than build large collections in London; to create a national open access statistics collection including both official and non-official statistics from the UK, Europe and international bodies; to link closely with other British Library information services, particularly the Business Information Service and Health Care Information Service; to offer free and priced information services based on CD-ROMs; online searching; a strong reference collection; displays of current reports, journals and newsletters; a major statistics collection; and up to three-year runs of UK social science monographs; and to complement, rather than compete with, existing services outside the British Library and to offer a gateway to them. (Grayson, L., 'British Library Social Policy Information Service', *Assignation*, **13** (4), July 1996, pp. 32–4).

The new service, formally launched in December 1996, became an OP&SS responsibility which was transferred from Humanities and Social Sciences to the Science Reference and Information Service and renamed Social Policy Information Service (SPIS), on the grounds that the worlds of business and the social sciences were converging and over-lapping in such areas as crime, the environment, housing, employment and transport. OP&SS had long participated in SRIS' Business Information Service, providing a back-up service for legal and statistical information. Moreover, there had been a marked shift away from pas-sive curatorial function at SRIS towards a more active exploitation of its collections.

The plan for the new service was first revealed in J.M. Grimshaw's 'OP&SS Transformed into SPIS', a two-page A4 document, circulated in the last week of April 1996:

> the first priority is to create the collections on which the new service in social policy will be based. The existing classified reference stock is being systematically upgraded. Out of date material is being withdrawn and new abstracting and indexing tools, directories and general reference works introduced. New open access stock sequences are being created: (1) A statistics collection consisting of 5 year runs of official and non-official UK statistical series drawn from the legal deposit intake. Initially the collection will cover social and demographic statistics. It will be expanded at St Pancras to include trade and production statistics; (2) a browsing collection of new social sciences monographs drawn from the legal deposit intake; (3) a display of one year runs of core applied social sciences journals; (4) displays of current issues of newsletters, research reports and briefing papers in field; and (5) key CD-ROMs in the fields of applied social sciences and statistics.
>
> Following the development of these collections, new services will be initiated, *viz* an expanded CD-ROM service with printing facilities; a publications programme which will include production of a new journal, *Public and Social Policy* as well as literature guides and bibliographies, both free and priced; a seminar and training course programme; a priced research service available by phone, fax and mail; and a free enquiry ser-vice available by phone, fax and mail as well as to personal users in the reading room.

Alan Gomersall's 'British Library Social Policy Information Service', *Assignation*, **12** (4), July 1995, pp. 29–30 is an authoritative résumé of its conceptual basis and ethos:

> Emphasis in the new service will be placed upon active exploitation of the collections and by ensuring that users can make maximum use of

the collection on their own behalf. An enquiry answering service using both database resources and the open access stock is to be offered to both academics and practitioners and it is anticipated that there will be a market for a premium service from those organisations and individuals needing information rapidly and able to pay for it.

Richard H.A. Cheffins' 'Launching The British Library's Social Policy Information Service', *Assignation*, **14** (2), January 1997, pp. 19–21 delves into the background for an improved British Library service for social sciences practitioners, examines the reasons for subsuming it in the Official Publications and Social Sciences Service, explains why the new service was transferred to SRIS where 'the pro-active ethos . . . has been beneficial to SPIS' and discusses the first fruits of the new service and the plans for its future development.

SPIS quickly provided a free, quick enquiry service, an extended CD-ROM service and, in the summer of 1997, a fee-based Social Science Search service covering all aspects of the social services in depth. Unlike other applied social science information providers, which usually focus on specific issues, Social Science Search offers a comprehensive service covering the whole field, in the form of literature surveys either to on-site or remote users, a current awareness service, document supply, briefings on key areas or subjects, with a range of delivery options (post, courier, or fax) and an expert translation service. Details of the expertise available, examples of some recent searches and notes on how to use the service, may be found in 'Social Science Search', *SRIS News*, no. 28, Autumn 1997, p. 4.

Linking research, policy and practice, the first issue of *Public and Social Policy* was published by the British Library in association with the London Research Centre in July 1996. Each issue contains news and views of important social science issues, detailed summaries of new reports from major research institutes and a bibliography of recent report literature. Its purpose and thrust was precisely defined:

> *Public and Social Policy* will review each quarter the response of academics, politicians, journalists and writers to the themes and ideas thrown up by this debate [i.e. the unprecedented wealth of assessments of changing British social, cultural and political life] and will focus on a particularly current topic each issue. The reader will be guided through current thinking and from all sides of the argument and directed to the original sources of published and semi-published materials. Currency

will be a key factor and historic analysis will be left to the publications of academics. However, sources of statistical material, government reports etc. will appear in the bibliography.

Health Care Information Service

Until the late summer of 1995 responsibility for medical and health care information provision within the British Library was dispersed between the Medical Information Centre (MIC) at Boston Spa and SRIS in London. In the first stage of restructuring MIC was closed and its functions, services and products were incorporated into a new Health Care Information Service located in SRIS's Holborn Reading Room. A unit remained at Boston Spa engaged in subject indexing and database compilation. HCIS offers an extensive reference collection of printed and electronic biomedical and health care literature encompassing books and journals, registers of practitioners and of medical products, health statistics, major indexing and abstracting services, and medical dictionaries and textbooks.

HCIS publications inherited from MIC include monthly bibliographies on specific medical topics drawn from MEDLINE and from AMED (Allied and Alternative Medicine Database) which covers literature in Complementary Medicine and Allied Health disciplines. *BSE and Prion-Related Diseases* was added to the MEDLINE update series in October 1996 and is issued quarterly in printed format and floppy disk. A detailed account of AMED and its series of current awareness bibliographies, its indexing system and thesaurus headings, its software and its language coverage, is printed in Judith A. Crowe's 'Alternative Medicine Information', *Online and CD Notes*, May 1994, pp. 6–8.

Coinciding with the start of HCIS, the British Library launched *Guide to Libraries and Information Services in Medicine and Health Care* (1995, 162pp.), a directory compiled by Peter Dale listing 660 information sources including hospital libraries, professional associations, company libraries, charities, voluntary bodies and support groups willing to provide information. Data supplied include full address or contact details; telephone, fax and E-mail information; opening times; information on the type of organization and its objectives and purposes; its library stock and subject coverage; its publications; and its services and facilities.

Environmental Information Service

In partnership with the Confederation of British Industry, the Environmental Information Service (EIS) was launched in 1989 to provide companies involved in environmental issues with a comprehensive package of current awareness, research and document supply services, coupled with a seminar and publishing programme. Recent publications include a second edition of Nigel Lees and Helen Woolston's *Environmental Information: A Guide to Sources* (1996, 180pp.). First published in 1992, its contents cover technical, government, business and patents information; UK and EC legislation; environmental auditing assessment and policy; sources of information on pollution, waste disposal and recycling, energy, transport, conservation, agriculture and food; and detailed appendices and indexes.

Lesley Grayson and Ken Young's *Quality of life in Cities: An Overview and Guide to the Literature* (1994, 160pp.) is arranged in two sections. Section one is divided into separate chapters, examining the debate about what constitutes quality of life; the question of how to measure this, its determining factors as experienced by individuals. In section two, five separate chapters focus on the issues and policy implications behind local factors: the safety and security of one's person and belongings; adequate and affordable shelter; a well-planned 'user-friendly' and humane place in which to live; a safe and healthy environment, and public services which help to sustain all these elements. Each chapter starts with a detailed overview of the topic followed by an extensive list of references to other information sources. Detailed author, corporate body and subject indexes are provided.

Grayson's *Channel Tunnel – The Link to Europe: An Overview and Guide to the Literature* (1995, 215pp.) focuses on the negotiations between Britain and France, the building of the Tunnel, the development of transport infrastructure, how the Tunnel operates and its likely economic and regional impact. Chapters include: Overviews and studies; Project management and finance; Design and construction; The transport system; Safety and security; Infrastructure links; Economic impact; and Regional impact.

Israel Berkovitch's *Energy Sources and Policy: An Overview and Guide to the Literature* (1996, 186pp.) covers the main issues in energy policy from UK, European and international perspectives. Each chapter contains a short bibliography – including some of the less well-known report literature, and the guide includes a useful list of UK and international organizations in the energy world (with full address and contact details).

Brokerage Services

SRIS's brokerage services whereby information brokers undertake research and locate information on clients' behalf, to precise specifications and in time to meet deadlines, researching in printed reports and journals, online databases and CD-ROMs, within a price limit, are outlined in 'Information Brokerage Services at SRIS', *SRIS Newsletter*, no. 24, May 1995, pp. 4–5. Client benefit, online costs, the specialist information on hand, SRIS's unique resources, and the quality of the research work are the topics covered. 'For Information Expertise Ask SRIS', IBID., no. 27, Winter 1996, p. 10, names The British Council, the European Commission, and the Department of Transport, being among an increasing number of organizations who have contracted SRIS to work with them on long-term information projects.

9

SPECIAL COLLECTIONS

In common with other service and support directorates Special Collections has experienced the impact of the new technologies but, unlike other directorates,

> the Special Collections of the British Library are for the most part private in their origin and unpredictable in the manner and timing of their acquisition. We are not, therefore, in the position of being able to foresee or systematically to plan for large accessions of unpublished, electronically generated material.

Alice Prochaska's 'The British Library and the Challenge of Electronic Media: a view from the Perspective of Special Collections', p. 167–73, *Electronic Information Resources and Historians* (St Katherine, Scripta Mercaturae Verlag, 1993) examines the problems digital technology poses to the directorate in its role as a provider of original source material for historical research.

Large scale Ordnance Survey mapping is a prominent case in point. In 1997 the Ordnance Survey ceased to produce this in analogue form and transferred to an entirely digitized output and, although this provides customers with a vastly enhanced and continuously updated database, it undoubtedly presents difficulties for the legal deposit libraries. Currently the Map Library receives new microfiche editions of Ordnance Survey mapping under the provisions of the Copyright Act 1911.

> We receive it free of charge, but pay a substantial sum for jacketing the fiche. From 1997 onwards, as matters stand at present, we would have to pay probably well over ten times that cost in order to receive the equivalent digitised output. We also have to take account of capital investment in the necessary equipment and extra staff and of the commercial interests of Ordnance Survey, which might well wish to have a

say in regulating the way in which the material is used in our reading rooms.

Far from enhancing the supply of original source material to future historians, digitization in this instance could in fact lead to a deterioration in the standing of the Map Library as the leading source for the national topographic record. 'How are we to ensure that the comparative information they need over time will be available to them on the same comprehensive basis as before?' Circumstances of this nature explain why the British Library is seeking the extension of legal deposit to non-print materials.

Conversely, digital technology opens up opportunities for collection development. Collaborative schemes with other institutions could lead to an exchange of digital copies of various physically separated complementary collections to distinct scholarly advantage. Already computer-assisted photography has advanced text enhancement almost beyond belief, allowing researchers and scholars unprecedented access by 'producing a videotape from the electronic camera, which is then digitised and used on an image-processing computer to enhance the image.' But even here a circumspect approach is necessary.

> While the opportunities seem almost infinitely seductive, there are difficulties arising from costs, from relationships between the Library and publishers, where rapid technological changes could outstrip long-term undertakings and from considerations of preservation. The cost factor will always loom large in determining priorities. Electronic advances have to be balanced against the priority of maintaining the necessary level of acquisitions, for instance. It is likely that most electronic publishing based on the Special Collections of the British Library will be undertaken in partnership with other publishers . . . Inevitably therefore, commercial considerations will govern the great bulk of our electronic output. Any large-scale projects for electronic scanning which might be expected to yield high academic but low commercial benefits, would need to be supported by special grants.

An imponderable feature of the electronic revolution is how far physical survival is guaranteed. Acquisition signifies preservation for future use but, as yet, ways of preserving and making use of non-print media have not received the attention that will soon be required, especially computer tapes and discs of the 1970s and early 1980s. 'Our curators', Prochaska concludes, 'will face special challenges explaining and making available computer-generated materials. They will also find themselves at the centre of the debate over which sources are published and which are not.'

WESTERN MANUSCRIPTS

Western Manuscripts holdings, continuously augmented by donations, bequests and by purchase, now total some 300,000 items. Most are designated Additional Manuscripts, catalogued and indexed in a series of volumes covering the period 1756 onwards, the latest being *Catalogue of Additions to the Manuscripts 1986–1990* (3 vols., 1995). Catalogues of named collections are also published, for example, *Catalogue of Additions to the Manuscripts in the British Library: the Cecil of Chelwood Papers* (1991). By the end of the decade the databases should be available for consultation via JANET.

Rachel Stockdale's 'Automated Cataloguing of Manuscripts at the British Library' (*European Research Libraries Cooperation*, 1 (4), 1991, pp. 402–7) describes in detail the automated cataloguing database system introduced in the Manuscript Collections in 1986. Two different methods of automation were adopted for the constituent parts of the catalogue: word-processing for the descriptive matter and a database for the index. Microsoft Word software was used for the word-processing, not only because it was easy to use and user friendly, but crucially because it carried three specific typefaces, bold, italic and small capitals, traditionally used to distinguish data on the printed page.

Despite current cataloguing of Western Manuscripts material being fully automated, many of its older catalogues fail to provide adequate information. For example it has proved impossible to determine how many illuminated manuscripts there are in the collections, thus handicapping efforts to ensure they are properly stored and preserved. To remedy matters a Survey of Illuminated Manuscripts is now in hand to produce a customized database. Starting with a pilot project in November 1995, the Survey embraces all pre-1200 AD manuscripts, all pre-1600 manuscripts with illumination, and post-1600 items relating to the history of early and illuminated manuscripts. By the end of Phase 1 of the project, in the year 2000, there will be electronic records of an estimated 20,000 items. Plans for later phases of the Survey include a full electronic index to illuminations in the manuscripts, with CD-ROM, hard copy and Internet publications envisaged.

'The Department of Manuscripts', *The Book Collector*, **45** (1), Spring 1996, pp. 9–23 is a benevolent essay recalling Sir Frederic Madden who 'has never been given full credit for all that he did to make the Department of Manuscripts what it is today'. Madden's reputation has, of course, long suffered because of his clashes with Panizzi. Keeper of the Department of Printed Books for almost two decades (1837–56)

> there was hardly a feature of its accommodation and work that he did not examine, test and improve, devising routines that have stood the test of time. Acquisition and deposit, shelving and binding, the rules for staff and readers, precautions for security against fire and theft – no aspect of his charge was too small to escape the rigorous examination that he gave it before establishing the routines that have lasted so well.

Then, switching abruptly from Madden's era to the formidable cataloguing problems which beset the Department from the 1950s onwards, the author describes in readable detail how, with the assistance of the Library's Computing and Telecommunications directorate, they were overcome by the adoption of digital computing techniques. Beyond this, there

> lies a still more exciting prospect, the conversion, using improved optical character recognition technology, of the catalogues of the entire collection from 1753 to 1955. This has already been the subject of a feasibility study lasting six months; this showed that records thus generated could be automatically transferred into MARC format with all but total accuracy. A modest investment of staff-time and in equipment could achieve a startling *aggiornamento*, just in time before the collections themselves move to St Pancras.

But, sadly, the resources to achieve this visionary project vanish as 'everything, all at least that does not contribute directly to the task of moving into the new building, is at risk of delay or outright cutting . . . Something so vital cannot be allowed to stumble, or fall, for want of the support it needs now.

In October 1996, the British Library was awarded a grant of £358,000 from the Heritage Lottery Fund towards the cost of converting over 30 of its manuscript catalogues to automated form, thus significantly expanding the database.

> The project which can now be realised . . . will use pioneering scanning technology and specially devised parsing programmes to convert the

printed catalogue text and indexes into data which can be stored and searched on the computer. [And, further,] full automation of the range of the Department of Manuscripts' mainstream catalogues will open new avenues to research for British Library readers who currently make over 17,000 visits to consult more than 70,000 manuscript items per year and for users at a distance who in the same period of time address more than 28,000 enquiries by letter and telephone to the specialist staff. Not only will the British Library be able to enhance its services to individual researchers with more flexible on-line access to the catalogues compiled over two hundred years, it will also be able to share this unique information more readily with other libraries and archives throughout Britain and the world. ('Lottery Fund Grant Makes Library Collections More Accessible', *British Library News*, no. 208, November 1996, p. 2).

As part of the British Library's Initiatives for Access programme, Computing and Telecommunications evaluated Excalibur EFS (Electronic Filing System), an integrated system for indexing the textual content of an electronically scanned document and searching it, using Adaptive Pattern Recognition technology. One of the London trials in 1994 was the digitization of the Library's *Catalogue of Seals*. Published in 1887 this describes the Library's' collection of over 100,000 seals under a classification scheme reflecting the type of holder, kings, archbishops, ministers and other leaders, but contains no index or other assistance by different criteria. To complicate matters further, the entries contain a number of not always consistent specialist abbreviations and symbols. Consequently subject searching was difficult, tedious and sometimes unsuccessful, but EFS allows whole pages of data to be digitized and indexed in a few seconds. The trial's technicalities, scanning (the preparation of digital images of the catalogue pages by electronic scanning of the printed copy) and interpretation and indexing (the recognition of words and phrases using Optical Character Recognition software, followed by the preparation of an index which allows EFS to locate them rapidly); retrieval facilities; image quality; OCR zones; and relevance ranking, are all outlined in Steve Brown's 'Playing at 'Give us a clue' with a British Library Catalogue' (*T.I.P. Applications*, 8 (8), February 1995, pp. 3–5). His conclusion was: 'EFS is a very suitable system for searching the Catalogue of Seals and similar printed volumes. The thoughtful experiments performed at the British Library have already highlighted a number of practical issues that will need to be resolved before a working system is implemented.' It was an encouraging start and it was believed that readers in its Manuscripts Students Room might soon be able to search an experimental computerized version of the *Catalogue of Seals*.

One of the most noteworthy recent acquisitions was the purchase in 1994, with grants from the National Art Collections Fund and the Friends of the National Libraries, of the manuscript known as *Dugdale's Book of Monuments*, a pictorial record of monuments, stained glass and inscriptions, made for Sir William Dugdale, Garter King of Arms, who foresaw the coming of the English Civil War and the destruction of church monuments by the victorious Puritan army. Accompanied by William Sedgewick, a heraldic draughtsman, Dugdale travelled through England in the years 1640 and 1641, recording many monuments, which were either subsequently defaced or destroyed.

Made possible by a £300,000 grant from the National Heritage Memorial Fund in 1996, the British Library secured the Lansdowne Archive from Bowood House. Comprising the private and political letters of William Petty, 1st Marquess of Lansdowne, Prime Minister under George III; those of his son, the 3rd Marquess, who twice declined the premiership; and the papers of the 5th Marquess, whose ministerial career spanned fifty years from Gladstone to Asquith, the archive was reunited with the papers of Sir William Petty (great-grandfather of the 1st Marquess) purchased in 1993 and with the Lansdowne Manuscripts acquired in 1807 and recorded in *A Catalogue of the Lansdowne Manuscripts in the British Museum* (2 vols., 1812–19).

With the assistance of a £1.45 million grant from the National Heritage Memorial Fund, the British Library was able to purchase the John Evelyn archive in 1995. Consisting of 605 numbered manuscripts and papers (half bound in volumes), 80 foolscap boxes of loose letters and papers, a trunk, 15 thick bound volumes of correspondence and a large number of other items, this very substantial archive spans several generations, casting light on almost all aspects of social and public life of sixteenth- to eighteenth-century England. Funded by a gift from John Paul Getty II, Collections and Preservation Staff embarked upon a year-long project in 1997 to conserve the archive. 'John Evelyn's Archive at the British Library', *Book Collector*, **44** (2), 1995, pp. 146–209 which examines its principal contents, is reprinted in *John Evelyn in the British Library* (British Library, 1995, 96pp.). Also included in this erudite study was Nicolas Barker's 'The Sale of the Evelyn Library 1977–78' which narrates in detail how complex legal problems threatened the break-up and dispersal of the library, the ensuing public outcry, and how the British Library was able to reunite the Evelyn manuscripts with the nucleus of his library of printed books. Michael Hunter's 'The British Library and the Library of John Evelyn' traces the formation of Evelyn's library, its decline in the eighteenth and early nineteenth centuries, and ends with an alphabetical list of books from the Evelyn library now in the British Library's holdings.

The archive's significance to scholars is neatly summed up by Anthony Kenny in his foreword:

> If the newly acquired papers consisted only of the writings of Evelyn himself, they would form one of the most significant collections in the British Library. But Evelyn inherited, from his wife's ancestors, papers of Queen Elizabeth's Earl of Leicester and other valuable material about the Elizabethan Navy, as well as the archives of diplomats and civil servants of the age of Charles I. Exploring the vast uncharted riches of this newly acquired collection will involve demanding and rewarding work by the British Library's expert staff and provide challenging and exciting opportunities for the British Library's learned readers, well into the next millennium.

The purchase of the Kenneth Tynan papers in 1994, assisted by a grant of £155,000 from the Shaw Fund, reaped an unexpected return. An initial contact between the University of Salford's Department of English in relation to the Tynan archive eventually led to a collaborative agreement which aims to bring together those who are participating in current debates regarding the nature of research on manuscript material at postgraduate and post-doctoral level in English Studies. From the Library's point of view it was a superb opportunity to put into practice one of its strategic objectives, outlined in *For Scholarship Research and Innovation* (1993), to make a positive and significant contribution to the overall effectiveness of the national library network, underlining its support of academic researchers, students and libraries of higher education. The Director of Special Collections at the British Library said at the signing

> This new agreement is further proof of the Library's commitment to co-operative projects with the academic community following the report of the Joint Funding Council's Library Review Group chaired by Professor Brian Follett which stressed the importance of co-operation between the

national library and the universities in developments concerning academic research and information technology.

Acquisition is one thing, the possible enforced transfer of irreplaceable documents to disgruntled claimants elsewhere is quite another. A potentially horrendous scenario moved a tiny bit closer after a media campaign mounted by members of Newcastle City Council culminated with the tabling of a House of Commons early day motion by a group of northern MPs, 24 February 1997, supporting the return of the seventh-century *Lindisfarne Gospels* to Durham Cathedral where they were seized by Henry VIII's commissioners. The British Library promptly rejected such a move: 'if you start with the Lindisfarne Gospels there is no telling where you will end up', Alice Prochaska, Director of Special Collections, was quoted as saying in Nick Howard's 'Henry VIII stole our Gospels: We want them back', *Mail on Sunday*, 29 June 1997, p. 17. The proposal undoubtedly represented a not so very thin edge of a very substantial wedge.

In fact, the *Gospels* had returned to the north-east the previous summer when they were the centrepiece of an exhibition of Anglo-Saxon art in the Laing Gallery in Newcastle. As the *Daily Telegraph* reported: 'the *Gospels*, painstakingly copied in Latin and Anglo-Saxon were sent to the British Library in the eighteenth century and have been exhibited outside London only four times since. The book is being displayed under tight security', ('Lindisfarne Gospels home after a thousand years', *Daily Telegraph*, 43840, 1 June 1996, p. 9). It had taken the gallery two years to persuade the British Library to loan the *Gospels* for the three months exhibition.

A Leader in *The Times* suggested that the British Library adopt a generous attitude by allowing the Gospels to go to Durham on loan.

> Seen in their places of origin, such historic documents increase their numinous aura and attract new admirers who may never go to Bloomsbury . . . Fortunately, modern computer technology also makes it possible for viewers to turn the pages in virtual manuscript-reading. And modern digital arts can now make the holy images widely available everywhere ('Unholy Row', *The Times*, no. 65932, 3 July 1997, p. 25).

Having already digitized the Gospels in a series of CD-ROM discs, the British Library was in no position to dispute this last point.

A number of recently published studies have broadened our knowledge of the British Library's early manuscript collections and have added detail to Edward Miller's splendid and authoritative *That Noble Cabinet: A History of the British Museum* (André Deutsch, 1973). M.A.E. Nickson's 'Books and Manuscripts', included in *Sir Hans Sloane, Collector, Scientist, Antiquary, Founding Father of the British Museum*, edited by Arthur Macgregor (British Museum Press, 1994), is mainly concerned with Sloane's printed books although Nickson also examines the manuscript collection which was especially strong in medieval medical material and in sixteenth- and seventeenth-century travel accounts. These latter included contemporary records from the northern and southern hemispheres and cartographical items of great historical interest. Although the riches of the Sloane manuscript collection have long been known to scholars, Nickson regrets that no adequate catalogue of them has ever been published.

Equally erudite in concept and execution is Colin C.G. Tite's *The Manuscript Library of Sir Robert Cotton* (The British Library, 1994), the illustrated text of his 1993 Panizzi Lectures. In the first of the series Tite presents an account of the highlights in the formation and development of Cotton's library, principally in his own lifetime, but continuing when it passed to his son and grandson, until it finally entered the British Museum in 1753. Perhaps the most fascinating passages of his second lecture, which examines the record of the Cotton librarians, among them Richard James, James Ussher, John Selden and William Dugdale, are those in which he assesses the professional input of Cotton himself, meticulously collecting, editing, cataloguing, indexing, abstracting and supervising the binding of his manuscript collection, and consciously assembling an unparalleled research resource for future historians to exploit. A reconstructed library floor plan, its dimensions, the arrangement and sequence of the book presses, and Cotton's contemporary reputation as an antiquary and collector, are the two main themes of the third lecture.

Sir Robert Cotton as Collector. Essays on an Early Stuart Courtier and his Legacy, edited by C.J. Wright (The British Library, 1997) contains 17 extensively annotated individual studies which collectively illustrate the many different facets of Cotton's life, draw attention to the variety of his collections and attempt to shed new light on their dispersal and subsequent fate. Learned and scholarly in nature, it is probably not suitable for casual reading, pitched as it is at a high professional and expert level, but it is nevertheless immensely rewarding for the light it casts on one of the British Museum's foundation collections.

James P. Carley's 'The Royal Library as a Source for Sir Robert Cotton's Collections: A Preliminary List of Acquisitions' explores the provenance of ten manuscripts which appeared on a 1542 inventory of 910 books housed in the Upper Library of Westminster Palace and examines the direct or circumstantial evidence of their subsequent acquisition by Sir Robert Cotton. On the same tack, Janet Backhouse's 'Sir Robert Cotton's Record Of A Royal Bookshelf' notes the existence of a small cache of books placed in one of the private apartments in Whitehall in the time of Elizabeth I. 'During the early years of James I's reign Cotton enjoyed the royal favour and was a frequent visitor in the palace of Whitehall. It was probably at this time that he saw and listed the cache of manuscripts in the privy closet. His interest was doubtless not untinged with covetousness.'

E.C. Teviotdale's 'Some Classified Catalogues of the Cottonian Library' considers a group of catalogues copied when the Library belonged to Sir John Cotton, the collector's eldest grandson. Colin G.C. Tite's 'A Catalogue of Sir Robert Cotton's Printed Books?' deals with their history, character and present whereabouts and examines a list of printed books bearing on its preliminary folio the title 'Catalogus librorum Robert Cotton' found in BL Add. MS 35213. Conversely, Tite's 'Lost or Stolen or Strayed: A Survey of Manuscripts Formerly in the Cotton Library' traces volumes which departed from Cotton's collection in significant numbers, either by gift or exchange, by loans not returned, the dispersal of duplicates, or by the sale of unwanted items.

Andrew Prescott's 'Their Present Miserable State of Cremation: The Restoration of the Cotton Library' records the long history of the conservation and restoration of the Cotton manuscripts lost or damaged in the fire at Ashburnham House, 23 October 1731. Today, 260 years on, 'the story of the restoration is not yet ended, Indeed it may be beginning afresh . . . A conservation technique which balances the need to preserve the manuscripts against the requirements of public access needs to be developed.' Simon Keynes's 'The Reconstruction of a Burnt Cottonian Manuscript: The Case of Cotton Ms. Otho A.1.' (*British Library Journal*, **22** (2), Autumn 1996, pp. 113–60), which includes 176 references and notes, is a masterpiece of bibliographical investigation and deduction.

An indication of the full range of Western Manuscripts' musical and literary archives is revealed in Anne Summer's 'Sources on Twentieth-Century British Cultural History in the Department of Manuscripts of the British Library' (*Contemporary Record. Journal of Contemporary British History*, **9** (1), Summer 1995, pp. 220–7). She deals in turn with manuscript collections focusing on correspondence and papers illustrating the processes of production in the arts and the interchange between artists and the mainstream social and political life of the nation. In particular she examines the records of the Society of Authors, the archives of the Royal Literary Fund, the Macmillan archive, the correspondence and memoirs of C.P. Scott, the Northcliffe Papers, the Marie Stope archive, the Lord Chamberlain's Plays and Correspondence files, and the records of the Royal Philharmonic Society. Lastly, she turns her attention to some finding aids to the collections.

Continuing the first location project, covering British literary authors of the twentieth century, published in two volumes, in 1988, the *Location Register of English Literary Manuscripts and Letters Eighteenth and Nineteenth Centuries* (2 vols., 1995) includes 35,000 entries indicating the whereabouts of manuscript material of over 1500 British poets, essayists, novelists, dramatists and men and women of letters, who flourished 1700–1900. The register covers all publicly accessible collections in the British Isles, over 1000 in all and includes not only holograph items, but also typescripts, amanuenses' copies, photographs and microfilms.

ORIENTAL AND INDIA OFFICE COLLECTIONS

Two projects of international importance have dominated OIOC's activities over the past decade: the International Dunhuang Project and the early birch bark Buddhist scrolls.

OIOC's Stein Collection of over 20,000 pre-eleventh century woodchips and woodchip fragments, with Chinese writing and Tibetan and Tangut manuscripts, Pakrit wooden tablets in the Brahmi and Kharosthi scripts and Khotanese, Uighur, Sogdian and Eastern Turkic documents, were recovered from various sites along the Silk Road in Chinese Central Asia in the early years of this century. Over half were discovered by Sir Aurel Stein in a walled-up library in the Caves of the Thousand Buddhas, near Dunhuang, an important administrative and cultural centre in Gansu Province. The full story of their discovery is related in Peter Hopkirk's *Foreign Devils on the Silk Road. The Search for the Lost Cities of Chinese Central Asia* (John Murray, 1980) and in Annabel Walker's *Aurel Stein. Pioneer of the Silk Road* (John Murray, 1995).

INTERNATIONAL DUNHUANG PROJECT

The International Dunhuang Project (IDP) had its beginnings in 1987, when visiting scholars from the Institute of History, in the Chinese Academy of Social History, proposed that a facsimile edition of the secular Dunhuang manuscripts should be produced from existing microfilms of the British Library's Dunhuang collections. It was soon apparent the microfilm quality was not up to scratch and a large proportion of the manuscripts had to be photographed, using high contrast film, to ensure legibility. Considerable effort by the British Library's Preservation Service, and by Chinese academics and craftsmen, was expended in preserving the remaining 'fragments' (some are 20 feet long!), in arriving at a clear text and, in choosing a long-life, acid free, non-reflective and insect-proof paper. Great care was especially taken on preservation since previous attempts earlier in the century had not proved entirely successful.

The techniques used, involving the discovery of the chemical components of the yellow dye used on many of the finest Buddhist manuscripts in the collection, the development of liquid secondary ion mass, and fast atom bombardment mass spectrometry, ink analysis, the search for a true 'acid-free' paper etc., are described in Susan Whitfield and Mark Barnard's 'The International Dunhuang Project: Re-uniting the World's Earliest Paper Archive' (*Paper Conservation News*, no. 75, September 1995, pp. 8–10). The facsimile publication, *Ying zang Dunhuang wenxian* (Dunhuang Manuscripts in British collections: Chinese Texts Other Than Buddhist Scriptures) is published by the Sichuan Peoples Publishing House in 14 volumes (1990–95). A final volume, containing supplementary material, essays and an index, is in preparation.

A leap forward came in October 1993 at a conference, 'Preservation of Material from Cave 17', organized by Peter Lawson, Conservator at the British Library, held at Sussex University and attended by Dunhuang scholars, curators and conservators from six countries, to discuss the preservation of the pre-eleventh century paper documents in their care. The conference papers were printed in *Dunhuang and Turfan. Contents Conservation of Ancient Documents from Central Asia*, published by the British Library in 1996, the first of a series entitled British Library Studies in Conservation Science, intended to present the latest developments in the field and to provide an insight into conservation practice, methods and theory. Here the most relevant papers are Frances Wood's 'Two thousand years at Dunhuang'; Mark Barnard's 'The British

Library's Stein Collection: its conservation history and future preservation'; and Susan Whitfield's 'Epilogue: the International Dunhuang Project'.

On their return from the Conference, three senior British Library staff determined to establish a steering group to ensure that the momentum was maintained. Its first meeting took place in April 1994, when the International Dunhuang Project was formally established, with a mandate

> to promote the study and preservation of the Dunhuang legacy through international cooperation. IDP has six key objectives: (1) to establish the full extent of the documentary legacy from Dunhuang and other Central Asian Sites and to share that information through the development of an international database; (2) to develop new techniques for the preservation of the original documents through close collaboration with research chemists and paper technologists; (3) to promote common standards of preservation methods and documentation; (4) to catalogue the material according to common or compatible standards; (5) to store the documents in the best possible environment and reduce handling to a minimum; and (6) to stimulate research on the material and increase accession through the production of surrogate forms, facsimile publications, microfiche and computer stored images.

In effect, what IDP is embarking upon is the international reassembling of the entire corpus of Dunhuang manuscripts, by exploiting the increasing sophistication and storage capacity of modern computer systems and the Information Superhighway, to create an online database of the manuscripts. Later the database is set to expand to include material from other Central Asian sites, relevant bibliographical material, site descriptions, and high-resolution images of the manuscripts themselves. This will facilitate research on the manuscripts by allowing scholars access to the reassembled collections in their entirety and also aid their preservation, two objectives that could so easily prove mutually inimical.

IDP's first-year activities, including the production of a brochure with an English and Chinese text, and plans to establish an International Centre for Dunhuang Studies at the British Library, are reviewed in Susan Whitfield's 'The International Dunhuang Project. A Successful First Year' (*OIOC Newsletter*, no. 52, Spring/Summer 1995, pp. 12–13). Details of the work still to be completed on the cataloguing and conservation of the documents, of the anticipated more powerful and comprehensive techniques to maximize their availability when computerized, of the international cooperation now firmly in place, and of the British Library's building up a library of reference and secondary material on the Dunhuang collection and its efforts to publicize its existence, may be found in her 'The International Dunhuang Project. An Initiative in Cooperation' (*IIAS Newsletter 4 – Supplement*, 1995, pp. 26–9). This also presents a detailed account of the circumstances surrounding the documents' discovery and clarifies their historical importance.

Frances Wood's 'The Dunhuang Manuscripts Project' (*OIOC Newsletter*, no. 45, Autumn/Winter 1990, pp. 11–12) and her 'From Central Asia To London: The Stein Collection of Manuscripts' *Committee on East Asian Libraries Bulletin*, no. 101, December 1993, pp. 93–95) add further detail on OIOC's efforts to make publication possible in collaboration with Chinese scholars. Fruition of this dream came measurably closer when, in June 1997, the Heritage Lottery Fund granted the IDP £148,000 for the cataloguing and digitization of the Dunhuang manuscripts, thus continuing the initial work sponsored by the Chiang Ching-Kuo Foundation for International Scholarly Exchange. Following its earlier support, the Foundation has provided a further award of US$80,000. Together these funds will enable the IDP to fulfil its aim of making information about all the documents in the Stein Collection available for study worldwide on the Internet by the middle of the year 2000.

IDP News. Newsletter of The International Dunhuang Project was first published as a single newssheet in May 1994, but by its second issue, dated January 1995, it had been transformed into a more permanent format, on more durable paper, and had doubled in size. It immediately embarked upon a series of articles devoted to the Dunhuang material held in various institutions overseas. The Summer 1996 issue carried a report on the Second International Meeting, held in Paris, 5–7 February 1996. Other regular features include news of specific Dunhuang topics, for example, the Queens University, Belfast, research on the Dunhuang Star Chart, circa AD940; the launching of an IDP page on the Internet in October 1995; symposium and conference reports and news of relevant publications.

An unfortunate, but not entirely unexpected, result of tests carried out by Kenneth Seddon, Professor of Chemistry at Queen's University, Belfast, on the chemical constituents of the *huangbo* dye, believed to be the source of colour in most yellow pre-tenth century Chinese paper, was the discovery that up to 600 of the British Library's 'ancient' Chinese manuscripts were twentieth-century forgeries. Dalya Alberge's 'Hundreds of fakes found in library's Chinese collection' (*The Times*, no. 65923, 23 June 1997, p. 7) quotes Susan Whitfield

> that some may have been manufactured in a massive forging operation run by a Chinese collector whose eminent reputation gave him a respectability that buyers did not question. Shengduo Li's activities lasted from 1911 until the 1950s and began when he persuaded a Chinese official to divert to his house an ox cart transporting a large collection of real manuscripts from the Silk Road site of Dunhuang to the National Library of China.

See also Jojo Moyes' 'The ancient Chinese texts that failed test of time', *The Independent*, no. 3331, 24 June 1997, p. 8.

Buddhist Birch Bark Scrolls

In 1994 OIOC acquired a set of birch bark scrolls whose significance at first escaped attention. Only after painstaking work in close cooperation with American scholars and experts were they recognized as being as important for Buddhism as the Dead Sea Scrolls are for the Judaeo-Christian tradition. Consisting of some 60 fragments of about 25 texts, from various parts of the Buddhist canon, written in the ancient Kharosthi script in Gandhari, the ancient language of the Gandhara region, an important Buddhist centre in present-day northern Pakistan and Afghanistan, the scrolls were reputedly discovered inside an inscribed clay pot which dated them to the first or second century of the common era. They are probably the earliest Buddhist manuscripts ever to be discovered.

Birch bark, although providing a natural writing material, copiously available from the forest slopes of the Himalayas, is nevertheless one of the most fragile writing surfaces ever used by early scribes. On arrival at OIOC the scrolls had all the appearance of badly rolled cigars. They were dangerously brittle and almost visibly crumbling. The task of unrolling them was infinitely delicate and complex but skilled attention by the Oriental Conservation Studio's expert staff succeeded in unravelling the scrolls (mostly written on both sides) after they were ultrasonically humidified with water and silica gel. They were flattened between sheets of glass to wait for research into preservation methods suitable for such a brittle medium.

Interpreting the text, which includes fragments of Buddha's sermons, poems and treatises on the psychology of perception, believed to be part of the long-lost canon of the Sarvastivadin sect, is the task of the Early Buddhist Manuscript Project, jointly established by the British Library and the University of Washington in Seattle. According to Professor Richard Salomon, director of the project, the text may lead to a better understanding of Buddhism's transition from an oral to a written tradition. Two postgraduate research assistantships have been created in the University but it may take years for the scrolls to be completely deciphered and interpreted.

To avoid further unnecessary handling of the scrolls the Information for Access Electronic Asia digitization programme was established.

> Digitally scanned images can be enhanced and manipulated in various ways without damaging the birch bark scrolls themselves, so digitisation is a crucial part of the project. Professor Salomon and his colleagues are essentially aiming to arrange and catalogue the manuscripts . . . In this particular instance there is the added problem of deciphering texts written in a very obscure script . . . Clearly it is imperative to understand how the pieces fit together (quite literally), identify the text they contain (as far as they can be matched against existing versions in other languages) and then order them in the most meaningful way and finally catalogue them so that they can be easily accessed. 'Buddhist Dead Sea Scrolls' (*Initiatives for Access News*, no. 4, Autumn 1996, pp. 1–2).

Simon Shaw outlines the methodology used in his 'Electronic Asia', *Information Services and Use*, **16** (3/4), 1996, pp. 175–7, detailing how the Library's Document and Image Processing team enhanced and manipulated the scanned images.

Michael O'Keefe's 'A British Library Early Buddhist Manuscripts Project', (*SALG Newsletter*, no. 43, January 1996, pp. 9–16) sets the Library's acquisition of the scrolls in the context of the development of early Indian Buddhism at the time they were written, noting especially the extreme paucity of written records of this remote period; examines how much material for reconstructing Buddhist history survives; and describes how they were deciphered. In summary,

> the Project will involve several scholars in years of study. Decipherment, analysis, comparison with existing texts and palaeographic research will

be required before publication is complete. The editorial process will be assisted by image digitisation of the manuscripts, an invaluable technique never before applied to Central Asian manuscripts. Just completed, in cooperation with the British Library's Computing and Telecommunications Directorate, this undertaking represents a meeting of the oldest South Asian manuscripts with the newest in image capture and manipulation technology.

Graham Shaw's illustrated article, 'Buddhism Unrolled', *OIOC Newsletter*, nos. 53–4, Summer 1997, pp. 2–5 sketches the scrolls' known history and provenance, their conservation, their content, current research and identification of the texts, the effect of digitizing the scrolls, future publication plans and the worldwide media interest. Following this article, 'A Note on Kharosthi' (p. 5) explains what it is (a script, not a language), its origins and its construction of vowels and consonants.

Other important acquisitions

Thanks to £25,000 from the National Art Collections Fund, in 1995 the Library acquired 23 albums of Indian, British and Chinese paintings, collected by the 1st Marquess of Hastings when Governor General of Bengal 1813–23, including eight containing an almost continuous series of illustrations taken during Lord and Lady Hastings' journey from Calcutta to Delhi and back in 1814–15. These albums had only recently come to light with the rediscovery of Lord Hastings private papers. Other opportunities to augment OIOC's collection of drawings and paintings by 'Company artists', the native Indian artist who, in the eighteenth and nineteenth centuries, 'modified their traditional style in order to accommodate techniques and compositional methods introduced from England' are expertly related in J.P. Losty's 'New Acquisitions Of Indian Art' (*OIOC Newsletter*, no. 52, Spring/Summer 1995, pp. 1–4). Included in these acquisitions are natural history drawings, portraits of Mughal emperors, court scenes, and detailed decorative views done in various styles.

David Blake's 'OIOC Acquires Clive and Curzon Collections', *OIOC Newsletter*, nos. 53–4, Summer 1997, pp. 29–30 records OIOC's purchase of the private papers of two towering figures of British India. Clive's papers include his correspondence with colleagues in the East India Company and their impact on Indian political, military and commercial history; his home correspondence with leading English politicians; a group of papers concerned with Clive's campaigns; and papers relating to his defence of his conduct in India at the parliamentary enquiry of 1772–73. The Curzon collection of about 1500 volumes is particularly valuable for its documentation of his Viceregal administration and correspondence with Edward VII, the Prime Minister and the Secretary of State for India. This, too, is frequently mined by researchers.

Historical photographs

In the summer of 1993 the Getty Grant Program of Santa Monica, California, awarded OIOC £160,000 to produce a detailed computer catalogue of 'what is certainly the most comprehensive single collection of historical photographs from the Indian sub-continent'. Some 450 hand-coloured views of Calcutta, Madras and Ceylon, made in the early 1850s by Frederick Fiebig and purchased by the East India company in 1856; an important collection of original large-format calotype negatives of Agra and Delhi just before and just after the Mutiny; 34,000 photographs accumulated by the Archaeological Survey of India; and the personal albums of Lords Elgin, Curzon, Reading and Hardinge, are among the highlights of the collection which presents an evocative record of the social life of India at every level. Previously this important historical resource had been accessible only through a card index. The cataloguing project now made possible

> will provide a detailed computer listing of over 200,000 photographs and will supply additional indexes arranged by subject, named portrait, event, geographical location and photographer's name. It will also record the physical condition of albums and collections as they are cataloged and this conservation assessment will mark up future priorities for the treatment of material in fragile or deteriorating condition' (John Falconer, 'Photographs of India in The British Library', *Friends of The British Library Newsletter*, no. 15, April 1994, pp. 6–7).

The series of photographs of monuments, architecture and sculpture, taken under the auspices of the Archaeological Survey of India, set up by the British Government in India to document and preserve the Buddhist, Hindu and Muslim heritage, represents a fully documented record from the 1850s to the 1920s. J.P. Losty's 'Much in a Small Compass' (OIOC *Newsletter*, no. 52, Spring/Summer 1995, p. 10) provides historical notes and reports the publication of *Archaeological Survey of India Photographs in the India Office Collections, Microfiche edition* (Haslemere, Surrey, Emmett Publishing, 1993) which contains 34,000 photographs on 230 black and white microfiches plus a printed guide and index.

OIOC's catalogues

The full complexities of OIOC's western-language printed book catalogues, including the historical background, and the introduction of OPACs, are revealed in 'The Printed Book Catalogues – the future, the interim and some mysteries explained' (*OIOC Newsletter*, nos. 48–9, Autumn 1993, pp. 4–6) and in 'Entangled In Their Mazes: more notes on OIOC's western-language catalogues', IBID., no. 52, Spring/Summer 1995, pp. 22–3. An admirably pragmatic approach to the types of catalogue needed for OIOC's multifarious collections is evident in J.M. Sims' 'Developments in the Bibliographical Control of South Asian Collections in the British Library' in *Planning Modernization and Preservation Programmes for South Asian Libraries*, edited by Kalpana Dasgupta (Calcutta, National Library, 1992, pp. 168–72):

> For IOLR, with its wide range of different types of material, each of which presents its own particular problems, there can be no uniform approach and the keyword has to be flexibility. In some cases online catalogue access is essential, in others it is unnecessary or simply impractical. In the new British Library building much of the IOLR stock will not be accessed through the OPAC and reliance will still be placed on printed, hard copy or fiche catalogues. There is, however, considerable scope for automation of shelf lists so that items identified in non-OPAC catalogues would be requested by pressmark through the Automated Book Request System. This would be of benefit to readers in terms of speed and ease of requesting and to the Library in gaining maximum benefit from the automated systems for document supply and collection management.

Historical Studies

G.E. Marrison's 'The British Museum, The British Library And South Asian Studies' (*SALG Newsletter*, **41**, January 1994, pp. 3–9) investigates the origins of South Asian studies in seventeenth century England and examines those institutions specifically established for the purpose in the nineteenth century, describing the growing Oriental collections in the British Museum Library and the formation of the Department of Oriental Manuscripts in 1867. Finally, he recalls his own times in the Department of Oriental Printed Books and Manuscripts, witnessing the emergence of the British Library, and the advent of computerization which posed special problems, namely the use of oriental scripts, the standardization of Roman transliterations, and the expense of adopting the new technology foremost among them.

Yu-Ying Brown's 'Japanese Books and Manuscripts', *Sir Hans Sloane*, edited by Arthur Macgregor (London, British Museum Press, 1994, pp. 279–88) focuses on the Japanese Library of Engelbert Kämpfer, the German physician and traveller, who spent two years in Nagasaki (1690–92) as medical officer to the Dutch East India Company. Kämpfer's papers and library, consisting of 32 individual works in 54 volumes, ten maps and seven important archival documents, were acquired by Sir Hans Sloane, included in the British Museum's foundation collections, and now reside in OIOC. Yu-Ying Brown had earlier written a six-page folded leaflet, *Engelbert Kämpfer First Interpreter of Japan*, produced to accompany the exhibition held at the British Library, 11 October 1991 to 17 May 1992, which included a list of 55 items from the Kämpfer and related collections and also 'Kämpfer's album of famous sights of seventeenth century Japan' (*British Library Journal*, **15** (1), 1989). Detlef Haberland's full-length study, *Engelbert Kämpfer 1651–1716. A Biography* was published by the British Library in 1996.

Perceiving three crucial factors differentiating the British Library's Tibetan collections from similar collections elsewhere, notably their composite nature, deriving from their dual descent from the India Office Library and the British Museum's Department of Oriental Printed Books and Manuscripts; the concentration of Imperial political interest and military activity in Tibet's southern and central regions; the intermittent acquisition of Tibetan material depending on political events; and the lack of continuity of specialist and dedicated staff, Ulrich Pagels' 'The British Library Tibetica: A Historical Survey' (*SALG Newsletter*, no. 43, January 1996, pp. 1–8) outlines the development of the Library's collection over the past 150 years, while simultaneously describing some of the principal items and types of material procured.

Among the main topics of this magisterial paper are private and institutional donations, the revolution in Tibetan studies brought about by 'the unprecedented flood of Tibetan manuscripts and xylographs' deposited in the India Office Library in the years leading up to and following the 1904 Younghusband 'mission' to Lhasa, the Stein Collection of Central Asian manuscript fragments and wood chips, their subsequent fifty years neglect, a comparative analysis of the IOL and Department of Oriental Printed Books and Manuscripts' holdings and their respective acquisition policies, the far-reaching consequences from their administrative merger in 1991, creating one of the largest single collections of Tibetan material in the Western world, and the consequent new found urgency for a coordinated conservation programme.

> During the past 100 years, [the collection] has witnessed long periods without specialised curatorial care, the collapse of three cataloguing projects and severe difficulties in terms of conservation and access. But even if history should repeat itself and the many thousand manuscripts and blockprints are, once again, left unattended, no one will be able to place the blame on a collection ranking among the finest holdings of Tibetan books worldwide.

An unexpected area of OIOC's vast collections is the material devoted to southern Africa vividly and comprehensively brought to life in Jill Geber's 'Southern African Sources in the Oriental and India Office Collections of The British Library' (*African Research and Documentation*, no. 70, 1996, pp. 1–35). In effect this constitutes an integrated chronological and thematic descriptive calendar broken down by format and topic. If this material was little used in the past, it will surely now be quarried much more often.

MAP LIBRARY

In the recent period the story of the Map Library has virtually been that of its catalogues. A printed cumulation, the *Catalogue of Cartographic Materials In The British Library 1975–1988* (K.G. Saur, 3 vols., 1989), described at the time as 'the most complete up-to-date bibliographic resource in the cartographic field'. This catalogue reflected

> the wide acquisition policy of the Map Library, covering antiquarian and modern materials in all forms: terrestrial and celestial atlases, globes, maritime charts, sheet maps and map series covering the entire world, as well as an extensive collection of monographs about cartogra-

phy and related subjects acquired not only on legal deposit from UK publishers but by donation and extensive international purchase. Also included . . . are records for some 260 digital cartographic and remote sensing databases in the UK, located as a result of a project carried out by Birkbeck College and sponsored by the British Library's Research and Development Department.

More significantly, the new *Catalogue* included, for the first time, entries for the map and atlas holdings of other parts of the British Library, notably the Department of Manuscripts and Oriental and India Office Collections.

In retrospect, converting the Map Library's catalogues from hard copy print to electronic form has all the appearance of an idea whose time had come. No doubt the desire to create and maintain a single file from the series of date closed catalogues, with historical files kept separate from current files, and with arbitrary cut-off dates, played a part but, overriding all other considerations, was the need to come to terms with the automated systems of the new St Pancras library. Serious discussions about conversion first took place in 1989 although it was not until April 1992 that the British Library signed a contract with Research Publications International (RPI) to publish a map catalogue on CD-ROM, by which RPI received exclusive rights to the British Library Cartographic File for 15 years, with the Library enjoying cheaper keyboarding charges and a share of the profits.

For a full understanding of the issues at stake and of the procedures followed, it is necessary to consult two papers by Tony Campbell. Topics discussed in 'Retroconversion of the British Library's Map Catalogues: the Art of the Possible' (*ERLC*, **3** (1), 1993, pp. 1–6) include the project's 93-page detailed specification drawn up to guide the keyboarding bureau; the tendering process and the awarding of a contract; and a justification of why the Library followed the retroconversion route, involving the merger of a comparatively small number of recent records created with machine readability very much in mind and a much larger number of older descriptions designed for traditional access, rather than a complete retrospective cataloguing programme. 'Even with extra staff (a dream!), it could still take 50 or more years to recatalogue those items that were described before the 'bible' became available – in our case the Anglo-American Cataloguing Rules.'

Making no apologies for committing itself to a less than perfect but practical end-product and acknowledging the deficiencies of the existing printed catalogues, mainly resulting from the vagaries of generations of cataloguers over a long time-span, namely omitted information on many pre-1940 catalogued items, including details of publisher and of the scale of the map; inaccurate information; data expressed the wrong way involving differing styles of title transcription; and structural problems such as information presented in the wrong sequence, the British Library preferred to go ahead, using the old descriptions and without re-examining the original items. Exactly how the printed text was transformed into machine-readable data, controlled by the Data Conversion Specification, is the principal theme of 'Conversion of the British Library's Map Catalogues: The Keys to Success' (*Inspel*, **28** (1), 1994, pp. 67–72).

At the end of the day, the Library claimed, the CD-ROM catalogue would provide significant improvements to the content of earlier entries. Besides the benefits of interactive access, added thematic elements where these were previously lacking and a concordance for country codes, normalized places of publication, the metric sizes of manuscript maps, and syndetic internal links, would also be gained. At the very least the converted catalogue would be no worse than its printed predecessors. To strengthen this distinctly faint praise, Campbell asserted that 'it is more important to have some kind of record for every map than a perfect record for some of them'. Moreover the Library reminded its users of the differences between a bibliography and a library catalogue. Whereas a cartobibliography distinguishes similar maps and provides a clear statement of the bibliographical relation between one map and another, a library catalogue's prime task is to provide access to the content of its holdings. 'The British Library Map Library now makes a clear distinction between bibliographical and topographical value. Minor sacrifices of bibliographical detail can speed up the cataloguing process, thus making more maps available. We see it as our task to lead the user, quickly and helpfully, to anything that might be of relevance. Thereafter, it is up to them to examine the items for themselves.'

The British Library Map Catalogue on CD-ROM (Reading, Primary Source Media, 1998), the fruit of the Map Library's endeavours and the first catalogue on CD-ROM of any of the world's major map libraries, brings together all 19 published volumes of the Library's catalogues of printed and manuscript maps and the automated files of post-1974 accessions. Entries can be retrieved by searching on a combination of different fields, including geographical area, period, theme, cartographer/

publisher, title, country or place of publication, physical form, or range of scales, many of which could not previously have been extracted from the printed catalogues. Again, in Tony Campbell's words, 'automating our printed map catalogues is akin to alchemy – transforming a simple, fixed sequence into do-it-yourself multi-access. Needles will not remain hidden in this haystack, arguably the finest historical map collection in the world.'

The new map file had already been added to BLAISE. John West-mancoat's 'The new British Library Maps file – how to get the best from a Blaise search', *Select*, no.21, Winter 1997, pp. 4–5 instructs potential users on search techniques, the geographic headings for specific or sophisticated searches, and how to search by date, all with sample searches.

However, this is not the end of the story, simply the completion of a single stage in a 15-year programme involving the enhancement of records already held in the file and the addition of a large number of historical records. Creating a comprehensive file is the long-term aim, incorporating map records from the British Library's book collections dispersed in RSCD, Western Manuscripts, SRIS and OIOC, entries in general library catalogues, entries in manuscript catalogues of specialized map collections and other material never previously catalogued. As neither the British Museum Library nor the British Library ever commanded the necessary resources to catalogue its large collection of atlases analytically, it welcomed the offer of Rodney Shirley to record the contents of its pre-1800 atlases. These records will also eventually be added to the file. 'The ultimate aim is for comprehensive and unified access to the 300,000 identified cartographic entities spread throughout the various BL departments.'

Peter Barber's illustrated feature 'Maps in the British Library' (*Friends of the British Library Newsletter*, no.20, Winter 1995/96, pp. 4–7) is an authoritative account of the transformation of the Map Library from what it was thirty years ago, little more than the map section of the British Museum Library's Department of Printed Books, when it was considered natural that the Museum's map holdings should be scattered among its various departments, to a distinct entity within the Special Collections Directorate, 'recognised as being the centre for cartography within the British Library and possessing degrees of authority over all of the Library's maps though these continue to be included in the collections of most of its sections'. Situated in more adequate accommodation at St Pancras, readers now enjoy the benefit of studying maps form across the British Library's collections without administrative hindrance. The Map Library's development as the national centre for the study of the history of cartography is also underlined.

Barber also turns his attention to a number of important individual maps, atlases, and early map collections housed elsewhere in the Library, notably the Department of Western Manuscripts' Anglo-Saxon world map drawn in the first half of the eleventh century, Tudor and Stuart Maps, and maps and atlases that arrived with the Old Royal Library presented by George II in 1757. Also in the Department are the large collection of eighteenth- and early nineteenth-century maps of South America brought together by the Spanish cartographer, Felipe Bauza and the manuscript maps of the Royal United Services Institution. OIOC's outstanding collection of maps include the archival collections of the former India Office, many descending from the East India Company, and examples of native mapping from its language sections.

Not that the Map Library's own treasures are overlooked: historical items of immense significance from the King's Topographical and Maritime Collections, presented by George IV in 1823, many of which were inherited from the collections of earlier monarchs; the 'Roy Map', the first detailed survey of most of Scotland, 1747–52; its comprehensive holding of Ordnance Survey maps, invaluable research sources for UK genealogists and local historians, solicitors and surveyors; its collections of old and modern globes; its remote sensing maps; and about 50,000 sheets of non-current foreign mapping deposited annually by the Ministry of Defence; to say nothing of its collections of cartographic postcards, tourist maps, coins and medals, or the archives of leading figures in British cartography. With massive understatement Barber concludes: 'maps in the British Library thus simultaneously reflect the past, the present and the future, as they should in any research library.'

Barber also examines the provenance of some of the Library's official maps in his extensively documented 'The Ones that Got Away. Maps of government and administration in the British Library' (*IMCOS Journal*, no.54, Autumn 1993, pp. 11–17), which focuses on the two national map archives, the Public Record Office, 'a vast quarry of official mapping most of which is still waiting to be discovered and exploited' and the Library, 'generally regarded as the appropriate place of deposit for official maps that had escaped from official guardianship'. Naming and describing some outstanding individual items included in the Old Royal

Library, presented to the British Museum in 1757, Barber emphasizes that some maps deemed indispensable for government were withheld and only arrived in the Library 60 years later when the King's Topographical and Maritime Collections were deposited. Even then the military maps remained at Windsor while the maritime atlases and charts were taken over by the Admiralty. The fact that since the 1840s these maps have gradually been transferred to the Library illustrates how the library authorities can afford to take the long-term view and patiently wait for separated items to be reunited in the fullness of time.

In some instances, however, time cannot heal the wounds. It was George III's practice to retain for his library maps and drawings enclosed with colonial governors' annual reports, with the consequence that 'the despatches survive in the Public Record Office with sad notes recording that the enclosures were missing while the British Library has the maps without the text that clarifies them'. Other topics Barber pursues here include the maps received from the Cottonian Library (Sir Robert Cotton was not above 'collecting' official government maps); maps from the papers of other civil and military office-holders; and maps deposited by the government or by the great departments of state, notably the Ordnance Survey's archive of preparatory manuscript maps and sketches.

With justifiable pride the British Library announced, at the end of May 1997, the purchase of the Mercator *Atlas of Europe*, made possible by a generous grant of £500,000 from the Heritage Lottery Fund. Incorporating one of only four surviving examples of Gerard Mercator's original wall map of the British Isles, dating from 1564, the atlas provides the earliest detailed and reasonably accurate geographical representation. 'It shows an enormous increase in the number of place names compared with earlier maps, with 2,500 names in all and 1,250 for England and Wales alone, including Stratford-upon-Avon in the year of Shakespeare's birth' (Peter Forster, 'The £700,000 book that put Britain on the map', *The Times*, no. 65902, 29 May 1997, p. 12).

The *Atlas* was compiled by skilfully cutting and pasting together multiple copies of maps of Europe and the British Isles to produce overlapping segments. Found in a Brussels bookshop in 1967, it was auctioned at Sotheby's in 1979 when the British Library was the underbidder; its acquisition almost two decades later was especially gratifying to the Map Library's curatorial staff. It was placed on public display immediately with plans to provide electronic access. 'It puts the world's crown on the library's collection of early maps, which is the finest in the world. Even to non-scholars it is a document of beauty and romance, charting a step up the ladder of the intellectual advance of man' ('Mercator's Perfection', 3rd Leader, *The Times*, no. 65902, 29 May 1997, p. 21).

The Map Library currently stocks two documented information sheet series: The British Library Map Guides include *How to Find Estate Maps in the British Library* (1996, 4pp.); *Cartographic Sources for Dating Houses in England and Wales* (1996, 5pp.); *A Brief Guide to Large Scale Ordnance Survey Maps of Great Britain in the Map Library* (1995, 9pp.); and *A Brief Guide To Large Scale Ordnance Survey Maps Of Ireland In The Map Library* (1994, 7pp.). Select Reading Lists on the History of Cartography comprise *General* (1995); *Great Britain* (1995); *Ordnance Survey* (1995); and *Ireland* 91995). *Sample Shelfmarks Found In Map Library Catalogues* giving pressmarks, description (i.e. interpretation) and location, is also issued.

Some interesting cartographical titles are currently on the British Library's publication list. Peter Whitfield's *The Image of the World: 20 Centuries of World Maps* (1994) contains reproductions of 70 maps produced in the ancient and medieval worlds, the age of discovery, the heyday of the Dutch cartographers in the late sixteenth and seventeenth centuries, and world cartography form the late 17th century to the present day.

Rebecca Stefoff's *The British Library's Companion to Maps and Map making* (1995), first published by Oxford University Press in New York, can hardly be faulted as an introduction for the general reader. Its 350 plus entries, some mini-essays, others definitions and explanations of cartographic or geographic terms, cover map-making techniques, regional surveys of exploration, brief biographical sketches of explorers, mapmakers and geographers, and geographic and cartographic organizations. But it is not a guide to the British Library's cartographic collections as some might suppose. Ian Mumford, for one, was especially critical:

> There is surely sufficient curatorial expertise in the British Library to produce a reliable guide to maps and mapmaking as revealed in its own important collection, whatever the level required, without misrepresenting a shallow American product . . . This book is certainly not a companion to the British Library's own map collection, nor is it the comprehensive international reference it claims to be; it sits as a cuckoo in the nest of the Library's own worthwhile publications on maps and mapping (*Bulletin of the Society of Cartographers*, **29** (2), 1995, pp. 32–3).

P.D.A. Harvey's *Mappa Mundi. The Hereford World Map*, published jointly with Hereford Cathedral in 1996, views the Mappa Mundi in the context of other detailed maps from the twelfth to the fourteenth century. Extensively illustrated with newly commissioned photographs, including 30 colour plates, this 64pp. booklet examines the map's origins and the sources from which it draws upon for its geographical outlines. Two appendices list the inscriptions on the map's frame and reproduction of the map itself. A select bibliography is included. Peter Whitfield's *The Charting of the Oceans. Ten Centuries of Maritime Maps* (1996) has sections on navigation before charts, sea-charts and the age of exploration, Europe's maritime age and war, empire and technology in the last 200 years. No excuses are made for its being an entirely Euro-centred study since the charting of the world's oceans was a European enterprise.

The British Library has also published Donald Hodson's *County Atlases of The British Isles Published after 1803: A Bibliography Vol.III Atlases Published 1764–1789 and their subsequent editions* (1997). This important reference tool aims to provide a detailed reconstruction of all atlases published after 1703 through original research partly based on an analysis of map and atlas advertisements in eighteenth-century newspapers. Volumes one and two, examining the periods 1704–42 and 1743–63, were published by the Tewin Press in 1984 and 1989 respectively and are now distributed by the British Library.

PHILATELIC COLLECTIONS

Totalling over eight million items, including postage and revenue stamps, specimen issues, postal stationery, artwork, essays, covers and entires and postal history materials, the British Library's Philatelic Collections cover all countries and periods. The Library also holds a major collection of philatelic literature, numbering over 30,000 volumes, of which 4500 comprise the Crawford Library bequeathed to the British Museum in 1913 by James Ludovic Lindsay, 26th Earl of Crawford and Balcarres. The importance of this library of books, journals and pamphlets is reflected in the imposing *Catalogue of the Crawford Library of the Philatelic Literature at the British Library*, first published in 1911 as volume 7 of *Biblioteca Lindesiana*, under the title of *A Bibliography of the Writings General, Special and Periodical forming the Literature of Philately*, and in a revised edition by The Printer's Stone Ltd., in association with the British Library, in 1991. It incorporates British Library shelfmarks for the easy identification of specific items and also includes Sir Edward D. Bacon's 1926 *Supplement* and *Addenda* printed as a supplement to the March 1938 issue of the *London Philatelist*. Retained in this revised edition are the Earl of Crawford's Introduction outlining the development of his collection and Bacon's preface detailing the use of his bibliography. D.R. Beech collocates and updates various historical and technical matters in a new preface.

An authoritative paper by R.F. Schoolley-West, presented to the Royal Philatelic Society London in December 1988, considers the Collections' past, present and future, and is a convenient overview for the non-philatelist reader. The first proposals for the formation of a collection of postage stamps were made to the Trustees of the British Museum by Dr John Gray, Keeper of Zoology, and William Vaux, Keeper of Coins and Medals, in the 1860s.

> This initial enthusiasm to form such collections does not appear to have been pursued by the Trustees, as no evidence of any remain today and it was not until 1891 that the collections we know today were established at the British Museum and the special relationship between the Institution and the Philatelic Society, London, later to become The Royal Philatelic Society, London, was formed and which the British Library still enjoys today.

Perhaps the chief value of Schoolly-West's paper is his survey of the British Library's policy for the acquisition of philatelic material which traditionally has been to accept country rather than thematic collections. Consequently, 'it is virtually impossible to offer a service to the thematic collectors'. No change in this policy is foreseen 'and there is no intention to collect in that manner or accept material that has been collected for that specific purpose'. Current work focuses on

> strengthening the base for the philatelic researcher of today and the future by concentrating on the assemblage of information in every possible way . . . the maintenance of the existing collections and the expansion of their coverage by the acquisition of new material of all forms . . . best exemplified by the development of the collections of postal administration pre-issue publicity leaflets and photographs of items in other collections or sold by auction or public treaty. Whilst they have some significance today, they clearly have a considerable future and should prove invaluable to our successors.

Within its restricted financial and spatial resources, the Philatelic Collections strains to acquire all new significant literature, irrespective of language, to assemble duplicate literature for exchange purposes and to provide access to the collections to the general public, either by way of permanent gallery displays (within the past five years the British Library's commitment to this had been seriously doubted), by personal visits by appointment, or by the supply of information by post or telephone.

Peering through the St Pancras murk, not an easy task in 1988, Schoolley-West was able to conclude his paper by remarking that

> Planning is already underway to bring together all of the philatelic literature and to introduce a unified pressmark to make the material more readily identifiable. The automated retrieval system to be adopted should represent a substantial saving of time for readers. [He continued,[the major task for the future is the long-term conservation work on the Collections, which will also include remounting and captioning in standard form. The conservation quality of the materials we use will have to be carefully monitored to ensure that the best possible techniques are always used for the long-term storage of the Collections. [And, finally,[publications work must be expanded to produce more information for the public and be related to the history and contents of our collections ('The British Library Philatelic Collections', London Philatelist, 98, May–June 1989, pp. 91–9).

Important individual collections are both numerous and various. Pride of place goes to what might be called the foundation collection, the Tapling Collection, formed by Thomas Keay Tapling, MP, of more than 100,000 stamps, assembled in the short span of 25 years and bequeathed in 1891. Covering the first 50 years of the adhesive postage stamp era, 1840–90, its scope is worldwide and it is virtually complete in all standard issues besides boasting a good number of recognized rarities. A detailed account of its antecedents, provenance and history may be found in James A. Mackay's The Tapling Collection of Postage and Telegraph Stamps and Postal Stationery (British Museum, 1966) or in a series of articles in Gibbons Stamp Monthly, June 1966 to February 1967:

> The Tapling Collection may be regarded as a national institution – and as such it has long been fashionable to criticize it. In mitigation I must point out that one must not be too critical by present-day standards and

remember that it represents the form of philately which was in vogue in the late nineteenth century. [He continues,] in spite of its limitations and imperfections [poor, faded and cleaned stamps] the Tapling Collection is a remarkably fine one nonetheless and is, in fact, to be ranked amongst the most outstanding acquisitions ever made by the British Museum.

The Keeper of Printed Books at the time, Richard Garnett, remarked 'extraordinary as it may appear, it is unquestionable that never since the bequest of the Grenville Library (in 1847) has the Library of the British Museum received a benefaction remotely approaching the pecuniary value of this collection' (*Gibbons Stamp Monthly*, **39** (10), June 1966, p. 166).

Paolo Vaccari's 'The Tapling Collection. Philatelic Collections. The British Library – London' (*Vaccari Magazine*, **7** (16), 1996, pp. 33–7) is important for its brief career profile of Tapling and for its short account of his mounting style and system:

> first a complete issue in mint condition, then a range of shades and varieties of perforation and watermark . . . A curious feature was the inclusion of reprints, imitations (official and non-official) and forgeries, as a demonstration of his culture for stamps. As a collecting conception, Tapling did not follow the fashion of his time in that he loved cancelled stamps too, which were virtually neglected . . . moreover, he was particularly interested in blocks and strips.

Other British Library collections are listed in Pamela Morgan's 'The British Library Philatelic Collection', *Stamp Lover*, April 1985, pp. 187–8 and in Eric Glasgow's 'Stamps that the Nation Owns', IBID., **83** (1), February 1991, pp. 20–1. These include The Supplementary Collection, comprising mainly British Colonial mint stamps and proofs 1900–22; the Crown Agents Collection, covering the period 1922 to date; and the extensive Crown Agents Philatelic and Security Printing Archive, consisting of essays, artwork, proofs, colour trials and associated records for postage and revenue stamps, postal stationery, covers, postal orders and paper money, from 1900 to recent date.

Great Britain collections include the extensive Board of Inland Revenue Stamping Department Archive, postage and revenue proof material, 1710–1950s; the H.L'Estrange Ewen Collection of railway letter stamps 1891–1912; and the H.G. Fletcher Collection of postal history and postal stationery, covering a 300-year period, over half of which is pre-adhesive stamp material illustrating the development and operations of different postal services.

James L. Grimwood-Taylor, 'totally unprepared for the scope and quality of the material', examined a couple of dozen of the collection's 162 volumes in his 'Fletcher Collection Now Accessible at the British Library', *Stamp Lover*, April 1990, pp. 46–7. An important collection of British pre-stamp correspondence, known as the Treasury Excise Correspondence Collection, comprising about 750 letters between the Treasury and Excise dated mainly between 1826 and the 1840s, presented to the British Library by the Board of Customs and Excise in 1992, complements the Fletcher Collection.

In 1890 the Colonial Office determined that an official collection should be formed of an example of every postage and revenue stamp issued in the overseas Empire together with examples of postal stationery. In 1992 this collection, now known as The Foreign and Commonwealth Office Collection, was transferred to the British Library. Correspondence relating to both these events is reprinted in D.R. Beech's 'The Foreign And Commonwealth Office Collection', *London Philatelist*, July/August 1993, pp. 210–14.

A further portion of the HMSO Collection of archival National Insurance, Revenue, Income Tax, Medicine and National Savings stamps was also transferred to the British Library in 1992. The Collection is mainly of proof and registration sheets showing the development of these issues of stamps from the 1930s to the 1950s. It complements the Board of Inland Revenue Stamping Department Archive and the Davies and Kay Collections of Revenue material already held by the British Library. The last issue of National Insurance Stamps and related material was transferred by the Contributions Agency a year later. Other items presented include the 1992/93 National Insurance Cards to which the stamps were affixed and a Grovering Machine used to cancel the completed cards.

But, for all their standing and importance as the national collection, within the British Library the Philatelic Collections are relatively obscure although, from time to time, they have attracted controversy and critical comment. In 1984 Kenneth Lake investigated how active the British Library was in exploiting its collections. Were they accessible? Were they on display? What plans were there for the future? When attempting to find answers to these questions, in a one-to-one discussion with the Superintendent of the Philatelic Collections, Lake ran up against a familiar brick wall, government cuts in public expenditure. Although the Philatelic Collections were recognized as a separate department of the British Museum in 1961, the staff still numbered no more than the Superintendent, two full-time staff, one of whom was occupied almost entirely mounting and recording Universal Postal Union material and a clerical officer. In these circumstances full public access and long-term plans were aspirations rather than expectations. However, a number of projects had been initiated: the systematic collection of announcements and brochures from all stamp-issuing countries in the hope that some day they might be bound; and the permanent recording of every item in photographic form. Many of the collections could then be transferred to colour microfiche both for sale and for research use in the Reading Room.

As for knowledge of what the Collections include:

> Well, you can go and see for yourself! Of course, you can't wander into the strongrooms, or browse among vast quantities of material – today's security-conscious society precludes such fantasies. The system is quite simple: you write or telephone and explain what you would like to see . .
>
> and you call at a suitable time to view it. [A member of staff] sits with you while you work – he'll even help or advise you if you wish and will happily put you in touch with others doing similar or parallel research, provided they agree, so that you can cut corners and save time.

Storage and conservation problems to date had been tackled on a short-term basis. The Library had invested in temperature and humidity controls and had created its own 'mounting package' catering for virtually all types and sizes of stamps, covers and miniature sheets, but the photography project was estimated to need half a million photographs and would take three years to complete. The gum time-bomb – 'every gum will in time cause damage to the paper on which it is found, so that stamps and covers alike will deteriorate and ultimately disintegrate if something drastic is not done about it' – can be neutralized in a variety of ways but at a cost.

Display of the British Library's collections presents its own problems. Not all the material – archival items, records, specialist studies – would have little visual interest to the casual visitor. Such displays that were mounted were aimed at a non-stamp collecting audience since it was estimated that only 5% of British Library visitors were philatelists. Whether this point would remain valid if the Philatelic Collections enjoyed more spacious accommodation is open to debate. In different circumstances more philatelists, greater both in numbers and in proportion to the total number of visitors, might be encouraged to exploit the Collections in the course of their research.

> So that's the British Library, [Lake concluded,] one of the world's major repositories of often unique philatelic material, available by prior arrangement to any inquirer who will also find he is offered personal service, an interested and informed guide and help and advice in pursuing his personal task ('This Philatelic World of Ours', *Gibbons Stamp Monthly*, **14** (10), Mar 1984, pp. 85–6).

Writing in the same journal five months later, John Holman took issue with Lake's bland acceptance of the British Library's good intentions regarding public access to its collections. In May 1983 he had written to the Director General of the British Library's Reference Division, volunteering to write an article on the future plans for the philatelic collections. A reply was received from the Superintendent declining to cooperate in preparing such an article:

> This type of information is not normally publicised in this manner and, in the past, has been circulated either verbally to those persons or bodies who would be interested in specific projects or by way of a press release which would be distributed by The British Library Press and Publicity Officer.

Although the results of research undertaken by philatelists on the Library's collections were published in the philatelic press 'we would not wish to extend this to matters concerned with internal work or policy.' Most library and information professionals would no doubt sympathize with the Superintendent's stance on not publicly discussing internal policy matters but Holman was convinced that 'there can be no real justification for not wanting to let the public about the collections and the plans for their future'. Plainly, they were at cross-purposes.

Holman wanted to know what had led to a change of heart and the interview with Kenneth Lake. Was it possible the British Library Board had been made aware of concern about the direction of the Philatelic Collections' plans? Few philatelists, he declared, were satisfied with the progress made in the previous decade especially with the lack of display facilities. The De La Rue archives were withdrawn by the De La Rue Company when it discovered that the archive was on view only by appointment and was given instead to the National Postal Museum. He took his enquiries further and contacted his Member of Parliament. Eventually he received a letter from the British Library's Chief Executive informing him that the Library was determined to make the collections as accessible as practicable and cited the photographic project as evidence of this. Although mollified Holman was not entirely placated, arguing that Library visitors could see the originals of the Magna Carta or Shakespeare folios. 'If the National Postal Museum and many other museums throughout the world can display original stamps why cannot the British Library.' And, in the absence of adequate display facilities,

> could not the British Library publish a handlist or short guide to its philatelic collections as an interim measure? Even if the stamps are not to be put on general display such a listing would be of use to the collector contemplating visiting the Library to see stamps by prior appointment.

He had written to the Chief Executive offering to prepare such a guide himself but his offer brought no response.

While congratulating the Superintendent for his admirable work on conservation, Holman contended that conservation was only part of his role:

> his major duty must surely be to ensure the public is aware of and able to see the material he is responsible for. Indeed, it could be argued that display policy and public relations are the main function of a head of section, technical aspects such as security and conservation are best left to a senior but subordinate officer. However important security and conservation may be, they cannot justify long-term withdrawal of items from display ('The British Library Philatelic Collections – Is All Well?', *Gibbons Stamp Monthly*, **15** (3), Aug. 1984, pp. 71–2).

In retrospect this squabble was simply a minor manifestation of the age-old conflict between conservation and access. No doubt the Superintendent would have preferred to improve access but his options were obviously constricted by the resources available to him both in terms of accommodation and in staff time. With a professional team of three, one of whom was almost continuously occupied on a single operational task, the scope for delegation at a senior level was limited. Holman's Parthian shot in this particular episode was a proposal that the British Library Board should appoint a small committee of experienced philatelists to advise the Superintendent. Not surprisingly there was no take-up on that offer either.

Ten years forward Holman was in a more contented frame of mind in his 'Forty Million Stamps. The British Library Philatelic Collections', *Gibbons Stamp Monthly*, **25** (5), Oct. 1994, pp. 64–5. 'Happily common sense prevailed and selections from the Tapling and other collections were on display again by the end of 1985' and the previously implied policy of restricting access to photographic reproductions had not been implemented. The bulk of this article is, in fact, given over to notes on the contents of ten display cabinets, totalling some 80,000 items on 6000 sheets. Although these represent only a small percentage of the Library's collections, they include material from several major collections. David Beech's 'The British Library: An International Philatelic Resource', *Friends of the British Library Newsletter*, no. 20, Winter 1994, pp. 4–5 considers where philatelic material is to be found in other parts of the Library.

The first issue of the *Philatelic Collections Newsletter* was distributed in the Spring of 1997. Its front page was given over to news of the Collections' impending move to St Pancras. 'Moving the thirty-six principal Collections, comprising over 8 million items and all that supports them will be the largest move of philatelic material ever.' Once there, 'all of our collections will be housed in carefully controlled environmental conditions including temperature and relative humidity. We shall enjoy, for the first time, a large strongroom situated next to the office and the time saved in commuting between the two.' A new Philatelic Students Room provides access for researchers to material not on display. Other features include a summary article on the Tapling Collection and a useful column on published research on the Collections, a precedent which other British Library newsletters might profitably follow.

MUSIC LIBRARY

The British Library holds the national reference collection of manuscript and printed music, some 1½ million items of printed music and thousands more manuscripts for reference, ranking as one of the outstanding collections in the world. The music section at the Document Supply Centre has a collection of 125,000 music scores. Malcolm Turner's 'Music Library, Notable Acquisitions 1985–1994', *British Library Journal*, **21** (2), Autumn 1995, pp. 289–313 demonstrates that the Music Library . . . has continued to maintain the pre-eminence of its existing collections by a vigorous programme of acquisitions ranging widely both geographically and temporally... made possible by continuing support for the Music Library's purchase budget from the Directorate of Special Collections.

Its main section, First And Early Editions of Printed Music 1596–1982, listed chronologically, is followed by Editions with Covers Designed by Modern Artists, Opera Full Scores, and First Editions of Nineteenth-Century Viennese Dance.

As if to prove that the Music Library has its roots deeply planted in popular taste, Turner notes that

> the Music Library as part of the national library has always seen itself as having a responsibility to document British musical life by collecting as complete an archive as possible of British publications and of other appropriate published material, such as foreign compositions setting texts by British writers or related in some way to British composers or performers. This involves the acquisition, quite cheaply, of much popular and relatively ephemeral music, especially of nineteenth-century songs, salon music, arrangements of favourite arias from popular operas and the like . . . during the period in question the Music Library purchased over 800 such items from one dealer alone and the total acquired from all sources must certainly be double this quantity. The Music Library was also able to buy a collection of 2,085 sets of parts of dance band and light orchestral music formerly in use in the Tower Ballroom, Blackpool. [Overall,] the principal criterion for inclusion in this, necessarily highly selective, list is the intrinsic interest or importance of a given item, but secondary consideration has been a desire to reflect the diversity encompassed by the Library's collecting policy.

Sundry Sorts of Music Books. Essays on The British Library Collections Presented to O.W. Neighbour on his 70th birthday, edited by Chris Banks, Arthur Searle and Malcolm Turner (The British Library, 1993) contains 29 essays by various hands including 'Tim Neighbour: an appreciation' (Alec Hyatt King and Hugh Cobbe); 'The Nonsuch Music Library' (John Milsom); 'Problems in three Mozart Autographs in the Stefan Zweig Collection' (Alan Tyson); and 'American Music in the British Library: a preliminary survey' (James Fuld).

Continuing Malcolm Turner and Arthur Searle's 'The Music Collections of the British Library Reference Division', *Notes*, no. 38,

1981/82, pp. 499–549, Searle's 'Music Manuscript Acquisitions at The British Library Since 1981', *Brio*, **31** (2), Autumn/Winter 1994, pp. 69–78 describes in detail some of the more important additions, 'some of superlative importance'. The full significance of the Zweig Collection is underlined while other sets and collections mentioned include the scores of Haydn's London symphonies purchased from the Royal Philharmonic Society in 1988; the Royal Musical Association's archive; some exceptional Vaughan Williams manuscripts, 'almost all the result of the continuing interest and generosity of Mrs. Vaughan Williams'; and the manuscript of *Rose Lake*, Michael Tippett's orchestral work, first performed as part of Tippett's 90th birthday celebrations, together with earlier unpublished works and notebooks.

Chris Banks' 'From Purcell to Wardour Street: A Brief Account of Music Manuscripts from the Library of Vincent Novello now in the British Library', *British Library Journal*, **21** (2), Autumn 1995, pp. 242–58 attempts to identify all the music manuscripts which were written or owned by Vincent Novello, together with the details of how they came into the Library's collections. The manuscripts derive from three sources: manuscripts presented to the British Museum by Vincent Novello during his lifetime; those he had already given to friends and institutions subsequently acquired by the Library; and the large number of manuscripts presented by the publishing firm that still bears his name to the Library in 1986 and 1987. A brief sketch of Vincent Novello's life and of the publishing firm, puts the material into its historical context.

Made possible by an appeal mounted jointly by the Library and the Purcell Centenary Trust, the British Library was able to purchase a unique autograph manuscript of keyboard music, including pieces by Henry Purcell (1659–95) written in his own hand, five of them previously unknown. The manuscript first came to light in November 1993 and was subsequently put up for auction by Sotheby's in May 1994. The Secretary of State for National Heritage withheld an export licence in September 1994 to enable a national institution to equal the purchase price. This is the first instance of an export licence for a music manuscript being withheld on grounds of national importance. The Purcell section amounts to 21 pieces written on 22 pages and, in addition to the five previously unknown pieces, four others are previously unrecorded arrangements for keyboard of his theatre music and the remainder are known movements from his keyboard suites.

A year later the Delius Trust and the British Library announced the donation by the Trust to the Library of its unique collection of auto-graph scores of the composer, Frederick Delius. Hugh Cobbe, Music Librarian of the British Library, commented

> This donation is the fourth of a series of remarkable gifts made to the nation over the last 35 years by composers' estates as a result of which the British Library holds the overwhelming majority of the autographs of Elgar, Holst, Vaughan Williams and now to complete that genera-tion, Delius. These great collections are complemented by comprehen-sive collections of many of the next generations of British composers, notably Britten, Tippett and most recently Maxwell Davies. So we are immensely grateful to the Delius Trust for their generosity in thus filling what was hitherto a serious gap.

In June 1996 the Library announced the purchase of all the extant origi-nal manuscripts of Benjamin Frankel (1906–73) widely regarded as Britain's leading symphonist. His output comprised eight symphonies, the opera *Marching Song* and notable film scores such as *The Night of the Iguana*. They join the Frankel Manuscripts which the Library acquired some years ago, among which is his Violin Concerto of 1951, composed for the Festival of Britain. Chris Banks, Curator of Music Manuscripts, affirmed that Frankel's manuscripts joined 'an ever-growing collection of the music of 20th century composers held by the Library, including, of his own generation, Bernard Stevens and Humphrey Searle. The unpub-lished and sketch material in the collection will be a particularly valuable research resource for those wishing to study Frankel's compositional process.'

Published by Bowker-Saur in 1993, *CPM Plus, The Catalogue of Printed Music in the British Library to 1990 on CD-ROM*, which provides instant fingertip access to approximately 1 million entries and cross-references for printed music published between 1503 and 1990, brings together data from the *Catalogue of Printed Music to 1980* (London: K.G. Saur, 62 vols., 1980–87) plus previously unpublished records from the CPM *Supplement* (pre 1987 imprints acquired since 1980) and the *Current Music Catalogue* (c.4000 records a year since 1980). Oliver Neighbour's 'CPM: Some Quirks and Caveats', in *Music Publishing and Collecting. Essays in Honor of Donald W. Krummel*, edited by David Hunter (Graduate School of Library and Information Science, University of Illinois at Urbana–Champaign, 1994, pp. 205–14) relates historical events and decisions which shaped the Catalogue and accounts for some discrepancies and inaccuracies in its entries for the period 1801-32.

NATIONAL SOUND ARCHIVE

Currently holding over a million discs, 160,000 tapes and a growing number of videos and laser discs, the National Sound Archive is a unique resource for the study of all kinds of music, literature and the social and zoological sciences. Its character and structure have altered little since the British institute of Recorded Sound entered the British Library as the National Sound Archive in 1983. Its agreement with the British Phonographic Industry Ltd (BPI), by which it received copies of most discs and cassettes published in the UK still stands, although moves are afoot within the Department of Culture, Media and Sport to extend legal deposit to non-print publications. NSA activities and services, initiatives and publications are best followed through the pages of its bulletin, *Playback*, circulated free of charge three times a year.

'Collections and Acquisitions' (*Playback*, no. 7, Spring 1994, pp. 2-8) provides a structured overview of its specialist sections, summarizes their more important existing holdings and gives an update on 1993 acquisitions. Pop Music section is largely concerned with Anglo-American pop music on published discs received under the BPI agreement.

> Receipts from larger companies are usually part of a promotional copy distribution, so by now we have archived countless rarities in the form of remixes, 'special shape' discs and packaging and other small-circulation items aimed at disc jockeys. [Moreover,] since 1987 the Musicians' Union has passed on to us all the promotional videos it receives for vetting . . . since many of these are never broadcast, let alone re-edited for sale, we have acquired much that is unique.

Andy Linehan's 'Pop videos. The NSA holds the national collection' (*Playback*, no. 14, Summer 1996, pp. 4-5) goes into more detail on this point, underlining how difficult it would be for the NSA to ensure a comprehensive collection in the absence of any central organization to coordinate production.

Wildlife Section, the most extensive of its kind in the world, with more than 100,000 recordings of all classes of animals from every zoogeographical area, is solidly based on a complete set of the BBC Natural History Sound Archive recordings and on unique collections of unpublished tape recordings contributed by amateur and professional recordists. The collection is scientifically organized and documented and enjoys a wide recognition in bioacoustic and zoological circles. Although funded by the British Library the section is supported by the Friends of Wildlife Sounds at the National Sound Archive so that it can more easily expand its activities, finance overseas recording expeditions, produce new cassettes and CDs, and develop further as an internationally respected centre of recorded sound. The first issue of *Wildlife Section Newsletter*, to be produced on a twice-yearly basis, is dated August 1997. Its purpose is to inform users and contributors of important accessions, to report on significant developments and to disseminate general information about bioacoustic activities.

The International Music Collection, currently consisting of 100,000 items, is the Archives specialist collection of non-western art music, variously described as traditional, ethnic, folk or world music. Its holdings include the unique collection of 2000 ethnographic cylinders, originally collected by Sir James Frazer, recorded on expeditions to Australia, New Guinea, India, Africa and South America in the period 1898–1914. British folk music in its heyday is well represented and when a need emerged for a systematic and coordinated approach to the preservation of recorded sound collections in private hands, the NSA was widely perceived as the only institution with the necessary credibility and facilities for preservation, storage and accessibility to undertake this task.

As the largest public reference collection of its kind in the country, IMC's primary concerns are active participation in commercial and educational work and involvement in research and technical advice regarding recording and fieldwork techniques. An historical perspective is printed in the Spring 1995 issue of *International Music Connection. The Newsletter of the International Music Collection*. This six-page, thin paper, quarterly newsletter is published to keep people informed of IMC's activities; to provide updates on recent acquisitions, internal developments and special projects; to increase awareness of the archive as a resource for scholars and students; and to encourage potential depositors. Forthcoming events with an IMC input are chronicled. Articles of particular interest include 'Selection and acquisition in IMC' (no. 4, Winter 1996) and 'IMC policy on music from the British Isles' (no. 8, Winter 1997).

NSA's enthusiasm when the British Library's Digital and Network Services Steering Committee was formed in 1993 to investigate how the Library might take advantage of digital technology by funding a series of projects collectively designated Initiatives for Access is seen to best advantage in Peter Copeland's 'Project Digitize: an initiative for access', *Playback*, no. 8, Summer 1994, pp. 5–7 which specifies three ways whereby digital technology could be of service to NSA: original recordings, once digitized, can in theory be copied indefinitely without loss of quality, permitting indefinite preservation; access to the recordings can be improved because they can be sent by digital telecomms links with high quality and low cost; and NSA is in a position to use the experience of other parts of the British Library to digitize artefacts such as record sleeves and so reduce wear-and-tear on originals. He emphasized that digitization is not simply an engineering process, before digitization starts there has to be a careful study of the source material, gremlins have to be ironed out at a very early stage, tests have to be devised without damaging the original recordings. Before choosing a digital recording system NSA must be certain that it offers the best balance between longevity, cost, reliability, quality and ease of playback.

Concentrating on two International Music projects, the NSA put forward a successful proposal 'aimed at exploring all the issues surrounding the conversion of analogue recordings to digital . . . engineering and archival policy issues, documentation of the results and automated access to them'. First it had to be determined what exactly should be preserved: 'the surviving recording the way it is . . . the recording as it would have been heard by the original recording engineer . . . the sound the artiste would have most liked, or a version which reproduces the original sound most accurately, irrespective of the wishes of the engineer or artiste'. Finding a way ahead was also subject to the pressures of priority. Media at risk, recordings liable to decay to the point of unplayability if treatment is not urgently forthcoming, frequently demanded top priority. Nitrate discs, acetate-based recording tapes, of which the NSA holds thousands of reels and wax cylinders all fall into this category.

The NSA takes a pragmatic view when considering such material, contending that its responsibility is to ensure that the actual recording is preserved for future researchers, not the original carrier medium, wax cylinders, acetate tapes, or whatever. 'It's the job of the Science Museum to preserve examples of media such as shellac 78s for posterity' is the line it invariably adheres to.

Also by Copeland, 'Project Digitise', *Information Services and Use*, **16** (3/4), 1996, pp. 199–208, more specialist in appeal, enumerates the full aims and objectives of NSA's pilot project: to test collection management methodology regarding the provision of service and conservation versions and backup copies; to develop the skills of NSA technical staff in analogue/digital transfer procedures including (where appropriate) segmentation and data reduction; to gain experience which would enable the accurate sizing of a large-scale digitization project and propose a costed programme of further work; to gain 'hands-on' experience of working with a wide range of digital carriers in order to assess their potential suitability for a large-scale programme; and to establish a set of digitized recordings and develop an experimental online playback service. He also elaborates on the collection management methodology, the analogue/digital transfer procedures and the digital destination media.

Paul Fisher's 'Making a sound investment for the digital future' (*DT Connected*, pp. 8–9. Insert in the *Daily Telegraph*, no. 44105, 8 April 1997) is based on the theme that

> digitisation means two things for libraries: one, material is easier to store and get at; two, it is damn near immortal. Time is frozen into utterly stable accretions of noughts and ones that will be cloned onto future storage media with no loss of quality. Along with this curatorial commonplace comes the prospect of new ways of distribution, consumption and, finally, new ways of thought.

Reporting NSA's aims, activities and philosophy, Fisher also explains why it has established CDs as the national storage medium:

> It applied the Arrhenius test, which heats a material and predicts its lifespan by extrapolating from rates at which chemical reactions take place, to give the CD half a century before the onset of the smallest degradations. The same test revealed that well-kept optical discs would endure for 400 million years. The NSA says there are more CD players in the world than there are years in an optical disc and, with an eye to the future, has plumped for what's cheap, reliable, plentiful and common.

CADENSA

NSA's cataloguing database, initially known as NIPPER, came into operation at the end of September 1995, but when publicly launched in June 1996, the homely NIPPER had been translated into the more exotic CADENSA (Catalogue Access and Data Entry for the National Sound Archive). This is an online catalogue and collection management system, whose 24-gigabyte database index includes 900,000+ recordings, scheduled to be doubled within twelve months as more historical data are entered. Designed to facilitate rapid and trouble-free browsing, CADENSA can carry out instant complicated data searches otherwise requiring hours of expensive research time. It has the capacity, for example, to perform keyword searches on any term in the database; to find recordings by name, title, place or subject; to browse indexes of names, titles, subjects or keywords; to display recordings by date or date range; to show recordings held for a given category; to show spoken or sung recordings by language or translation; to list holdings on a given format; to list releases on a given label by serial number, album title and release date; to sort listings by title, artist and recording date; to display copyright information; and to show details of NSA conservation.

This speed, flexibility and comprehensive capacity will undoubtedly provide an effective platform for NSA's access and information services at St Pancras. A longer-term aim is to integrate the catalogue with the recordings so that researchers can access a digitalized collection without having to play the originals on conventional equipment.

Details of CADENSA's architecture, how exactly the NSA has transformed its record creation 'into a fully-catalogued, integrated archival collection in which the key processes of accessioning and cataloguing (including conservation logging) are governed by a cohesive system' are readily available in Chris Clark's 'The National Sound Archive IT Project: Documentation Of Sound Recordings Using the Unicorn Collections Management System', IASA Journal, no. 5, May 1995, pp. 7–24. This authoritative, well-structured account by the Head of Documentation and Public Services at NSA proceeds step by step through the procurement of a collection management package: customization (the NSA's requirements pushing the Unicorn Collections Management System's flexibilities to the limits); the conversion of retrospective data; the wide involvement of NSA staff in record creation, and the derivation of catalogue records from external sources including the Mechanical-Copyright Protection Society's National Discography, the BBC, and The Gramophone database. There are four annexes: Table of NSA MARC codes; Updating Unicorn; Navigating the OPAC (including searching the NSA online catalogue, browsing and LINK terms); and a replay of a typical OPAC session. For less computer literate users the NSA has produced an information sheet on how to navigate CADENSA.

On arrival at St Pancras, NSA assumed responsibility for developing the shape of recorded sound services there. The Listening and Viewing Service offers playback access to sound and video recordings to users by appointment although there are plans for a self-service automated system as demand increases. An NSA Recorded Sound Information Service deals with subject enquiries in literature and drama, wildlife sounds, language and dialect, sound effects, the study of recording technology and the broadcast and record industry. An integrated Music Service, comprising the Music Library and the NSA's recorded music services, covers selection, specialist cataloguing, reference work and exhibition support. Integration with existing services on a subject basis is the key approach including acquisitions and collection management. Recorded sound holdings are stored at St Pancras although the processing, conservation and technical sections relocate to Micawber Street.

A transcription service for radio stations, record companies and institutional users; spectograms of wildlife sounds made to order; a research and consultation service; studio and other technical facilities hire; and training courses in oral history and wildlife sound recording, comprise NSA's range of charged services, outlined in *Services from the National Sound Archive*, an introductory leaflet distributed to coincide with NSA's arrival at St Pancras.

PART III

SUPPORT SERVICES

10

COLLECTION MANAGEMENT
Acquisitions, Processing and Cataloguing

In the final stage of restructuring Acquisitions, Processing and Cataloguing (AP&C) will merge with Collections and Preservation (C&P) to form a new directorate, Collection Management. AP&C is currently responsible for acquisition procurement and processing and for record creation and catalogue control, while C&P's responsibilities are in the field of pressmarks, labelling, storage, collection security and preservation.

A short passage from Andrew MacEwan's 'LCSH and the British Library: an international subject authority database?', a paper given at a Cataloguing and Indexing Group seminar at Libtech, at the University of Hertfordshire, September 1995 and printed in *Catalogue and Index*, no. 120, Summer 1996, pp. 1-6 may be regarded as the prime *motif* of this chapter.

> The key structural change has been the creation in 1989 of a centralised directorate for Acquisitions Processing and Cataloguing to take responsibility for the cataloguing operations previously carried out in the separate collections areas of the Library. The new AP&C directorate has provided a focus for defining a strategy that will lead towards a single unified catalogue for all the Library's collections.

If successful efforts to reach agreement with the Library of Congress over an Anglo-American Authority File and the harmonization of US-MARC and UKMARC, both affecting the UK library community, are added, then the activities and responsibilities of AP&C since its formation are clearly defined and comprehended.

ANGLO-AMERICAN AUTHORITY FILE

The first problem tackled was the creation of an Anglo-American Authority File (AAAF) of headings used in common by the Library of Congress and the British Library since

> searching authors' names to find a list of their works is by far the most common way of finding books and the lack of common forms between the two major catalogues has acted as an obstacle between users and the collections at a time when many more are accessing catalogues remotely through computer networks ('Anglo-American Cooperation', *Select*, no. 13, Autumn 1994, pp. 11–12).

In May 1993 the two libraries agreed to converge the US National Authority File and the British Library Name Authority List. Three principal benefits to librarians and library users were adduced: exchange of bibliographic records would be simplified; compatibility between access points in remote databases would be enhanced; and duplication of authority records would be eliminated.

These benefits would not materialize immediately but significant obstacles had been overcome, notably the British Library and the Library of Congress had agreed on the interpretation of AACR2 with regard to the formulation of access points. Implementation of the AAAF would take place in three phases: the resource file, the joint authority file, and retrospective convergence. Progress towards the AAAF, the methods adopted, system problems and the signing of a Cataloguing Policy Convergence Agreement early in 1996, are recorded in Alan Danskin's 'The Anglo-American Authority File – Completion of Phase 1', *Select*, no. 17, Spring 1996, p. 11; in 'A Declaration of Inter-dependence', no. 18, Winter 1996, pp. 10–11; and in his 'The Anglo-American Authority File – Completion of Phase 2', no. 20, Spring 1997, p. 13.

The project also caught the eye of *The Times*: in a third leader, 'What's in a Catalog', it wryly observed:

> The decision to standardis(z)e the names of authors may be a big stride for the book world. But it is only a small step towards that Cloud-Cuckoo-Land where everybody speaks and writes English according to the same rules. A world without its rich national varieties and dialects would be a poorer place. Even in the narrower world of libraries, universal standardised English would make it impossible to identify the source of a text. Luckily, it is not going to happen. While the British Museum

is blowing its own trumpet over the joint catalogue, the Library of Congress still prefers already to blow its own horn over the joint catalog. (*The Times*, 64967, 30 May 1994, p. 15).

LIBRARY OF CONGRESS SUBJECT HEADINGS

Library of Congress Subject Headings (LCSH), first added to BNB-MARC records in 1971, were deleted in 1987 as a result of the *Currency with Coverage* policy recommendations to reduce record creation costs. Although successful in this respect and in effecting a rise in the hit rate figures, the absence of LCSH was a constant source of friction between the British Library and other large research libraries. When it became clear that there was a genuine demand for their reinstatement, the British Library relented with as much grace as it could muster and AP&C reintroduced them from January 1995. At that time the Library took the decision not to provide headings for fiction and juvenile literature, but in October headings were assigned to juvenile literature, leaving fiction as the only category not to accord with Library of Congress practice. By virtue of contributing new subheadings to LC's authority file, the British Library is now a partner in the Subject Authority Cooperative Program, a partnership mainly consisting of major American libraries.

To quote MacEwan again: 'by subscribing to the subjects authority file we are buying into the only standard for subjects with a wide enough currency to be a meaningful counterpart to cooperation over names'. He expands on the British Library's future role:

> It is important to reiterate that LCSH belongs to the Library of Congress. We are adopting their file and their system and their editorial control. We cannot expect to change that system just to suit our needs, perhaps leaving out the things we do not like and indeed there would be little point if our aim is to provide a standard record valuable here and in America, Canada, Australia, etc. By contributing authority work of our own, in the form of proposals for new headings or for changes to old headings, we will be able to influence and improve the content of the authority file itself. Work of this kind has already begun through our participation in the Subject Authorities Cooperative program and, so far, 89 new proposals and 45 change proposals from the British Library have been accepted on the LCSH file at the Library of

Congress. [Moreover,] Our resources for expanding our role are limited in the immediate future by our need to pursue and complete an internal training programme in LCSH indexing for all cataloguers within AP&C and in other parts of the Library. Adopting LCSH as a library-wide system for access inevitably means that for a period we are focusing heavily on our internal needs, rather than on our wider role.

MARC HARMONIZATION

Staff from the British Library and the Library of Congress met on 21 June 1994 to review principles for harmonization of the USMARC and UKMARC formats in an effort to increase their compatibility. The UKMARC and USMARC formats were designed primarily for the communication of machine-readable records, which may comprise bibliographic, name authority or other information necessary to describe items of library material. The UKMARC format has diverged in a number of respects from the archetypal USMARC, which was originally developed by the Library of Congress in the 1960s. The following statement was issued:

> This was the first step in a continuous effort to develop a more simplified cataloguing system that would decrease the redundancy of work required to create records and facilitate the sharing of bibliographic records. Presently both the Library of Congress and the British Library must maintain conversion programs to process each other's records. The participants also proposed the inclusion of Canada's CANMARC in the integration process and discussed the relationship between the Anglo-American Cataloguing Rules (AACR) and MARC formats. Both libraries, [it was emphasised], would extensively consult with MARC users before considering any proposed changes.

An open meeting at Library Association Headquarters, 21 July 1995 discussed a background paper distributed to all those accepting invitations to attend. It transpired, to nobody's surprise, that some wanted immediate implementation, whilst others wished to adopt a softly, softly approach. In the mean time, the British Library gave notice that

> (1) certain features of USMARC will be proposed for incorporation into UKMARC in the very near future. Regrettably, these will not include – as had been hoped and was announced at the meeting – amendments to

the name fields in advance of implementation of the Anglo-American Authority File (although the schedule for AAAF remains otherwise unchanged), but will cover fields which the Archives and Serials communities have pressed to be adopted; (2) the British Library is commissioning a cost-benefit analysis of the harmonisation process, with a view to having this ready in the autumn. This will inform the decision that the three libraries should be taking before the end of the year on whether to proceed and how to set about resolving the significant differences that exist; and (3) format users will continue to be kept informed about developments.

At a meeting in December in Washington the British Library, the Library of Congress and the National Library of Canada, agreed formally to harmonize their national MARC formats. At the same time, a consultative paper was issued listing all the major areas of difference between UKMARC and the two North American formats. The British Library promised to heed users' views when planning its strategy prior to negotiations. Concerns expressed by UK users encompassed three particular areas: subfield encoding based on International Standard Bibliographic Descriptions (ISBDs); software-generated punctuation; and the treatment of individual volume information.

After a further meeting in Washington, in February 1997, it was announced that USMARC and CANMARC were to be fully harmonized, but that the British Library's stance on the three areas of users' concerns had proved insurmountable for UKMARC to participate. Nevertheless, to ensure formats should not diverge further, a MARC Harmonization Co-Ordinating Committee would coordinate new developments in the UKMARC and harmonized USMARC and CANMARC formats; seek further opportunities for harmonization; ensure that future development would take other international standards into consideration; and explore the impact of technological change on MARC formats. It was the best that could be achieved. Clearly

> the goal of full harmonisation across the Atlantic may not have been reached in the short term, but there will be many benefits to be gained from a programme of increasing convergence. Each step will make format conversion easier, as will the wider availability of PC-based conversion software. In this way the original aim of increasing the pool of records available to libraries for copy cataloguing and resource sharing

activities can still be achieved (Stuart Ede, 'LandMARC Decision', *Select*, no. 20, Spring 1997, p. 3).

UK MARC MANUAL

Incorporating all changes and amendments since the third edition was published in 1990, *The UKMARC Manual: A Cataloguers Guide to the Bibliographic Format* (4th ed., 1996) is extensively rewritten, redesigned and comprehensively updated. To give it more emphasis as a tool for cataloguers, technical data relating to exchange formats is largely excluded and appears instead in a new publication, *The UKMARC Exchange Record Format* (1997). *The UKMARC Updating Service* issues prompt updates when format changes are agreed. 'The New UKMARC Manual', *Select*, no. 18, Winter 1996, p. 11 takes the form of a dialogue between the editor and Cynthia McKinley who worked on the new edition.

CATALOGUING ELECTRONIC MEDIA

Faced with the possibility of extended legal deposit to floppy disks, CD-ROMs etc., the Electronic Media Group of AP&C, set up to develop a centre of expertise for the cataloguing of electronic publications, and to participate in the international development of cataloguing standards, investigated the problems looming up for AP&C should electronic materials arrive in large quantities. A test study, involving staff dealing with reader access, preservation, bibliographic services and storage, and undertaken by cataloguers skilled in monograph and serial cataloguing, concluded that cataloguing electronic items would be easy compared to installing them. Throughout the study detailed notes on the cataloguing process were recorded, the time taken, the technical difficulties, the system inadequacies, and the problems associated with the application of conventional cataloguing and classification rules. Sandie Beaney and Stephen Bagley's 'Towards a Policy for Cataloguing CD-ROMs and Other Electronic Media', *Select*, no. 19, Spring 1997, p. 12 and no. 20, Summer 1997, p. 14 reports at first hand on the latest developments.

Beaney and Leona Carpenter's 'The indexing and retrieval of digital items', *Information Services and Use*, **16** (4), 1996, pp. 209–21 is at pains to refute some popular misconceptions.

What our users may fail to realise, is that for us the greatest challenges of providing the services they need lie not in the technology, but in the intellectual endeavour required to make the technology useful, in the resource implications of being required to provide new or digitally-enhanced services while continuing to provide traditional services in a time when many libraries face severe budgetary restraints and in the necessity for international cooperation in defining and agreeing the standards which will ensure the quality of those services.

Underlining the enormous potential of digitization for the cataloguing of both electronic and traditional documents, with a consequent boost for record enhancement, including the display of associated images and attached graphics, they reiterate that should legislation be enacted for the legal deposit of electronic material, the British Library would have to consider how to offer access to this material. In the mean time AP&C 'are currently at an experimental stage in receiving electronic journals on deposit of cataloguing, to test the procedures which would become necessary as a result of extended legal deposit'.

LEGAL DEPOSIT OFFICE

Encompassing the progress of British legal deposit legislation, the processing and coverage of legal deposit material (the 1996–97 influx totalled some 300,000 items, comprising 80,000 books and 220,000 issues of 37,000 serial titles), the alert and recovery procedure for overdue items, and the possible introduction of legislation to cover the legal deposit of non-book materials, Wendy Frankland's 'Building the national archive – Legal Deposit at the British Library', *Select*, no. 21, Winter 1997, pp. 6–7 provides a rare insight into the work of the Legal Deposit Office at Boston Spa.

Collections and Preservation

BRITISH LIBRARY'S PRESERVATION POLICY

By far the most complete and illuminating summary of the British Library's preservation policy and programme and its role in a national preservation strategy through the National Preservation Office (NPO) may be found in 'Preservation Policy, Dilemmas, Needs', *Conservation Administration News*, no. 58/59, July/October 1994, pp. 1, 3–6; no. 60, December 1994, pp. 6–10; and no. 61, April 1995, pp. 5–8, which prints papers delivered by Mirjam Foot to a conservation forum sponsored by the Harry Ransom Research Center and Preservation and Conservation Studies/Graduate School of Library and Information Science at the University of Texas, Austin. Firmly linking preservation to the British Library's acquisition, retention and access responsibilities, and to the extent to which these can be shared, Dr Foot examined the Library's policy as it has evolved from the reorganization of its Preservation Service in 1986 when it was entrusted with more wide-ranging responsibilities, when greater curatorial involvement was encouraged in decision-making and in the setting of priorities for the preservation of the collections, and when more emphasis was placed on the amount of use the material was likely to get as an indicator for priority treatment.

Although not set in concrete, the British Library's policy is to ensure the preservation of the intellectual content and physical format of its collections; to ensure the security of its collections; to promote awareness of preservation problems and good preservation practice, nationally and internationally; and to aim at preserving material in need of conservation. Six descending areas of priority had been established: heritage material and unique or rare material, including manuscripts, certain special collections, archives, rare printed material, material of bibliographical or structural importance, or material classed as artefacts; the national collection of British publications; material that is heavily used now and has become fragile, or that may be expected to receive heavy use in the future and has already become or is likely to become fragile; material not available elsewhere; research archives; and low-use material too fragile to be consulted or copied.

In addition, the Library's intention is to develop through the National Preservation Office a national preservation strategy together with other libraries and archives in the United Kingdom, to encourage international cooperation in the field of preservation, to develop and invest in new preservation techniques, such as paper strengthening and recorded sound restoration, to encourage the use of archival/permanent paper and other sound structures by publishers in the United Kingdom, to encourage sound storage strategies and conditions, and to devise ways to encourage and support the maintenance and development of preservation skills.

Nowhere is this more evident than in reaping the benefit of experiments aimed at mass deacidifying and paper-strengthening treatments, the main thrust of Foot's second paper in the Preservation Policy. Dilemmas, Needs series. In 1980 the British Library commissioned the University of Surrey's Chemistry Department to investigate a treatment that would successfully deacidify bound books on a large scale and, in addition, would chemically consolidate paper deteriorating because of acid attack. Although Foot professes to make no attempt to describe the full chemical complexities of the experiments, or the range of problems encountered, her account is sufficiently technical to demand a good understanding of the chemical processes involved. No doubt the concepts of polymerization, gamma radiation, the homogeneity of the polymer deposition, graft copolymerization, monomer introduction etc. are familiar enough in the University of Surrey's Chemistry Department, and in the University of Manchester Institute for Science and Technology, where the chemistry of the treatment was verified, but the rest of us will be better advised to proceed without delay to the practical significance of the results of the various experiments and to the schedules drawn up for the mass deacidifying and mass paper-strengthening processes.

> A timetable per treatment cycle was established and realistic costs, including both direct costs and overheads, were worked out. On the basis of 200,000 books per year in two shifts per day, with a treatment cycle that allows 24 hours for equilibration, 12 hours for irradiation and 36 hours for ventilation, the all-inclusive cost is . . . much the same as that of most mass-deacidification processes and noticeably cheaper than microfilming. Moreover, the cost for the paper-strengthening processes includes all overheads.

In 1991 the British Library agreed with Nordion International, a Canadian firm engaged in producing radio pharmaceuticals and radio isotopes, that it should embark on a feasibility study of the chemical and engineering aspects of the processes for low-cost preservation of post-1850 books printed on poor-quality paper and explore their commercial viability. But, although the initial results were encouraging, the processes remain formidably expensive. However low the unit cost is and however favourably it contrasts with microfilming, the sheer number of books needing treatment means that no single library can afford the immense sums required.

> The only way . . . that such processes can be used, is if they are used on a national scale based on the national need . . . We cannot afford to duplicate or triplicate our efforts if we want to save the national printed effort and the national archives. It is therefore necessary to tackle the problem on a co-operative basis on a national scale . . . We must attempt first to formulate and then start to implement a national preservation programme. In order to do this we need published retention and preservation policies for all major university and research libraries; we need a truly national register of preservation surrogates, as well as a national register of preservation techniques, available technology and available skills. More ambitious still: we need a nation-wide register of material conserved and of planned conservation work.

Clearly, the British Library's preservation policy and programmes must be concerned not only with the conservation of its own unique collections, but must also relate to wider national responsibilities. As the national library

> it must be willing to undertake the preservation of those collections that no other major library can or wishes to preserve. It must be willing to understand the preservation priorities of other libraries and, though it may have to co-ordinate those priorities on a national level, it must not prescribe them. It must make the knowledge and expertise of its staff available to advise and help those who have not been able to develop such expertise.' Above all, 'it must lead the library community in its attempts to obtain funding'. The medium chosen to channel the British Library's knowledge, expertise and advice is the National Preservation Office.

NATIONAL PRESERVATION OFFICE

When established in 1984, after the publication of F.W. Ratcliffe's

Preservation Policies and Conservation in British Libraries: Report of the Cambridge University Conservation Project, which recognized the need for a national advisory centre, the NPO was entirely funded by the British Library both in terms of staff and accommodation. However, strictly speaking, it remained independent of the Library and operated under the guidance of the National Preservation Advisory Committee made up of representatives from national, research and public libraries, record offices, and institutions such as The Library Association, the Library and Information Science Councils and SCONUL. Despite its slightly ambiguous status the NPO worked well enough thanks to the close proximity of the British Library's Preservation Service and the continuing influence of its Advisory Committee.

Its functions were

> to offer free advice and a referral service on all aspects of preservation, disaster control planning and security . . . It lobbies for such things as the wider use of permanent paper in publishing and high standards in preservation microfilming. It acts as a publisher, producing an ever-increasing range of free publications on a variety of issues, as well as some priced products including a selection of videos. It maintains lists of conservators, suppliers and courses and a number of bibliographies. Most years it organises a major national conference . . . (Valerie Ferris. 'The National Preservation Office', *Paper Conservation News*, no. 70, June 1994, p. 6).

During the 1980s and early 1990s the NPO's work and development is described as

> a fascinating barometer of how preservation 'took off' as a key library discipline and responsibility . . . in producing common sense material the Office helped demystify the world of conservation. In producing high quality videos and other training aids the message of preservation found the perfect medium (Marie Jackson, 'A Decade of Achievement: a review of the NPO', *Library Conservation News*, no. 50, Spring 1996, pp. 4–5).

A notable inclusion in these training aids was a Preservation Training Pack, designed to back up library staff training by displaying the need for preservation; explaining why library and archive materials deteriorate; identifying areas where staff could contribute to the preservation effort; stressing the need for good housekeeping; and setting out good practice guidelines. The training text is supplied in a ring-binder and is accompanied by eleven black and white and seven colour OHP overlays.

Further efforts to advance practical co-operation by means of an agreed national preservation strategy were investigated by a meeting of preservation administrators from the national libraries, the Public Record Office, and the Consortium of University and Research Libraries (CURL), called by the NPO at the instigation of the British Library in 1994. Four working parties were set up to address significant issues in the development of a national preservation policy. These were the use of information technology; the identification of issues affecting the preservation of nineteenth century and twentieth century materials; the coordination of existing preservation policies and issues relevant for a national framework; and the assessment through existing preservation surveys of the national preservation problem.

A summary of the working parties' deliberations was announced via a press information sheet, 8 March 1996:

> The Working Party on a National Preservation Strategy had as its aim the provision of an independent focus for ensuring the preservation and continued accessibility of library and archive material held in the United Kingdom and Ireland.
>
> The Working Party envisaged that the National Preservation Office should be at the heart of this strategy . . . [it] has enjoyed considerable success in the promotion of preservation as a vital activity in libraries. The Working Party felt that the NPO should become independent of any one organisation so that it could act on behalf of the majority of institutions in response to their requirements and that joint funding be sought from the Legal Deposit libraries, CURL and the Public Record Office.
>
> It recommends a strategy to take the NPO forward with a programme supportive of the needs of the library community by undertaking work of common use and interest to all:
>
> to *develop and co-ordinate the national preservation strategy*;
> to *promote an information and referral service*;
> to *promote good practice through education and training*; and
> to *co-ordinate and initiate research*.

The NPO's terms of reference were revised accordingly. At the practical level, the five other legal deposit libraries, the PRO and CURL all agreed to contribute funds to support the NPO for three years. To confound those of a Machiavellian turn of mind who might be inclined to suspect the British Library of endeavouring to shed one of its financial commitments, the Library agreed to maintain its current level of funding for the same period.

Valerie Ferris' 'To Boldly Go . . . a new look for the National Preservation Office', *Library Conservation News*, no. 50, Spring 1996, pp. 1–2 outlines the issues to be addressed in the three-year period. They include

> guidelines for condition surveys of both library and archive collections; developing a register of collection strengths; development of the MARC format to include preservation information (and support for a national bibliographic utility to support its use); improving co-ordination with other preservation groups and organisations to avoid duplication of effort; providing a clearing house for advice about grants and research; and developing a strategy for more education and training to promote good practices in the preservation and security of collections.

The NPO will also

> develop closer links with the British Library Research and Development Department and other grant-awarding bodies. In this way we hope to be able to work towards better use of the available resources both by encouraging the use of relevant standards and by directing some funds to support the development of the national programme.

Stephanie Kenna and Vanessa Marshall's 'A New Future for Preserving our Past: BLRIC and the NPO' (*RIC Research Bulletin*, no. 17, Summer 1997, pp. 12–13) underlines that in the future the NPO and the BLRIC will work closely together to identify areas for research and to encourage potential researchers!

Currently the NPO is pressing for the adoption by publishers of permanent paper which

> during long term storage in libraries, archives and other suitable and stable environments, has a high degree of permanence. This means that it will not discolour or become brittle with normal usage, such as examination and copying. Permanent, or archival paper must be manufactured from chemically treated virgin fibre; recycled pulp cannot be used as it contains a mixture of acidic and other unsuitable fibres.

A leaflet, *From Rags to Ruin*, issued by the NPO and The Library Association (July 1995), recommends that

> Organisations should use permanent paper for all records and written material for long-term retention. Publishers of non-ephemeral books and journals should adopt the use of permanent paper as a matter of high priority. Authors should encourage their publishers to use permanent paper whenever possible. In this very simple way all can play a vital role in the long-term survival of our written heritage.

A major new initiative to develop a national strategy for preservation digitization and digital archiving was launched at a one-day conference at St Pancras, 28 April 1997, when the NPO announced the formation of a new Digital Archiving Working Group. Drawn from legal deposit libraries, higher education institutions, funding bodies, record offices, publishers, and data archives, DAWG will report to the NPO's Management Committee and to the Higher Education Funding Council's Joint Information Committee. Working within the context of the national preservation policy, with the collaboration of the Research and Innovation Centre, and acknowledging the need to determine technical and managerial standards, the NPO's objectives will be to co-ordinate the development of a national digital preservation policy and guidelines on practice; to promote awareness of the issues and strategies in preservation digitization and digital archiving; to identify training needs and provide instruction in relevant best practice and management; and to act as a clearing house for information. Quickly off the mark the NPO organized a seminar on Digital Archiving Emerging Practice at the Public Record Office at Kew, 16 July 1997, at which archivists and others from the UK, the United States and Holland focused on three crucial issues: costs, technicalities and the organization of digital archiving projects.

REGISTER OF PRESERVATION MICROFORMS

Progress reports on the Register of Preservation Microforms (RPM), a BLAISE-LINE database, set up in 1986 to record all items preserved on microfilm for which a microfilm master is available for purchase, are printed in Lynn Staggs' 'The Register of Preservation Microforms', *Newspaper Library Newsletter*, no. 16 Autumn 1993, p.5; Isobel Pickering's 'The Register of Preservation Microforms', *London Services –*

Bloomsbury Newsletter, no. 12, Spring 1995, p.5; and Staggs' 'Locating The Microform Master', *Select*, no. 15, Spring 1995, pp. 8–9.

Originally established to list the British Library's internal filming programme, RPM has developed into the national database for the Mellon Microfilming Project funded by the Andrew W. Mellon Foundation, New York. This Project is a co-operative scheme, administered by the NPO, whose Project Officer advises and monitors the programmes, whereby participants in the Project select and create archival negative microfilms of material of national and scholarly interest, and contribute records of the films produced to the Register. The *Mellon Microfilming Project Manual* (1992) is a practical handbook outlining preparation guidelines, targeting and technical specifications, the boxing and labelling of microfilm, storage, submitting records for the Register, and post-filming guidelines. A series of appendices include a list of organizations involved in the Project, tags and subtitles used in records for the Register, notes on using the RPM Online File, a list of materials, supplies and suppliers, and a BSI classified bibliography.

By October 1994 RPM contained 100,000 records including many of the Library's special collections. A notable case in point is the collection of Sir Joseph Banks, one-time President of the Royal Society, who accompanied Captain James Cook on his 1768–71 voyage to the South Seas, and whose extensive library on natural history was acquired by the British Museum Library in 1827. Another celebrated collection, The Thomason Tracts, pamphlets, newspapers and other extremely scarce ephemeral material printed in the Civil War and Interregnum periods, 1640–61, is also entered on the Register. Plans to extend its coverage to other areas of the Library are in hand. Once the current Newspaper Library catalogue is converted to machine-readable format, records of microfilmed newspapers will be downloaded. The Register is now incorporated in the European Register of Microform Masters, a co-operative venture with the Bibliothèque Nationale (Paris), the Biblioteca Nacional (Lisbon) and the Staats-und-Universitätsbibliotek (Göttingen) where it is accommodated.

'Microfilm revolutionised', *Initiatives for Access News*, no. 1, May 1994, p.8 reports on the Ageing Microfilm Project set up to examine the feasibility of digitizing some of the Library's microfilm holdings. First to be decided were the criteria by which films would be selected. Hazel Podmore, the project manager relates, the chosen set had to be microfilm which had been produced some time ago and which therefore would not necessarily be of the same archival quality as that produced today, with a print quality and subject matter likely to provide a good test for the equipment. We wanted to use a set which was in high demand by readers and outside users . . . so we would not only be providing easier access to the material for them, but also would be able to get an immediate reaction which would help us evaluate the project as it progressed.

The material selected, technical details of scanning and compression and the cleaning process, are also described.

Podmore's paper, 'Aims and scope of the Digitisation of the Microfilm Project', *Information Services and Use*, **16** (4), 1996, pp. 85–187 expands on the technical detail and spells out the project's precise objectives:

to identify the best possible uses of the Mekel microfilm digitising equipment within the Library, contributing towards establishing a preliminary portfolio of digital texts; to examine in conjunction with C&T (Computer and Telecommunications) the most appropriate storage medium for digitised material and the implications for its maintenance in the medium and longer terms; to examine the implications for staff resources and operations in producing digitised material and providing adequate indexing for access to it; to determine the technical and procedural implications of supplying material digitised from microfilm to readers in the Reading Rooms; and to learn lessons for the future about microfilming standards and their importance for microfilm digitisation.

BRITISH LIBRARY REPRODUCTIONS

A restructured British Library Reproductions, the reprographic and photographic service based on Reader Services and Collection Development, offers two basic types of copying service, paper and microfilm. Photocopies are supplied either from paper originals or from original microfilms brought in by readers. There is a general restriction on photocopying pre-nineteenth-century books because of the harm caused by handling and bright light. Postage stamps and other philatelic material, most music items, manuscripts and maps are also deemed unsuitable. This type of material, which cannot be photocopied, is first microfilmed and the film is then used to produce paper copies. Most material is considered suitable for microfilm copies which are produced in the Library's studios to the same standard of archival durability as copies made for its own use.

Copyright restrictions are rigidly adhered to and the Library follows an overall policy that, unless an author or illustrator is known to have been dead for more than 70 years, books published within the last 20 years are normally assumed to be still in copyright. It is also stipulated that copies may not be reproduced in any medium without express permission. If the item is out of copyright, permission will be granted on the payment of a reproduction fee.

Ben Bergonzi's 'The use (and non-use) of the British Library's photographic services', *Library Management*, **16** (7), 1995, pp. 25–9 gives details of a market research project to confirm or disprove that slow delivery times and high prices were deterring prospective customers. On the bright side, a survey showed that 'a viable constituency of potential customers exist'. Despite the tardy and uncompetitive picture service offered there was still a considerable measure of goodwill towards the photographic services. But many found that access to the collections was too often strangled with red tape. What was most unpopular was the requirement to pre-pay and the long delivery times, even the express service normally took two weeks. Nevertheless, it was apparent that there was a definite potential for converting occasional customers into regular customers. Efforts are now in hand to speed up technical processes and book delivery and to streamline administrative procedures. Moves towards providing a browsing service to on–site customers and an approval service to remote customers, are linked to instituting a hire service to complement the sale service.

A significant addition to Reproductions' resources arrived in January 1996 when it took delivery of a digital scanner which copies books face-up, rather than face-down and so subjects even fragile books to no more stress or damage than does normal desk use. Moreover, 'it is not necessary for operators to flatten pages against a glass sheet because the scanner has software to automatically correct the curvature of the page in the digital image before it is printed' ('British Library Reproduction News', *London Services - Bloomsbury Newsletter*, no. 14, Summer 1996, p.5). A further advantage is that the scanner can be used for remote orders and enables staff to provide off-site customers with a more rapid and better quality service. The Reprographic Service also allows access by appointment to a free picture browsing facility using the PIX project electronic photo-viewing system which holds in digital form several thousand images from across the Library's collections.

SECURITY

In common with other libraries, the British Library is more and more experiencing anti-social and even criminal behaviour. Occasionally some of the more flagrant cases of book theft surface in the press. An important seventeenth-century Japanese devotional manuscript in scroll form was returned to OIOC in 1994 after being stolen eight years earlier. Containing parts of the Lotus Sutra, written in gold ink on indigo blue paper, with an illuminated frontispiece of Buddhist parables and with gilt-decorated borders, it was recognized by a senior member of staff when asked by a New Bond Street dealer for her opinion when it was offered for auction. Legal proceedings followed and eventually the undamaged scroll was restored to the collections. The theft of 143 plates, which were not recovered, from Johann Weinmann's *Phytanthoza Iconographia* (1737–45) forced the Library to tighten its security arrangements in the shape of TV monitors and closed-circuit video cameras covering the North Library reading room before the move to St Pancras. ('Video security at BL', *Library Association Record*, **98** (8), August 1995, p. 410 has the details).

Michael Horsnell's 'Library thief plundered rare and precious books', *The Times*, no. 65487, 27 Jan 1996, p. 6 reported the case of a landscape gardener with a passion for antiquarian books who had systematically removed over 1100 plates from rare and valuable books, including Cecil Aldin's *The Sporting Garland* and from Theodore Henry Fielding's *Picturesque Illustrations of the River Wye*, both belonging to the British Library. A spokesman for the Library was quoted as saying:

> We do regard as a top priority taking care of material in the collection so it is available to present and future users. The missing plates from our books have been recovered, thankfully. This is part of the nation's heritage. We are making sure that it is not easy to plunder material from us in future.

Among the precautions he cited were the closed-circuit cameras, bag checking as readers left the Library, and regular security patrols.

Security mishaps on this scale were no doubt a shade embarrassing for the national library housing the National Preservation Office, especially since the NPO had published guidelines on crime prevention, *Security Matters: How to Deal with Criminal and Anti-social Behaviour* (1994). Concentrating on the necessity to devise a security policy setting out library priorities and staff responsibilities, on petty crime prevention, the importance of good communication skills when dealing with awkward or potentially dangerous situations, this pamphlet lacks cogent advice on curbing the activities of determined and knowledgeable thieves. There is, for example, no hard information on the benefits or costs of video cameras, where to site them and how to employ them to the fullest possible advantage. As a general guide to staff training and library procedures to obstruct anti-social behaviour *Security Matters* can be recommended for wide distribution, but it is not really of much consequence in thwarting the worst intentions of landscape gardeners nurturing a laudable but unrestrained passion for antiquarian books.

11

RESEARCH AND INNOVATION CENTRE

BRITISH LIBRARY RESEARCH AND DEVELOPMENT DEPARTMENT

In 1994 BLR&DD celebrated its twentieth anniversary as part of the British Library. At its open day in November the Department hosted a seminar so that those attending could discuss the future of library and information science research in the United Kingdom in general and the role of the Department as the major funding agency in particular. A full report of the seminar proceedings was published in October 1995 as *The Future of Library and Information Science Research in the United Kingdom*, no. 13 in South Bank University's Information UK Outlooks series. There were three principal contributors.

Jack Meadows examined past and likely future research trends and offered a personal proposal for BLR&DD's future role, stimulating innovation by using research funds for pilot studies, as seed corn money, for jointly funded prospects and for 'armchair' projects such as information policy studies. In addition it should adopt a new entrepreneurial role, putting its prestige, contacts and general know-how on the line to seek out and negotiate research bids and help to initiate, coordinate and advise research teams at other institutions in applying for research funds.

Stephen Robertson stressed the importance of re-examining the relationship of technology to research in library and information work. 'We must make sure that the technology-orientated research in this field is driven in the future, as it very largely has been in the past, by our sense of what we need to do, not by the machinery.' Tom Wilson suggested that an organized, systematic approach to forecasting was needed, with a corresponding attention to the importance of technology. More effective lobbying for funds and political activity was also required. In the course of the discussions there was general agreement that it was becoming increasingly difficult to define BLR&DD's role, especially in the light of competition and possible overlap with other funding bodies.

After reflecting on the day's proceedings Meadows, Robertson and Wilson posed four questions to move the debate forward. (1) Is it now time to set up a high-powered review of the support given to the whole of the IT/information/library field? The field is diffuse and is partly covered by a number of funding bodies. (2) Should BLR&DD itself now have the status of a research council, which would at least allow it to compete for funds on a level playing field? (3) Is it now time for BLR&DD to reappraise its own approach to developing and supporting research? (4) What is the role/contribution of the profession in helping BLR&DD to improve its position? How can the LIS community play its part in helping to secure better funding for research activity?

An internal working group was already reviewing the Department's operations. It was plain that it was itself evolving from a funding agency into a centre of advice on the potential and viability of research proposals and as an information point on work already in progress. At the same time the British Library was being forced to review its services by cuts in government funding necessitating a 13% reduction in its research grants budget. Although it was planned to restore research funds to their previous level the following year, the Department was clearly approaching a watershed in its history.

Externally, a new player was on the park, the Library And Information Commission, an independent body sponsored by the Department of National Heritage, was assuming responsibilities for developing a strategy for research and development for the information community and for seeking the necessary funding. At one point it seemed that the Department was on its way out of the British Library's orbit altogether. That doomsday scenario was averted but an end of an era atmosphere persisted.

RESEARCH AND INNOVATION CENTRE

A wide-ranging programme of changes to the structure and functions of the Department was announced in April 1996 and in July came the news that it was changing its name to the Research and Innovation Centre (RIC), whose aim was to promote, support, manage and disseminate high-quality research, innovation and development in information, library and related fields. The decision to change the Department's name was made primarily to reflect its new role more accurately. Specifically, the old name was often misunderstood by those not familiar with the

Research and Development Department; the changes in function mean that it will become more of an analytical centre for research; 'development' is no longer as important as it was, owing to the arrival of the Library and Information Commission and the disengagement by the Research and Development Department from funding projects which have clear market potential; and new significance will be attached to innovation and good practice in the Centre's Research Plan and in its growing role in support of research activities throughout the British Library.

A Mission Statement for the Centre, 'to advance UK information and library services by promoting and funding research, development and innovation' was printed in the Summer 1996 issue (no. 14) of an attractively reset and redesigned *Research Bulletin*:

> The Centre is the only UK research funding agency to have this specific task. Many other public, private and charitable organizations support, alongside their other activities, research and development concerned with the communication of information.
>
> The Centre will fund projects which complement such related work and will, in conjunction with the Library and Information Commission, the National Preservation Office, the Higher Education Funding Councils and other bodies, seek to promote coordination and cooperation in this field among the various funding agencies.
>
> In order to ensure that the maximum benefit is gained from research, the Centre will undertake and support a programme of research evaluation, synthesis and awareness-raising aimed at disseminating information primarily (but not exclusively) to policy makers, senior managers and information professionals. (p. 3)

For 1996/97 the Research Grants and Awards Plan, designed to allow proportionately more funds to be allocated directly to research rather than to staff and administration, included seven programme areas:

1   the Digital Library programme explores means whereby technology can be applied to improve library and information service provision. Networking, including use of the Internet, document delivery, electronic publishing and copyright and legal deposit, the digitization of information resources and the automation of library processes, are all encompassed within this crucial area;

2 Information Retrieval investigates the basic principles and processes of retrieval in order to develop more effective and efficient systems, with emphasis for the moment on image retrieval search;

3 Management of Libraries and Information Services assists managers to make the most of new opportunities by stimulating research on the management techniques and issues of current concern including strategic planning, evaluating the systems and structures used to achieve a quality service, securing more resources through income generation and identifying and motivating an appropriate work-force;

4 Value and Impact of Libraries and Information Services researches *inter alia* into how individuals can benefit more effectively from the use of information resources;

5 Library Co-operation subsumes regional issues with emphasis on the outcomes of cooperation and how it can lead to improved service provision;

6 Preservation covers research contributing to the development of a national preservation strategy, studies concerned with electronic archiving and innovative preservation techniques. This programme is undertaken in close cooperation with the National Preservation Office; and

7 Providers and Users of Information covers the relationships between various parts of the information chain (publishers, database producers and providers, booksellers, etc.), how users of information interact with the system, the information needs of specific groups including, particularly, the health care and business communities and the effectiveness of the services provided for them. All seven programmes were maintained for 1997/98.

Taking on board the views of both researchers and practitioners in the information community, this new strategy is intended to commit funds to assist innovation at the sharp end of the information industry. In addition a budget will be reserved for unsolicited projects across the whole menu of the Department's areas of interest. Conversely, those proposals which are seen as not yielding sufficient gain, either in terms of know-how, or innovation, will fail to gain support as the Research Plan redirects funds to the selected programme areas.

While continuing to promote high-quality research, development and innovation in information and related fields and to disseminate its results, this new approach will also facilitate the ordination of intelligence on the sources of research and development funding available in the UK and Europe and has the added advantage of encouraging close links with other research institutions. Not least, the Department will further develop the consultancy service which handles contracts for the British Library. A stronger programme of research relating in particular to company and industrial information services and the wider issue of the communication and use of business, commercial and technical information, will be given a high priority. The information needs of small and medium-size enterprises are expected to figure more prominently.

To reflect the Research Grants and Awards Plan a new matrix staff structure has been introduced. In the place of project managers, a team of Research Analysts will each be responsible for one of the identified programme areas, whose remit will include keeping the information community aware of developments, controlling the awards programme and liaising with other agencies, including the Library And Information Commission, with regard to related funding programmes. In addition they will each monitor developments in a particular sectoral field. A skilled and specially trained support staff, using improved office automation and deploying revised standardized procedures, will provide professional, administrative and financial expertise, unshackling the Research Analysts from routine research grants administration. These responsibilities are outlined in 'New Staff Structure' (RIC Research Bulletin, no. 14, Summer 1996, p. 5) and updated in 'Changes to Staff Structure' (no. 15, Autumn 1996, p. 6).

Dissemination of research programme results has often caused problems. In the past various methods of publication have been adopted according to the size and nature of the anticipated audience. Three categories of publications will be continued: available on demand from the British Thesis Service at DSC (previously known as deposited reports); from the award holder's institution; or from commercial publishers. Summaries of results will rapidly be made available over the Internet and will also be printed in the expanded Research Bulletin distributed without charge to a wider audience.

> An internal task group has been set up to examine new approaches to publication and dissemination within this overall framework . . . with the emphasis being on speedy, focused and targeted transmission of research outcomes and on the provision of guidance in finding and

negotiating with publishers for those award-holders without easy access to publishing facilities. ('New approaches to Publications and Dissemination', *RIC Research Bulletin*, no. 14, Summer 1996, p. 8).

The launch of RIC was reinforced by home pages on Portico, the British Library's World Wide Web server, which provides a guide to its resources and services. These pages will be increasingly used to disseminate information, not least on completed research projects. Already Portico has the full text of key publications, notably *Guide to the Preparation of a Research Proposal: General Conditions of Grants for Research*; and *Research Grants and Awards Plan for 1996/97*. A full list of R&DD and RIC funded research project reports and of current projects, will be added along with application forms so that applicants may apply for grants electronically.

RIC's *Research Plan April 1997 To March 1998*, a six-page A4 document 'sets out the priority topics and sectors which will guide the way the research grant is disbursed' *viz*. the value and impact of libraries; the importance of preserving the nation's heritage and memory (this covers the importance of the appropriate use of funds especially from the Heritage Lottery Fund and the Higher Education Funding Councils); techniques to promote excellence in information management in special libraries; and best practice in public library management. Details of the existing research programmes are reprinted and there are notes on the importance of an international dimension in research projects, the dissemination and awareness raising of research results, calls for proposals, unsolicited proposals, the size of awards; joint funding of projects and of other award-giving activities within RIC's remit. The *Plan* ends with a statement on RIC's links with other professional bodies and institutions.

DIGITAL LIBRARY PROGRAMME

RIC is leading the British Library's Digital Library Programme (formerly the Digital Library Development Programme) which derives its origins from the Library's third strategic plan, *For Scholarship, Research and Innovation. Strategic Objectives for the Year 2000*, published in May 1993. Recognizing the increase in electronic publishing and the changing nature of scholarly communication, one of the objectives outlined in that document was to maximize access to services through the full use of new techniques on site and over electronic networks to other major networks and users. The term 'digital library' is generally accepted shorthand for 'the use of digital techniques to acquire, store, preserve and provide access to information and material originally published in digital form or digitised from existing print, audio-visual or other forms'.

As is explained in 'The Digital Library Development Programme' (*RIC Research Bulletin*, no. 15, Autumn 1996, pp. 1–2),

> the British Library will be able to enhance the services provided to our current core user base and also to reach new users. The number of people able to use our services will expand, as digital infrastructure capabilities allow the Library to handle large volumes of requests quickly and at low cost, without regard to the user's location. Digital collections and services will enhance rather than replace the traditional collection and services. Most reading room users will combine electronic with paper use and most remote document delivery will be from electronic sources.

Five areas have been given priority: the establishment of an infrastructure capable of supporting the extension of UK legal deposit legislation to electronic materials; the expansion of British Library document supply services built on article alerting and improved requesting and delivery from a digital store; the expansion of patent services; improved access to the Library's historical collections through services to researchers, schools and the general public; and integration of these developments into the mainstream of British Library collections and services. 'In particular, there is a substantial shared requirement for common digital library technical, process and management infrastructures if the Library is to achieve its objectives effectively.' Early developments will include providing access to a wide range of digital material on CD-ROM in the reading rooms and expansion of the new Inside current awareness and document supply service to encompass delivery via the Internet.

What exactly makes the networked digital collection a 'library' is a concept difficult to grasp. The British Library perceives four crucial factors:

> the digital collection may be created and produced in a variety of different places, but will be accessible as if it were a single entity; it will be organised/categorised/indexed for greater ease of access than is possible from its original point of production; it will be stored and maintained in such a way as to ensure that it will continue to be available long after

the period of its immediate currency; and a balance will be found between the copyright/intellectual property rights of the creators and the 'fair dealing' or scholarly requirements.

The Library's current digital collection stems from the digitization of material from its existing collections through the Initiatives for Access programme and the steady purchase of a large number of CD-ROM publications, including a substantial collection of audio CDs at the National Sound Archive.

Enthusiasts within RIC, and elsewhere in the British Library, are striving to establish a collection of digital material, comparable to the existing print collections for future generations of users. But the Government is unlikely to provide the necessary funding within its annual grant-in-aid for business development, the digital and technical infrastructure, or the commercial skills required to manage the risks and to deliver services. Consequently, an essential strand within the overall programme is the Digital Library PFI Development Project. The Private Finance Initiative (PFI) was launched by the Government in 1992 as a mechanism for financing public sector procurement based on the principle of allowing both private and public sectors to concentrate on their own expertise and activities.

The onus on the British Library is therefore to create an environment in which the private sector can find profitable opportunities which do not compromise the Library's objectives and to provide value for money for the UK Treasury, especially through the transfer of risk to the private sector partner. A major step forward came on 15 February 1997 when the Library published a Prior Indicative Notice in the *Official Journal of the European Communities* to initiate a market-sounding exercise for the Library to enter into discussions with the private sector on its broad requirements for the Digital Library. Key players in the hardware, software, multimedia, telecommunications, library system field were among the hundred plus firms who requested further information. In January 1998 the names of three bidders who would proceed to the next stage of negotiation under PFI were announced: Dawson-IBM Consortium; Digital Library Consortium (Blackwell, Chadwyck-Healey, MicroPatent, Unisys); and Elsevier Science. The selection of the preferred bidder was expected to be known 19 September 1998 and the new services are scheduled to begin in 1999.

DIGITAL LIBRARY RESEARCH PROGRAMME

Parallel with RIC's Digital Library Programme is its Digital Library Research Programme exploring ways in which digital and networking technologies can support and enhance library and information services. A call for research proposals, 13 December 1996, signalled priorities by inviting prospective researchers to address such questions as: How can access to networked resources be widened to include the whole community? How can digital information resources be integrated more effectively into library and information services? How can networking technology aid cooperation between different sectors in the library and information community? What skills will information professionals and users need? How can they be acquired? What will be the principal economic models for the digital library? What technical standards or evaluation methods will apply?

It was announced in August 1997 that RIC had awarded over £400,000 to libraries, universities and research institutions across the United Kingdom to assess the potential impact of digital and networking technology on library and information provision in the following two years. Grants have been made to a wide variety of projects. One will study the impact of the Internet on small and medium enterprises; others include the potential of the World Wide Web for encouraging children to read and the delivery of open learning resources and community information over the Internet. RIC will ensure that the research results of the projects awarded grants will be disseminated as widely as possible in a series of conferences, workshops, events and publications. Details of the 10 approved projects appeared in 'Digital Libraries research', *Library Technology*, 2 (4), August 1997, p. 67.

DIGITAL DATASTORE DEVELOPMENT PROJECT

Also part of the Digital Library Programme is the Digital Datastore Development Project, which began in 1996 to define the Library's business and technical requirements in developing its use of digital data. It registers four main aims: to supply the Digital Library PFI Project with sufficient information about the Library's business and technical requirements to enable it to produce a comprehensive specification; to ensure that the existing digital material within the Library's collections continues to be maintained, preserved and made available for use; to provide a suitable corporate framework for the continuing development of digital library activity at a directorate level which will accord with the Library's strategic developments as identified by the Digital Library Programme Board; and to consolidate and develop the technical expertise already present in the Library to ensure that it maintains its position as a major player in the national and international library information world.

Answers to 17 frequently asked questions and a list of current projects of the Digital Library Research Programme, upon which much of the foregoing is based, are available from the Project Manager of the Digital Library Programme.

PUBLICATIONS

A change in the publication pattern for RIC research reports has operated since September 1996 when the Centre ceased its in-house publishing. New titles and the backlist can be obtained from Turpin Distribution Services Ltd. Reports available on demand from the British Thesis Service at Boston Spa, those published by award-holders' institutions, and the commercially published series, are not affected by the change. Complementing Margaret Mann's *Complete List of Reports Published by the British Library R&D* (1988, 322pp.) is Nicholas Jones' *Complete List of Reports Published by the British Library R&D Department 1988–1994* (1995, 258pp.). *Research and Innovation Centre Publications List 1996* provides full lists of recent and forthcoming titles and a backlist of all research reports and other publications together with an author and a title index.

A sense of imminent change prompted R&DD to commission Jack Meadows' *Innovation in Information: Twenty Years of the British Library Research and Development Department*, published in Bowker Saur's British Library Research Series in 1994. To catch the tide it was written in four months, an almost superhuman effort in the light of the author's preoccupation with a major upheaval at his university. Not primarily intended as a straightforward narrative history – although an historical outline inevitably emerges – *Innovation in Information* is more concerned 'to study how a single organisation, not one over-generously endowed with funding, has managed to have a major impact on the development of library and information research'. In seven chapters, Meadows examines R&DD's origins, investigates the nature of research and the structure of the research community, outlines its contacts with libraries and users, looks at the impact of automation, follows this with an overview of the major research projects that attracted funding, expounds on the Department's support for conferences and other meetings, and ends with a study of its links within Europe, its role in the British Library's own research programme, its organization, funding and its immediate future. But perhaps the greatest virtue of this authoritative and definitive work is that it presents a complex story in terms that non-research specialists will appreciate, even injecting a little humour to lighten the text.

12

INFORMATION SYSTEMS

Information Systems directorate, formerly Computing and Telecommunications, is responsible for the development, operation, enhancement and maintenance of all corporate information systems services to meet the Library's strategic objectives. Its touchstone is the Library's Information Systems Strategy, addressing the whole range of its activities and whose leading objectives include improved access to the Library's collection, a collection of digital material and library services closely integrated with computer-based working. Supporting objectives are listed as efficient library and administrative processes; management information systems; partnership and cooperation; developing and retraining key IT skills; establishing a widely used infrastructure; and an effective management framework for IT. Three major groups oversee systems development.

CORPORATE BIBLIOGRAPHIC SYSTEMS

By 1999 the British Library intends to replace all its IBM based bibliographic systems, BLAISE-LINE, WLN (the cataloguing system used in AP&C), LOCAS and the BL Catalogue, which together cover almost every aspect of the creation and accessibility of the Library's catalogue records. Corporate Bibliographic Systems (CBS) replacement strategy is to assemble all the Library's separate catalogues into a unified database, which will not only improve bibliographic cooperation with other libraries, but also ease the path of the Library's cataloguers and enquiry desk staff. The principal advantage will be that amendments to the catalogues will be registered instantly and will also end the duplication of records on different databases.

CBS's plans, costing in the region of £2 million, unexpectedly became enmeshed in the Government's Private Finance Initiative, requiring public bodies to seek private-sector investment in capital projects costing in excess of £250,000. Proposals for the design, development and operation of the new bibliographic system were evaluated in the summer of 1996. A short list of service providers was drawn up and negotiations started in September, with the aim of awarding the contract in April 1997. A business case was delivered to the DNH at the end of February.

As announced in James Elliot's 'Corporate Bibliographic System Contract Awarded', *Select*, no. 20, Summer 1997, p. 5, the contract went to Axis Resources of Harlow, Essex. The system will be based on the AMICUS software, developed by the Canadian software house CGI for the National Library of Canada, which offers

> a fully-integrated data entry, online information retrieval and product generation system. When fully implemented in early 1999 the CBS will have the capability to support up to 2,000 concurrent users and handle up to 30 million authority and bibliographic records . . . Access will be offered through both WWW and Z39.50 search and retrieve interfaces, thus maximising the ability to connect to and search other online database hosts for copy cataloguing.

The new system, which represents the largest and most complex single IT procurement in the British Library's history, is based on Windows NT workstations and will have all the standard Windows text-editing features, incorporating mouse, menus and standardized function keys.

SYSTEMS DEVELOPMENT (BOSTON SPA)

Systems Development (Boston Spa) is responsible for four main areas of operation: the coordination of the Library's technical involvement with document and image processing (DIP), the management of DIP systems and the provision of a centre of expertise to guide and support DIP technologies and standards to all areas of the Library; the provision of expertise on matters relating to the Ingres databases and systems and on the support and development of serials systems; the control of the development and support programme for the document supply systems including those relating to Automated Request Processing and Inside; and the management of the financial, administrative and office support systems for the Planning and Resources, Public Affairs and St Pancras Occupation BL Estates directorates.

SYSTEMS DEVELOPMENT (LONDON)

Areas falling under Systems Development (London) include responsibility for the technical systems architecture for London based systems; the technical design, configuration and project management and business design of the St Pancras Information Systems development programme; and account management for London-based directorates and the organization of the relocation of Information Systems to St Pancras.

ST PANCRAS SYSTEMS

The development and installation of the St Pancras information systems and infrastructure, together with the planning for their continued operation and development, are the chief responsibilities of St Pancras Systems. Just what these are and what they entail, is outlined in Roger Butcher's 'The Application of IT in the St Pancras Building of the British Library', *Alexandria*, 7 (2), 1995, pp. 83–96. The design of the online catalogue was pivotal as it was intended that 'readers should be able to find records . . . within just a few minutes of sitting down at the terminal, without training or any other help from reading room staff'. Another challenge was the large character set used by the data in the catalogues, including Greek, Cyrillic, Hebrew, Old Church Slavonic, African phonetics etc. Whatever system was adopted, it had to be capable of handling over 800 distinct characters. This was not easy 'but it was made possible because modern computer displays have a high resolution and therefore allow distinctions to be made between similar characters'.

The Automated Book Requesting system will, it is hoped, ensure that at least 80% of requests will be made available to the reader within 30 minutes. Using the INGRES database management system, it will run on a combination of Digital computers running the Ultrix operating system and on IBM-compatible PCs running Windows 3.1. Mechanical Book Handling and Management Information systems will also beneficially impact on reader services. In the new building's operations IT will monitor environmental factors like temperature, humidity, light level, carbon dioxide level of the air, smoke in the air and unexpected high temperatures (for fire detection). The St Pancras building has a design life of at least 200 years. 'However, it will open at a time when computer systems often become out of date after only 200 days. It has therefore been a challenge to design IT systems that stand a chance of lasting even a small fraction of the life of the building itself.'

PLANNING DESIGN & QUALITY

Responsibilities of Planning Design & Quality encompass implementation of the Information Systems Strategy; overall systems design and interoperability in information systems planning; financial planning and the management information system for the directorate; coordinating developments in quality management across the Information Systems directorate, including a framework of methods, techniques and tools for project management and systems development; and the coordination of IS staff training and development.

OPERATIONS AND TELECOMMUNICATIONS

Falling within the Operations and Telecommunications sphere are the management of computer operations, including data centre systems management; operational support for internal systems and external FM mainframe services; the management of IT services including Operational Services (i.e. LAN management, datacomms and PC support for London directorates); the provision of a corporate electronic mail service; IT procurement services; advice, guidance and support for telecommunications and network technologies and standards to all areas of the British Library; strategic planning of the corporate network infrastructure; and corporate level management of the networks including capacity planning, network design and monitoring.

At St Pancras, PCs, the OPAC terminals, the Automated Book Request System and the Reader Admission System, are connected through underfloor cabling to the equipment racks and, from there, to the fibre-optic 'electronic backbone' linking all staff and reader areas to the system's 'nerve centres', the Computer and PABX (Private Branch Exchange) Rooms and the Telecommunications Room.

> In this way, users all round the building are linked to each other, to in-house computer systems and via external links in the PABX room to Boston Spa, other Library buildings and outside services. To . . . drive the transfer of data around the network and link the various parts of the system together . . . IS has selected a technology known as ATM on

the basis that it provides higher speed, better manageability and greater quality of service compared with other readily available systems. The combination of the cabling provided with the building and ATM technology supplied by the BL will result in a Local Area Network at St Pancras which not only meets the Library's current needs but is also capable of substantial enhancement in the future.

13

ST PANCRAS OPERATIONS AND ESTATES

In the run-up to the relocation to the St Pancras building, St Pancras Facilities and Estates Management (FEM), the main part of the St Pancras Occupation and Estates (SPOE) directorate and organizationally separate from Estates and Facilities Management (E&FM), was engaged in contracts and procurement for establishing the key support services; planning and implementing various construction works necessary for the completion, amendment or upgrading of the building and its systems; for the liaison and negotiations, with the Department of National Heritage's facilities management team then maintaining the building; for the planning and implementing of its early occupation; and for preparing staff relocation. FEM is organized into two units: House Management, responsible for cleaning, office support services and security, which provides 24-hour cover with the help of closed-circuit TV monitors; and Technical Services, responsible for the building fabric and for the operation and maintenance of the mechanical and electrical services, including air conditioning, lighting and power and the mechanical book handling lifts.

OVERALL STRATEGY

The British Library's overall estate strategy, stemming primarily from the need to house its collections and to deploy its staff as cost-effectively as possible, is to restrain any future growth to the St Pancras site in London, the Newspaper Library at Colindale in North London, and to its Boston Spa site in Yorkshire. Until then the Library plans a gradual programme of relocation from leased buildings to these designated sites. After an evaluation of accommodation requirements in the next decade, the Library's Management Committee determined to cancel Private Finance Initiative construction projects that would have expanded facilities at Colindale and Boston Spa; to negotiate extensions at the Woolwich store until the year 2007 and the Conservation Studio at Bloomsbury; to increase shelving capacity at Boston Spa; and to retain the temporary office accommodation to the north of the St Pancras site. Negotiations will continue with the Department of Culture, Media and Sport for the retention of the land to the north of the St Pancras completion phase for the future construction of additional reading rooms, a Conservation Bindery and other facilities.

However, possible problems loom. By the year 2007 the Library may be forced to re-examine its storage requirements should the collections continue to grow at an alarming rate (notwithstanding the effects of the Smethurst Review) and should the Micawber Street outhouse and a storage building close to the Newspaper Library, be vacated. Estates and Facilities Management Department is charged with the responsibility of developing the Library's broad estate strategy and also with the practical day-to-day management of the Library's buildings apart from St Pancras. Its current tasks are examining how the Library can best provide additional office accommodation at Boston Spa, improve environmental conditions at its two main outhouses, and adapt Micawber Street for National Sound Archive uses which cannot, for the moment, be catered for at St Pancras.

In the mean time, a concerted effort is being made to reduce the Library's overall energy bill. Although, at the moment, its energy use falls within a reasonable bracket, the aim is to reduce its costs by £135,000 over the next five years by conducting energy surveys and by investment in technical improvements. A monitoring and targeting system identifies areas of excessive water and energy use at all British Library sites so that resources may be allocated effectively.

PART IV

DIRECTORATE REPORTING DIRECTLY TO THE CHIEF EXECUTIVE

14

PUBLIC AFFAIRS

The main responsibility of the Public Affairs (PA) directorate (formerly Public Services) is to increase and widen access to the collections, with the remit of extending the Library's programme of temporary and permanent exhibitions and public events in the UK and overseas; educational services; publishing; the bookshop; media resources; corporate communications, corporate design and development functions; and a wider communication with the general public. Among the responsibilities of Visitors Services, set up within PA to run the 'front of the house' operations at St Pancras, is that of staffing the vitally important Information Desk in the entrance hall of the new building, providing tours of the building to visitors and operating a general enquiry service.

A two-monthly, 12-page illustrated programme, *What's On* is distributed. The September–October 1997 issue carried information on a permanent exhibition, two special exhibitions, lectures, gallery talks, a concert, an events diary, online information regarding the move to St Pancras and the closure of the Reading Room at Bloomsbury, recent British Library publications available in the bookshop, and notes on the availability of recorded information on exhibitions and events, the gallery talks, and wheelchair access.

Transferring to St Pancras in 1998, the ground floor Bookshop stocks a wide range of books, including paperback guides to the collections and exhibition guides, postcards, colour slides, calendars and other gift items. In the year 1996–97 Bookshop sales amounted to £595,600, a sum that may confidently be expected to rise dramatically as the St Pancras building begins to attract visitors.

PUBLISHING

British Library publications include scholarly and popular works based on the collection, general and scholarly bibliographic, research and development reports and library and information science titles. Publications are available in a number of formats: printed, bibliographical and educational full-text/images, CD-ROM, CD, cassette, disc form, microfiche, online and video.

The *British Library Publications List 1997* (A4 size, 48pp.) is a complete list of current titles mostly available from Turpin Distribution Services, Blackhorse Road, Letchworth, Herts., SG6 1HN, although the names and addresses of 14 other suppliers are also given. Titles are listed in 29 categories, indicating the range and width of the British Library list. Occasional descriptive catalogues are also published, *New Academic and Reference Publications in the Humanities* and *General and Illustrated New Titles and Selected Stocklist*. And, more significantly, as the publishing seasons come and go, *The British Library Multimedia Catalogue. New and recently published CD-ROMs*. An assessment of the Library's publishing programme appears in Jane Carr(e)'s 'Les Éditions de la British Library pour la profession et le grand public', *Bulletin d'Information de l'Association des Bibliothécaires*, no.172, 3e trimestre, 1996, pp. 82–3. The British Library is spending £5 million annually on its publishing programme, which has to be recovered by sales. Considerable investment will be needed for development.

EDUCATION SERVICE

The British Library Education Service was relaunched in 1991 with the aim of exploiting the Library's collections for the benefit of a wide audience not otherwise catered for within the Library's research or information services. Since then Education Service staff has doubled in size (from one to two) and it has taken on board a respectable number of projects and publications. An authoritative overview of its activities is conveniently to hand in Karen Brookfield's 'Behind the Bookcase. The Work of the British Library Education Service', *School Librarian*, **43** (3), August 1995, pp. 95–6.

Gallery talks and sessions to school groups on a broad range of themes relating to the history of writing provide a limited opportunity for direct contact. However, an annual series of workshops on a specific tradition of calligraphy, Islamic, Western and Chinese, has attracted over 600 pupils in each series, enjoying a mixture of practical work and gallery-based sessions under the guidance of specialist curators. Sponsorship has enabled this popular programme to be expanded. Promoting Library Exhibitions entails helping adult and junior visitors to gain the utmost benefit and enjoyment from the visit by means of leaflets, gallery talks, slide lectures and interactive computer animations, graphics and audio commentaries.

An educational publishing programme with an emphasis on English, history and religious studies, is the second main strand of the Service's programme for schools. This is by no means limited to print publications, the full range of materials includes video and audio cassettes, resource packs, and most ambitious of all, the interactive, multimedia CD-ROM, *Sources in History: Medieval Realms: Britain 1066 to 1500*. Funded in part by a National Council for Educational Technology grant under its CD-ROM Applications Development Scheme, the disc, which is available for PCs and Acorn Archimedes, contains over 1450 pieces of primary source material for use in KS3 History and is designed to enable pupils to search for information themselves. It is intended to be the first of a series that will eventually encompass all KS3 units. A second disc, *The Making of the United Kingdom: 1500–1750*, using digital images from the Library's own photographic service, was published in January 1998.

Unveiled in 1996 the Library's Young Person's Guide, an interactive multimedia prototype, was devised and developed by the Education Service and Audio Visual Sources, to attract young people, specifically between 10 and 16 years old and to encourage them to look beyond books in glass cases and get to know their national library. Kate Barnes remarks

> we need to think carefully how we target this age group, not just here in the galleries but through the use of IT to schools/colleges, or via the Internet. In developing the prototype for the galleries it was vital that we presented the basic information about the institution in an accessible and fun way, to engage the user from the start. ('Young Person's Guide to the British Library', *Initiatives for Access News*, no. 4, Autumn 1996, p. 3).

The Education Programme for schools in the St Pancras building, beginning in May 1998, is outlined in *Sources*, no. 9, Autumn 1997, p. 4. It will include self-directed visits to the exhibition galleries; one-day workshops on calligraphy, printing and bookmaking in the Workshop and in the Education Room which will also be used for half-day A level student seminars focusing on primary source material for research projects. Services for teachers will encompass advice and support for curricular work in the shape of activity sheets for visits, INSET sessions, open evenings and pre-visits for specialist groups, and all-format classroom publications. Full details of all the Education Service's activities are included in the Spring 1998 issue of *Sources*. This journal, published termly since January 1995, contains information on the Library's exhibitions, holiday events, forthcoming workshops etc. Each issue, except the first, has also included a feature on the Library's collections.

EXHIBITIONS

Committed to making its collections accessible to the public, the British Library's permanent exhibition in the Treasures Gallery 'celebrates and interprets the magnificent range and depth of the Library's rare and unique collections'. Sacred texts from religious faiths around the world, illuminated manuscripts from many different countries, famous English language literary works, significant developments in printing, (from woodblock printing in the Far East, to the invention of moveable type in Europe), manuscripts of famous composers, important works on scientific discovery, and celebrated historical documents, are all cited as areas of particular interest. The Treasures Gallery has been supported by a personal gift of £1 million from John Ritblatt, a member of the British Library Board, and will be called the John Ritblatt Gallery: Treasures of the British Library.

Concentrating on fifteenth-century manuscript illuminations, typesetting and printing, bookbinding, and the history of sound recording, the Workshop of Words, Sounds and Images explains, in a determined user-friendly way, the processes and practices of book making and sound from the earliest alphabets to the present day. It is intended to be a hands-on experience so that visitors may handle materials and watch scribes, printers and bookbinders at work, and also try out a computer-based programme on 'Designing with Type'.

Providing a link between the Workshop Gallery and the treasures on display, the Pearson Gallery of the Living Word features a themed exhibition focusing on children's books, the story of writing, images of Britain, the scientific record, and the art of the book. Special exhibitions will be mounted from 1999 onwards. A useful overview of the nature of the exhibition galleries is printed in *Sources*, no. 9, Autumn 1997, p. 4.

PRESS AND PUBLIC RELATIONS

No British Library exhibition, launch, lecture, award, contribution to a national or international event, *Annual Report*, commemoration, notable acquisition or publication, is complete without a *Press Information Sheet* being circulated by Press and Public Relations. Facts and figures and descriptions comprise its staple information, along with snappy quotations from (usually) senior staff, and notes for editors who may or may not be entirely *au fait* with the British Library's collections, services and activities. The Department excelled itself when celebrating the British Library's evacuation of the Round Reading Room, 25 October 1997. A Press information sheet, *The Final Chapter for Readers in the British Library's Round Reading Room*, was accompanied by a series of supplementary sheets on the history and design of the reading room, including its dimensions, colour schemes, opening hours and the book stacks; a list of celebrated readers and users; a report on previous moves; the career of Sir Anthony Panizzi, who was largely responsible for the reading room's circular design; the British Library at St Pancras; opening dates of services there; an overall description of the British Library; facts and figures 1996/97; and some amusing personal views of the reading room, all enclosed in a durable folder, *Moving the British Library*.

Under Section 4(3) of *The British Library Act 1972* the Library is required to present to Parliament an *Annual Report* of its performance as a recipient of public funds. In recent years the Library has taken advantage of this to prepare a substantial pictorial document reporting its achievements and, where appropriate, the problems it has faced, in the context of the benefits its collections and services afford to British intellectual life, business, industry and the public. The aim is to give a comprehensive account of its activities as a world-class institution. To do this it seeks to combine well-written, incisive text with striking images highlighting the collection and services. General and strategic developments are discussed at the beginning of the report, after this comes news of specific services for on-site and remote users, the collection, and of cooperation with other institutions worldwide. The report closes with a section containing figures, membership lists of committees etc. Throughout, the *Annual Report* adopts a corporate view of the Library rather than focusing too closely on the work of individual departments. A review of the *Report*'s style, contents and distribution, to ensure its continuation as a key communication tool, was initiated in March 1997, when Press and Public Relations enlisted the help of users, sponsors, and other Library contacts, to complete a questionnaire, in the expectation of producing an improved *Report* in future years.

Another of Press and Public Relation's responsibilities is the production of *Shelflife*, a monthly publication which keeps British Library staff up-to-date with developments across the library and provides them with a medium to make comments and air opinions.

PUBLIC EVENTS

The Public Events programme includes lectures, seminars, one-person shows, literary readings, musical performances, as well as management of the Library's new Conference Centre and the hire of spaces within the St Pancras building as an additional source of revenue. Whispers from usually well-informed sources suggest it was the Public Events Office that was responsible for one of the most bizarre scenes ever witnessed in the Round Reading Room. On 3 June 1997, a shadowy figure clad in a dark cape and clerical hat stalked the aisles. It was alleged to be Enoch Soames, a decadent and obscure poet who figured in a Max Beerbohm short story. Dismissed as being of no account by his contemporaries, he made a Faustian pact with the Devil, 3 June 1897, bargaining his soul for a return to the Reading Room, a hundred years later, to consult reference works to find out how posterity had treated him. Dalya Alberge's 'Happy ending as a ghost writer returns in spirit', *Times*, 65839, 17 March 1997, p. 9 and Nigel Reynolds's 'The ghost of Enoch Soames gives a spirited performance', *Daily Telegraph*, 44154, 4 June 1997, p. 6 aided and abetted this engaging tomfoolery. Elsewhere, it was remarked that witnesses 'were uncertain whether the eccentrically-attired figure was truly Enoch Soames, an actor, or one of the many lost souls that return to the Round Reading Room day after day, year after year'.

AFTERWORD:
THE FUTURE OF THE
ROUND READING ROOM

Fears that the legendary Round Reading Room of the British Museum would be transformed out of all recognition once the British Library vacated it were allayed in July 1994, when regardless of the strong recommendations of the House of Commons National Heritage Committee, made public only a few days beforehand, 'that the Round Reading Room should be retained in perpetuity as a public reading room that is an integral part of the British Library', the Museum revealed that it was planning a new cultural complex on the Bloomsbury site.

> The year 2000 will see the centre of the British Museum transformed into London's first covered public square. Under a wide-span translucent roof, a new cultural complex at the heart of the building will provide outstanding facilities for learning and relaxation. Designed by the distinguished architectural firm Sir Norman Foster and Partners, the Great Court will be open to all visitors from early morning to late evening. A new multi-level elliptical building, constructed around the Round Reading Room, will house a Centre for Education, exhibition galleries and much-improved public services including high-quality bookshops and restaurant space. The Great Court will be an important addition to London and a significant contribution to the celebration of the Millennium.

At the centre of the Great Court

> the Round Reading Room will be restored to its original decorative scheme and made permanently accessible to the general public for the first time in its history. All visitors will be able to walk around and experience one of the most famous rooms in the world, which has been an inspiration to so many. Part of the Round Reading Room will serve as a study area where any visitor wishing to learn more about the Museum's

collections will find a comprehensive reference library combined with the most up-to-date information technology, including computerised catalogues and multimedia programmes. (*The Great Court*, 4p. brochure, 1994).

Further details were unveiled in November 1994. The whole of the inner courtyard was to be covered with a lightweight transparent roof, probably a double-skin inflated pillow of fabric coated in Teflon, which would place the minimum weight on the stonework of the courtyard façade. Passage across the Great Court would be at ground and first-floor level.

Six months later James Fenton reassured his readers in *The Independent*:

> Another thing you notice about the museum people is that whenever they talk about the Reading Room, a note of cautious reverence enters their voices. They want you to be left in no doubt that there is absolutely no question at all of any kind of indignity being afflicted on the Reading Room [which] still retains its iconic status and its ability to cause passions to flare up. So the museum people handle it like a bomb. ('A grand project to look forward to', *The Independent*, no. 2668, 8 May 1995, p. 15).

When the restoration of the Reading Room is completed, its upper walls will be lined with books from the Museum's own collections. At ground floor level there will be a new public reference library of some 25,000 books, catalogues and other printed material, specially created for the Reading Room and focusing on publications relevant to the civilizations, cultures and societies represented in the Museum's collections. Designated the Paul Hamlyn Library, marking a generous benefaction from the Paul Hamlyn Foundation, the Library will accommodate some 300 seats as a working library and place for study which will remain open in the evening. Also within the present reading room will be the Walter and Leonore Annenberg Centre, largely financed by a £6 million grant from the Annenberg Foundation which will combine modern technology with traditional sources of information retrieval, giving access not only to the Paul Hamlyn Library but also to COMPASS, the British Museum's Collections Multimedia Public Access System, linking a highly computerized database with a sophisticated search facility.

A new six-page A4 folding leaflet, *The Reading Room*, distributed by the Museum, notes that:

Both the Paul Hamlyn Library and COMPASS are conceived as new public resources for those who wish to explore the Museum's collections in a variety of ways. Together they will bridge the gap between the general enquiry service offered by the Information Desks and the research facilities of the specialist Student Rooms and will be particularly helpful to the Museum's many regular visitors and to students using the Museum's collections as part of a programme of study. Facilities for the use of COMPASS by school groups will be provided separately in the Centre for Education, at the lower level of the Great Court.

It is a bold project and one which should stifle murmurings from diehards fearing that the atmosphere will be disturbed and dumbed down by hordes of untutored hoi-polloi congesting the Reading Room, ignoring the fact that those who simply wish to see its interior which, remember, belongs to the whole nation and not to a minute proportion of it, will have the opportunity to view it from a separate entrance.

However, not everyone was content. According to Marianne MacDonald's 'The final chapter for library classic', *The Independent*, no. 3156, 30 November 1996, p. 3, the news that the Reading Room would be cut in half by a glass screen, have computers installed and would be used for displays, prompted 96 letters, many from overseas academic institutions, objecting to the British Museum's proposals when they were before Camden's planning committee. But Camden had no wish to delay such an imaginative scheme.

Nostalgic farewells include Malcolm Bradbury's 'As the Reading Room goes, so does an era', *The Independent*, no. 3170, 17 December 1996, p. 13; David Lister's 'Last readers at the library of literary lions', IBID., no. 3437, 25 October 1997, p. 11; John Ezard's 'Last shout at the reading room', *The Guardian*, no. 47004, 25 October 1997, p. 5; and 'Farewell To The Round Reading Room', *Friends of The British Library Newsletter*, no. 26, Winter 1997/Spring 1998, pp.2–3.

APPENDIX 1

THE BRITISH LIBRARY
FACTS AND FIGURES, 1996/97

COLLECTION (LONDON & BOSTON SPA)

includes:

Monograph and Serial Volumes	15,515,000
Patent Specification	40,585,000
Philatelic Items	8,166,000
Cartographic Items	2,286,000
Music Scores	1,562,000
Newspapers (Volumes)	643,000
Manuscripts	293,000
India Office	260,000
Photographs	204,000
Total items added to the collection annually	1,420,000

READING ROOMS

Number of reader visits	475,826
Items consulted	5,401,705
Requests for information	658,317

DOCUMENT SUPPLY

Number of documents supplied remotely	4,450,375

Key UK customers include most of the FT top 100 including ICI, Glaxo, British Aerospace and Smith Kline Beecham.

Over 4 million documents are supplied remotely to more than 140 countries.

BRITISH LIBRARY USERS

Reading Room Visitors		Requests for Remote Supply	
Postgraduate	31%	University	42%
Academic Staff	21%	Industry/Commerce	21%
Writers	14%	Other Academic	14%
Other Professional	12%	Government	11%
Undergraduates	11%	Public Libraries	10%
Patent Researchers	4%	Other	2%
Other	7%		

(Reprinted from a Press Information Sheet issued by Press and Public Relations)

APPENDIX 2

TOWARDS THE DIGITAL LIBRARY: THE BRITISH LIBRARY'S INITIATIVES FOR ACCESS PROGRAMME

Towards the Digital Library, announced for publication in July 1997, in the event did not appear until late March 1998, too late to be noticed at length in this present work. It gives a detailed account of the projects carried out both by the Library and its external partners in the form of individual case studies. These include:

1   The *Initatives for Access* programme: an overview (Michael Alexander and Andrew Prescott)

2   Digital Imaging

Constructing Electronic Beowulf (Andrew Prescott)
The York *Domesday* Project (Meg Twycross, Pamela King, and Andrew Prescott)
Digitising the Gandharan Buddhist Scrolls (Simon Shaw and Andrew Prescott)
The Image Demonstrator Project (Cindy Carr)
The Digitisation of Microfilm (Hazel Podmore)
St Pancras Treasurers digitisation project (Leona Carpenter with Clive Izzard)
PIX project (Peter Carey)
Gallery applications and educational multimedia (Karen Brookfield, Andrew Prescott and Simon Shaw)

3   Document Management and Descriptive Data

Access to Patents (David Newton)
The CD Demonstrator Project: a case study in cataloguing CD-ROMs (Sandie Beaney with Stephen Bagley, Richard Moore, Sue Skelton and Anne Sykes)
Project Digitise (Peter Copeland)
The British National Corpus (Lou Burnard)

A database for cataloguing Chinese and Central Asian manuscripts: the International Dunhuang Project (Susan Whitfield)

Excalibur: image-based text storage and searching (Andrew Prescott and Malcolm Pratt)

Image – the future of text? (Brent Seales, James Griffiven and Andrew Prescott)

4   Network services and the way ahead

Portico: The British Library's online information server (Graham Jefcoate with additional technical material by Andrew Ford)

Network OPAC and One (Christopher Easingwood, Neil Smith and Jan Ashton)

Automated Request Processing (Andy Ekers)

INSIDE: an integrated searching, ordering and delivery service (Richard Roman, with a technical note by Lynne Chivers)

Developing the digital library (Brian Lang)

5   Places and Spaces – an afterword (Lorcan Dempsey)

With a Foreword (Sir Anthony Kenny); an Introduction (John Mahoney); a Glossary of Terms (pp.242–6); and Further Reading (pp.247–53).

INDEX